Rethinking Peace and Conflict Studies

Series Editor: **Oliver P. Richmond**, Professor, School of International Relations, University of St. Andrews, UK

Editorial Board: **Roland Bleiker**, University of Queensland, Australia; **Henry F. Carey**, Georgia State University, USA; **Costas Constantinou**, University of Keele, UK; **A. J. R. Groom**, University of Kent, UK; **Vivienne Jabri**, King's College London, UK; **Edward Newman**, University of Birmingham, UK; **Sorpong Peou**, Sophia University, Japan; **Caroline Kennedy-Pipe**, University of Sheffield, UK; **Professor Michael Pugh**, University of Bradford, UK; **Chandra Sriram**, University of East London, UK; **Ian Taylor**, University of St. Andrews, UK; **Alison Watson**, University of St. Andrews, UK; **R. B. J. Walker**, University of Victoria, Canada; **Andrew Williams**, University of St. Andrews, UK.

Titles include:

Roland Bleiker
AESTHETICS AND WORLD POLITICS

Morgan Brigg
THE NEW POLITICS OF CONFLICT RESOLUTION
Responding to Difference

Susanne Buckley-Zistel
CONFLICT TRANSFORMATION AND SOCIAL CHANGE IN UGANDA
Remembering after Violence

Karina Z. Butler
A CRITICAL HUMANITARIAN INTERVENTION APPROACH

Henry F. Carey
PRIVATIZING THE DEMOCRATIC PEACE
Policy Dilemmas of NGO Peacebuilding

Jason Franks
RETHINKING THE ROOTS OF TERRORISM

Sarah Holt
AID, PEACEBUILDING AND THE RESURGENCE OF WAR
Buying Time in Sri Lanka

Vivienne Jabri
WAR AND THE TRANSFORMATION OF GLOBAL POLITICS

Daria Isachenko
THE MAKING OF INFORMAL STATES
Statebuilding in Northern Cyprus and Transdniestria

James Ker-Lindsay
EU ACCESSION AND UN PEACEMAKING IN CYPRUS

Roger MacGinty
INTERNATIONAL PEACEBUILDING AND LOCAL RESISTANCE
Hybrid Forms of Peace

NO WAR, NO PEACE
The Rejuvenation of Stalled Peace Processes and Peace Accords

Carol McQueen
HUMANITARIAN INTERVENTION AND SAFETY ZONES
Iraq, Bosnia and Rwanda

S. M. Farid Mirbagheri
WAR AND PEACE IN ISLAM
A Critique of Islamic/ist Political Discourses

Audra L. Mitchell
LOST IN TRANSFORMATION
Violent Peace and Peaceful Conflict in Northern Ireland

Sorpong Peou
INTERNATIONAL DEMOCRACY ASSISTANCE FOR PEACEBUILDING
Cambodia and Beyond

Sergei Prozorov
UNDERSTANDING CONFLICT BETWEEN RUSSIA AND THE EU
The Limits of Integration

Oliver P. Richmond, and Audra Mitchell (*editors*)
HYBRID FORMS OF PEACE
From Everyday Agency to Post-Liberalism

Oliver P. Richmond
THE TRANSFORMATION OF PEACE

Bahar Rumelili
CONSTRUCTING REGIONAL COMMUNITY AND ORDER IN EUROPE AND
SOUTHEAST ASIA

Chandra Lekha Sriram
PEACE AS GOVERNANCE
Power-Sharing, Armed Groups and Contemporary Peace Negotiations

Stephan Stetter
WORLD SOCIETY AND THE MIDDLE EAST
Reconstructions in Regional Politics

Rethinking Peace and Conflict Studies
Series Standing Order ISBN 978-1-4039-9575-9 (hardback) &
978-1-4039-9576-6 (paperback)

You can receive future titles in this series as they are published by placing a standing order. Please contact your bookseller or, in case of difficulty, write to us at the address below with your name and address, the title of the series and one of the ISBNs quoted above.

Customer Services Department, Macmillan Distribution Ltd, Houndmills, Basingstoke, Hampshire RG21 6XS, England

War and Peace in Islam

A Critique of Islamic/ist Political Discourses

S. M. Farid Mirbagheri
Dialogue Chair in Middle Eastern Studies
University of Nicosia, Cyprus

First published 2012 by
PALGRAVE MACMILLAN

Palgrave Macmillan in the UK is an imprint of Macmillan Publishers Limited,
registered in England, company number 785998, of Houndmills, Basingstoke,
Hampshire RG21 6XS.

Palgrave Macmillan in the US is a division of St Martin's Press LLC, 175
Fifth Avenue, New York, NY 10010.

Palgrave Macmillan is the global academic imprint of the above companies
and has companies and representatives throughout the world.

Palgrave® and Macmillan® are registered trademarks in the United
States, the United Kingdom, Europe and other countries

ISBN: 978–0–230–22061–4

This book is printed on paper suitable for recycling and made from fully
managed and sustained forest sources. Logging, pulping and manufacturing
processes are expected to conform to the environmental regulations of the
country of origin.

A catalogue record for this book is available from the British Library.

A catalog record for this book is available from the Library of Congress.

In the Name of the Author of Peace

From a whim springs their war and peace
On a caprice is based their honour and shame

Masanavi, Rumi
(Translation of calligraphy on the front cover)

Contents

Acknowledgements

The idea of producing this volume found concrete shape at the ISA meeting in Montreal, 2004, when my learned friend, Oliver Richmond, the series editor, suggested it to me. Encouraged by him and by another friend and scholar, Costas Constantinou, I began to search for and to organise the material I needed for the task. It was a monumental challenge for me, much greater than I had anticipated. The slow process gave rise to more questions in my mind than it produced answers. I took my time to bring together those elements of the discourses that I wanted to interact, in a context that could yield new understanding and new interpretations. I tried, but only the readers can judge if and to what extent I have succeeded.

This work owes much to many individuals and organisations, without whose generosity – financial, intellectual and personal – it would have been almost impossible to bring to fruition.

The A. G. Leventis Foundation, sponsor of the Dialogue Chair in Middle Eastern Studies at the University of Nicosia, which I hold, deserves profound thanks. Its financial contribution allowed me the space and time needed for this volume. I am indebted to it for life.

The work also owes much to Oliver Richmond and Costas Constantinou, whose comments throughout improved the quality of the book. They have reliably provided advice and have enthusiastically discussed issues pertaining to this volume. I am deeply grateful to them. Peter Loizos also ought to be thanked here for his encouraging and incisive comments on some parts of this work. I am also thankful to Mahmoud Monshipouri for his incisive and decisive comments in the very early stages of this work.

My parents in Iran must be mentioned here. My father has been a patient and reliable source, not only in offering advice and comments on many Islamic texts, but in pointing many of them out in the first place. His expertise was a convenient and trustworthy tool that facilitated much of the analysis offered here. My mother has been enthusiastic and encouraged me all along. I thank them both with all my heart.

Access to many texts was made possible by the untiring efforts of my sisters, particularly the youngest, Leyla, who either shipped them or actually brought them to Cyprus for me. She also helped in researching some of the material used for this work. I have hugely benefited from my parental family's unconditional support in this project for which I can never thank them enough.

Many colleagues, friends and scholars with whom I have communicated over various items relating to this work deserve to be thanked. They are too many to be mentioned by name but have my gratitude for their support and assistance.

I should like to thank the Library of the University of St Andrews, where the very first pages of this work were written. I spent several weeks there and found the library a rich and useful source for my work. Also, the electronic sources available at the University of Nicosia proved a convenient tool, particularly when quick references had to be made or some sources had to be double-checked. I extend my thanks to them also.

I would also like to thank my assistant, Marina Pavlova, for her organisation and the willingness to help whenever it was needed. Louise Carroll also offered her services in the very last stages of this work in helping the text to conform to the publisher's requirements. I am grateful to her for that.

Palgrave Macmillan deserve special thanks for their understanding, patience and professionalism. In particular, Liz Blackmore, Renee Takken, Julia Willan and Ellie Shillito, as commissioning editors, afforded me all the support I needed, whenever I needed it.

Last but not least, as always, my family, my wife Maria, my son Danial David and my daughter Ariana Michelle, should get the highest praise and the deepest thanks. Obviously works of this nature require space that cuts into family time. This case has been no exception. Patiently and generously they have given the time that has allowed the completion of this work.

Any mistakes, factual or otherwise, and any erroneous conclusions or interpretations in this work are mine alone.

Preface

The late twentieth century witnessed a rise in violent political behaviour by actors operating in the name of Islam. At times this violence pervaded intra-Islamic milieus and involved potent Islamic states. However, the most ostentatious advent of what can be referred to as Islamist fundamentalism occurred in New York and Washington on 11 September 2001. Coming in the aftermath of an Islamic anti-American revolution in Iran in 1979 and an acute hostage crisis in that country the next year, and followed by a series of bombings against Western targets, including the ones in Madrid and London, and other similar events after 11 September, the Western world has found itself in need of a better and deeper understanding of Islam.

In particular the concept of *jihad* has appeared instrumental to utilise, guide and understand the primary factors responsible for extremist behaviour among young radical Muslims. Yet despite an increasing volume of literature much has remained unsaid on the significance and the true meanings of this precept in Islamic teachings. This work is an attempt to outline some of the most fundamental questions relating to the subject of peace and conflict in Islam vis-à-vis the West and examine them in the light of current international developments and with an International Relations (IR) perspective. This will be attempted in the context of Gnosticism in Islam and critical theory in the West.

Conventional systemic paradigms in International Relations, it will be argued, have consistently overlooked the role and the significance of the individual. Gnosticism in Islam, however, promotes the inner development of each person as a prerequisite to external action towards change.

This work will borrow, apart from the Quran and the *hadith*, from the works of leading experts on Islam and critical theory in IR. In conclusion an attempt will be made to bring main points together in an assessment of the arguments made on *jihad*, relating them to the general perspective of war and peace in Islam vis-à-vis the West. It is very much that premise that may lie at the root of current debates in what may be referred to as the Renaissance of the Islamic world.

Introduction: Framework of Analysis and Setting the Questions

A scholarly assessment of Islamic discourses on peace and war in their varieties, and their contextualisation in time and place in relation to Western paradigms and theories, would serve more than just an academic purpose. Such a study could potentially expose the ineptitude of current Western thinking on Islam and Muslims on the one hand and illustrate the instrumentalisation of Islam by Islamist fundamentalists and many Muslim politicians on the other. The analogy of Islamic and Western philosophies, in the field of war and peace, reflects the need in our time to engage the two in a dialogical intellectual discourse. The advance of critical theory in International Relations opens up space for Islamic tradition to register, propound and interact with the prevalent Western outlook on peace and war. Through such an interaction the Islamic tradition can trade, inform and learn from Western discourses. The school of Gnosticism in Islam in particular may be able to contribute to debates on origins, management and resolution of conflicts engaging when necessary Islamic political philosophy vis-à-vis Western thinking in the field. Thus Hobbes, Locke and Marx, as well as contemporary IR theorists such as Walts, Huntington, Nye and Cox, can be discussed in relation to Avecina, Averose, Farabi, Ghazzali, Ibn Khaldun and others. This dyadic intellectual exchange is a prerequisite to building a solidarist international community, as outlined by Linklater, where dialogic interaction takes place.[1] A true effort towards eradication of the sociopolitical causes of major conflicts in our world would at the very least require a mutual cultural and intellectual exposure of Islam and the West to one another. This work is an attempt in that direction. It aims to critique both discourses, Islamic and Western, in

1

relation to one another and to peace and war. This dyadic exchange of views and vision will take place mainly within the frameworks of, but not limited to, critical theory in contemporary IR and Gnosticism in Islam.

It will not be the first time that Islam and the West engage in such an intellectual trade. In the past they both profited from this kind of exchange. Ancient Greek philosophy was translated and edited by Muslims during the reign of the Abbasids, and Islamic scholars worked on it assiduously. Later on, during and after the Crusades, Islamic works were used by Western philosophers and scientists. In that sense, therefore, both Islamic and Western discourses have already interacted and learned from one another.

The richness of Islamic and Western civilisations does not limit either of the discourses within the bounds of any single framework. Conflictual paradigms, including Huntington's civilisational outlook, may help explain partially certain global developments and trends, as did Communism for a period in the twentieth century. However, their input must be viewed only in contextual terms and any textualisation of their contribution ought to be seriously avoided. Neither critical theory nor Islamic Gnosticism claim to be writing a text, nor do they offer a mono-contextual analysis of the text. They appear as fluid understandings of humanity, its origins, its interaction with the environment and with one another, its agitation for more and better, its wars and its peace,[2] and the question of why we have stopped asking why; in the process they de-monopolise access to knowledge and understanding, opening up space for *the other* and 'non-Western' explanations of the world we live in. The state-centric system that sustains international relations now is a legacy of the seventeenth century in Europe, when European powers established the Westphalian framework to end the bitter religious wars that had ravaged their continent. It was therefore a system devised for a specific time, a specific geography and specific circumstances. There is no reason why that system should be viewed as the final and ultimate system of governance, everywhere, all the time. That pretence would represent ignorance blended, perhaps, with a touch of arrogance. If humanity has a historical existence and is capable of improving and developing itself and its environment, then change is an indispensable part of its discourse. Stagnating humanity within the bounds of a rigid system, impervious to change and improvement, is like clipping the wings of progress and closing the door to the advancement of humankind. Such a system is as indefensible as it is regressive. In short, if human beings can develop and improve, so should, inevitably, their environment and system of governance. In the realm of IR, Islamic Gnosticism and critical theory can provide new contexts for group formations and for political communities to operate.

Unlike conventional perception among Muslims that Gnosticism[3] in Islam is preoccupied with God–human relations only and is detached from temporal affairs altogether, the teachings of Master Sufis and their works inform us of the importance of wilful human intervention in society based on the divine precept of justice mediated through our interpretation. The most salient example is Hallaj, the renowned mystic of the tenth century, who was executed in a most brutal fashion by the Abbasid caliph. Although the public by and large believes he was killed for his mystic, esoteric and allegedly 'heretic' pronouncements – such as 'I am God'[4] – new research highlights the perceived threat he posed to the structures of sociopolitical power at the time as the reason for his execution.[5] Islamic Gnosticism is therefore a discourse that can attend to real-life concerns of people. That, it must be emphasised, is not the same as claiming to advance a new brand of 'mystic or Gnostic politics' in Islam just as fundamentalists have put forward their idea of a 'political Islam'. If Gnosticism concerns itself with temporality, it is because it sees itself in the position of being able to critique human-made constructs in its sociopolitical environment and not because it has a claim to any particular brand of politics; it does not seek to politicise mystic and/or Gnostic tendencies.

Muslim Gnostics engaged in their community and its affairs in a variety of ways. That is attested by the life of one of the leading Gnostics, Molavi of Iran,[6] otherwise known as Rumi, who contributed to the well-being of his community in non-politicised ways.[7] Therefore, even though many a Sufi these days would prefer detachment from worldly affairs as much as possible, viewing Islamic Gnosticism as spirituality indifferent to the material world is incorrect. The customary separation from the material world in Sufism could be partially explained by the Mongolian invasion of Iran, where in the wake of their continued and systematic massacres, Iranians, unable to effect any change in their tragic plight, sought refuge in de-temporalised mystic tendencies that could perceivably provide them with some degree of spiritual comfort. The subsequent reign of the Safavid Empire in Iran and its fascination with this particular interpretation of mysticism firmed up its roots among many Iranians. The popularisation of Gnosticism in the context of Iranian history may thus have caused much distortion, which shall be alluded to later in this work. However, as the ultimate role model of Muslim Gnostics, the Prophet himself was as much engaged with temporal affairs as he was with spiritual ones. Dismissing Gnosticism, therefore, as a discourse completely detached from, unimpressed by, and indifferent to worldly affairs can be inaccurate and misleading. And in any event, even if the disengaging aspects of Gnosticism have prevailed in the contemporary era, it would be beneficial to all if this mystic spiritualism was re-engaged in human affairs.

As opposed to the Gnostic school in Islam, jurisprudential Islam, the bedrock of fundamentalism in the faith, where priority is given to *shari'a* (legal codes of Islam), places a human's duties before his/her rights. This stands in stark contrast to the West, where rights precede duties. The prescribed mastery of human beings over their affairs in the West and the ineffable command of God over concerns of humanity in Islam are taken as one of the major differences between the two. The precepts of individualism, rationalism, liberalism and secularism, the foundational pillars of the Western outlook, are anathema to a Muslim fundamentalist's view of earthly living. These significant differences between the two schools have been cited as partial causes of the violence that has tended to increase between them in the past decades. An instance of this difference in the contemporary period will be alluded to in Chapter 5.

Though surprising to some, Islamist fundamentalism and realism and/or neo-realism, the prevalent Western political doctrines in IR, have more in common than initially meets the eye. Two points are particularly noted here. First, they are both preoccupied with hard power and its primary role in human affairs. This has been noted in almost every country where Islamist fundamentalists are in power. One of their first tasks is the violent subjugation of their opponents in the country (and even outside their territorial borders) and those who may perceivably threaten their hold on power. The discourse of rationality in realism and neo-realism appears also to subscribe to power in a similar fashion. It was only the advent of liberalism that somewhat

critiqued realism's preoccupation with hard power (through emphasising the soft power of ideas and people) and managed to relatively
push it back outside the sphere of human rights, albeit only within
the borders of the democratic state; nevertheless attaining and maintaining hard power are indispensable aspects of those schools.

Secondly, both Islamist fundamentalism and realist doctrines
assume a universal mantle of leadership offering universal explanations for all of history. They often tend to offer polarised perspectives
of the contemporary world and world history to their followers. The
terms *mostaz'af* (the poor) and *mostakber* (the arrogant) used often by
the late Ayatollah Khomeini, for instance, or *mo'men* (the believer)
and *kafir* (the pagan) used among fundamentalists, indicate polarised views just as terms like 'free world' and 'evil empire' have done
in the West. The term 'West versus the rest' in today's civilisational
discourse may also represent the same syndrome.

International Relations[8] was established in the aftermath of World
War I with a liberalist drive and in an attempt to protect humanity
from the scourge of war. The ravages and the carnage of the Great War
had clearly highlighted the need for a different approach to international life to avert or contain armed conflict. Peace, therefore, has
been the ultimate aim of IR. All paradigms in the discipline appear
to focus the thrust of their argument on the question of conflict
in human community. Political theory also addresses and analyses
conflict as a core topic. Hobbes, Kant, Marx and others wrote on
the causes of violence in human relations and how war could be
avoided. However, the approach of Western powers today to conflict
has thus far concerned the removal or containment of the symptoms
of war rather than attending to its root causes. Poverty, discrimination, unequal distribution of wealth and the ideologisation of
religion stand in the forefront of today's main causes of conflict in
the world. Focusing on the symptoms alone, while overlooking the
deeper causes of war, is unlikely to lead to a durable peace.

Liberalism per se cannot withstand the tidal wave of frustration
and anger of the impoverished and the underprivileged in the world
as long as the prime motive of foreign policy formulation continues
to be the pursuit of national interests at the expense of international
ones. A liberal approach would have to apply in the sphere of international relations first before a direct and definite linkage between
liberalism and international peace could be established. The two are

not detached from one another and are in fact interdependent. What we are witnessing at the moment in the West are liberal societies practicing liberal doctrine domestically but applying realist policies outside their borders (liberal France, for example, killed hundreds of thousands of Algerians only because they also sought liberty). In a fast-globalising world, interdependence between the local and the global is more so than in the past. Liberal peace, therefore, could be boosted with parallel efforts to convert the local and the global simultaneously. A realist international system cannot support, sustain, or encourage a liberal foreign policy. It would be a contradiction in terms. The very nature of the state-centric international structure and its inefficacy as regards peace and the demands of today's international life are central to this debate.

Since the time of the Renaissance in Europe and the advance of rationality in human affairs there, two world wars have been started by Europeans. That raises the question of how in an era of rationality such a degree of carnage and misery could be inflicted by humans on humans, particularly on a continent where people have championed the cause of rationality in our time. Does that tell us anything about rationality? Is rationality not compatible with peace? It may be observed that rationality, though necessary, is not a sufficient condition for the prosperous management of worldly affairs. There is perhaps a need for inclusion of other elements, hitherto absent, in relations among communities. Islamic Gnosticism may be able to contribute to this debate via its 'self-negating' teachings, whereby individual self-seeking approaches give way to more holistic outlooks. As pronounced by Molavi,

> *Wondrous and wandering is love, nay rationale*
> *Goes only after self-interest wisdom, ay so banal.*[9]

Holistic outlook

The fledgling field of ecosophy calls for a holistic approach to address the question of environment in an era when local solutions can no longer remedy the situation.[10] Nowadays, other problems facing humanity, such as crime and terrorism, also acknowledge not just the benefit but the necessity of adopting a cosmopolitan approach. The pedantic rationality of seeking the local and the limited has now proven to be insufficient and in fact futile. In the realm of politics the application of pedanticism also has left a world divided along inter alia ethnic and economic lines. The majority of humanity does not share the benefits of globalisation and the advent of the global village has only reduced the gap in awareness between the rich and the poor. The poor now know what they are missing and the North more than ever is confronted with a potentially explosive South where the inequalities of opportunity, wealth and power threaten to dislocate the current political coordinates that make up the status quo. There is a serious need for introducing a holistic rationality.

The relative nature of rationality is axiomatic. The rational choice theory focuses mainly on what Herbert Simon calls 'bounded rationality' and not 'optimum rationality'.[11] Neville Chamberlain viewed his appeasement policy to be a rational choice only to be proven wrong a few years later. History abounds in instances where pedantic rationality has failed to secure long-term interests pursued by decision-makers. It is pedantic rationality that seeks and sustains an exclusion-based system, where interests find a mutually exclusive quality and one's rise may be achieved at the cost of *the other*'s demise, that is, pursuit of national interests defined in terms of power. Critical theory has now justifiably launched a serious challenge to conventional paradigms, clearly demonstrating the relevance and significance of normative approaches, where humanity as a whole is treated as a unit and not studied as a fragmented, disfigured and divided entity.[12]

The question of holistic rationality is one which is now seriously considered and addressed. The long-term interests of all are now seen to be in the interest of the individual also. A pedantic approach overlooking the global outlook and neglecting the holistic framework can be only of shortterm and limited benefit at best. At worst it can backfire into a dangerous discourse threatening world peace and security. Whether in relation to the environment, crime, terrorism, or migration, collectivism and not individualism seems to be the order of the day. The theory of chaos appears to have found more tangible edges in the early part of the twenty-first century.

Structure of the book

Islam is accused by some in the West of having spread the word by the sword.[13] The wars waged in the early years of Islam have been cited as evidence for this claim. Today, groups of Muslims who encourage, support and commit violence against who and what they consider enemies of their faith appear to add some weight to those claims. This work is an attempt to analyse the concepts of war and peace in Islam in relation to Western paradigms and assess the narratives of armed conflict in that religion. Although this is not virgin territory,[14] a study by someone who does not feel rigidly bound by either the East or the West, but is impressed by and interested in both, may contribute to the debate.

In this endeavour we shall set out to examine *jihad*; *jihad* is a religious term that represents a belief in purity and justice and in humanity's effort to achieve those goals. However, in the real world of politics, this term has been abused to promote and justify violence waged for temporal gains or carried out with political motives in mind. *Jihad* as a religious precept aiming for the reconstruction of humanity and society based on piety has been instrumentalised by many for purely political ends. Efforts at politicising *jihad* have usually been driven by temporal factors and often emanate from political sources. In attempting to assess and examine *jihad*, the following questions will be addressed: (a) What is the meaning of *jihad*? (b) Under what condition/s does Islam prescribe and proscribe armed conflict? (c) How important and significant is peace in Islam? (d) How can true peace be achieved through Islamic teachings?

At the outset it ought to be noted that Islam at times in this work may appear to be viewed and even assessed in Western terms. Of course that does not in any shape or form imply ownership of the analysis by the West, but rather an attempt to interact traditions and analyse them in a dyadic manner in order to yield a more accessible understanding for the reader. Equally, Western tradition may be seen in places to have been studied through an Islamic prism for the same effect.

The first task concerns the very interpretation of the faith itself. Our outlook on religion can very much determine the way we interpret and understand religion. Religion has meant different things to different people throughout history. Islam is no exception. The Sufis, for instance, have emphasised the significance of an individual relationship with God, through which spiritual elevation can be achieved and salvation attained.[15] However, in the clerical and 'official'/legal versions of Islam, there is a conspicuous dearth of any consequential reference to this aspect and there is instead heavy reliance on the social and collective facets of life.[16] The two stand almost opposite to one another. Similarly, Muslim philosophers have tended to over-look certain legal aspects of the faith in favour of greater breadth and depth of understanding.[17] Most interestingly, however, of late a new generation of Islamic thinkers, such as Abdolkarim Soroush and Asghar Ali Engineer, have offered novel interpretations of Islam, which defy the traditional scholastic reading of the text by the *ulema*, the religious scholars, in the seminaries. In this regard certain sets of questions deal with the very essence of religion itself and present epistemological and revolutionary challenges to religious traditions; they include: What do we mean by Islam itself? Is Islam a set of rituals and a collection of dos and don'ts unimpressed by social and political developments and devoid of historicity? Is jurisprudence the only outlet to Islam or are there other outlets such as Gnosticism and philosophy? Is Islam for humanity or humanity for Islam? Is a human entitled to rights or do his/her duties precede and overshadow his/her rights? Does Islam preoccupy itself with God–human relations or human–human relations? How does Islam deal with plurality in the world? Is the monopoly of interpretation by religious jurists the will of God? Is secularism unholy in Islam? Is 'the unholy' to be dispensed with in politics, that is, rational government? What is the definition of 'holy' in Islam? Is interpretation of the text the same as the text itself? Can reason, in the absence of direct communication with the Almighty, be counted upon as a source of decision-making for Muslim politicians? Part of the first chapter deals with this trend and such questions.

Also, a narrative outlining the discourse of Islamic revivalism leading in part to fundamentalism and in part to re-interpretation will form part of the opening chapter. From Abdul-Wahab in Arabia to Afghani in Iran to Mohammad Iqbal in Pakistan to Hassan al-Banna, Mohammad Abduh and Seyyed Qutb in Egypt, to Shari'ati and Khomeini in Iran,[18] an attempt shall be made to follow the path of religious discourse, its fluctuations, tours and detours, peaks and plunges across the Islamic world.

In Chapter 2 some epistemological and philosophical overlapping between Islamic Gnosticism and critical theory in IR is discussed. In addition, some observations are made with regard to claims by Islamic/ist groups into the nature of politics and governance. The quintessential element for change, the individual, is propounded here through the prism of Gnosticism; an individual, who can ascend beyond him/herself, past the dictates of the state or the directives of jurisprudence, in order to rediscover and reconstruct him/herself and his/her society, not based on self-interest but inspired by love and care for others.

Chapter 3 deals with the broad question of the definition of the terms 'war' and 'peace' both in Islamic and Western discourses and attempts to identify the constituent elements of each term. Thereafter it will aim to outline the views of Muslim thinkers on hermeneutics and the universalist claims of Islam in relation to that of the West. There is an incompatibility between the two which requires an analysis of the religious doctrine. It will be shown that the very definition of the term *jihad* can very much depend on the battle of hermeneutics and universalism in the religion. The military aspects of the concept of *jihad*, it will be explained, have been over-emphasised and taken out of context. The doctrine of martyrdom, 'kill if you can and get killed if you cannot',[19] believed by the fundamentalists to be the essence of a holy struggle, does in fact stand opposed to the views of many leading Islamic scholars. Many senior traditional clerical figures openly opposed armed struggle against ruling governments.[20] Peace, *solh* in Arabic,[21] as a precept and ideal in Islam has been overlooked by militants, whose exasperated frustrations may have led them to believe that war is a recipe for justice. In fact the level and the nature of violent acts committed nowadays by adherents of fundamentalist Islam lends weight to claims that they now pursue violence for its own sake.[22] Otherwise, and in the absence of a clear agenda, one is hard pressed to find any justification for the senseless killings of innocent people. Suicide bombing in itself is an act that does not receive the support of the vast majority of religious leaders.[23] Political Islam seems to have turned into a doctrine seeking political goals through violence and interpreting Islam in a way that suits the politics of aggression.[24] Some of the questions dealt with in this chapter are: are war and peace essentially legal matters for Islam or are they more political? Can peace be a sacred aim in itself? If so, can there be a wrong or an unholy peace in Islam? When and how does a war turn holy? Under what circumstances can aggression against non-Muslims be justified? What are the ultimate goals of war and peace in Islam?

The following chapter begins by probing for a robust and comprehensive definition of the term *jihad*, one that does not overlook the greater *jihad*: one's struggle within to overcome selfishness and greed and to seek piety. Here the Machiavellian concept of power is particularly significant since *jihad* first and foremost requires working to triumph over arrogance and over the desire to dominate others. The Gnostic aspects of *jihad*, the greater struggle, stand loftier than its external or jurisprudential aspects:, the lesser struggle. It is by the construction of a less self-centred human and the promotion of selflessness among people that *jihad* aims to pursue justice in the human community. Committing oneself to temporal aspects of *jihad*, without first having gone through its spiritual dimensions, can be viewed as an anomaly and may lead to undesired consequences. There may of course be instances, anywhere in the world, where resorting to arms is the only way to establish peace and justice. The war against Nazi Germany is a good illustration of that point. There is also in the Islamic faith the question of using violence when violated by others and when no peaceful action can perceivably defend the lives and dignity of the faithful. There are rules of engagement according to the doctrine, the most prominent of which strictly forbids the killing of innocent people.[25] It will be suggested, however, that the real *jihad* nowadays may in fact require adherents of the faith to engage in serious efforts to overcome obstacles to their progress. 'The progress of any religion depends on the progress of its followers', said Ali Shari'ati some 40 years ago;[26] if he is to be believed, the plight of Muslims these days can barely do their faith any justice. There are few, if any, Muslim countries in our world that have successfully met the challenges of modernity and embraced a democratic sociopolitical life. A real *jihad*, therefore, may have to do more with learning and understanding fundamentals of progress in the twenty-first century and applying modern and advanced principles of governance, support for individual and social freedoms, adopting new technology and promoting science, all within the framework of justice. That is a true *jihad* for a Muslim in today's world.

Moving on, in the final chapter, the book turns to two contemporary cases of conflict, real and potential, in the Islamic world. Iran and Iraq, both ridden with formidable challenges, are examined in terms of factors that can help explain their plight. To start with Iraq, an approach based on political philosophy will aim to analyse difficulties faced by the United States in establishing peace and stability there. It will be argued that the Western-liberal discourse rests on certain pillars that may not have been present in Iraq and any attempt, therefore, to impose a Western-style democracy would perceivably face stern resistance. In the case of Iran, after the revolution of 1978–9, both internal and external challenges will be studied separately. The struggle of internal forces to open up the political life and the concerns of outside powers to counter the Iranian government's moves towards nuclearisation will form part of this chapter.

In the Conclusion the point will be made again that our view of religion in general and how big a role we believe it should play in our lives can also determine our approach to whether or not armed conflict may be sanctioned (or disallowed as the case may be) by religious interpretation. The epistemology of religion and religious science plays a pivotal role here. And perhaps understandably many an old traditional Muslim and cleric will find any challenge to customary religious learning uncomfortable and in extreme cases even blasphemous. This, in the main, it will be stated, stems from political and not religious factors, for any challenge may weaken the grip of clerical establishment on people throughout the Muslim world and that in itself would be an unwelcome development for some. However, the global Muslim community is in dire need of rethinking and is desperately searching for new interpretations of the faith whereby it can successfully adjust to the needs of the modern world without feeling a threat to its identity or meaning. Muslims worldwide are gradually allowing themselves to think the unthinkable. Islamic fundamentalism and its armed struggle against change may be the last obstacle to be overcome in this *jihad*.

One point needs to be reiterated here. At times both Islamists and Western discourses are examined in the light of one another's approaches to humanity and our sociopolitical environment. This should not be viewed as reflecting an axiological orientation of this work. Rather it is an attempt to further open up the debate on Islamist discourses. This emanates from a belief in the utility of interaction in intellectual terrain. Another point to be made relates to the citations from the Quran and *hadith* (sayings of the Prophet) where no particular source for translations has been adopted. Usually a blend of translations has been used to best convey the meaning as understood by the author. There are also numerous references to the Iranian Master Sufi and mystic Jalla-eddin-Rumi (known as Molavi in Iran). The translations of the Quran and Rumi used here do not come from one source alone. A variety of sources have been used and Rumi's translation is particularly influenced by Reynold A. Nicholson's work.[27] If the entire translation is depicted word for word then the source is mentioned in the endnotes. Otherwise the author's blend of various translations, or his own translation, have been adopted.

The significance of Rumi's teachings can hardly be exaggerated as both Muslims and non-Muslims have attested to the importance of his holistic and spiritual wisdom. The following, by the great scholar, mystic and poet of the fifteenth century, Jami, on Rumi and his work, *Masnavi*, illustrates the point:

> *That figure, in the spiritual world, so unique*
> *Has Masnavi as the proof for those who seek,*
> *What shall I say on His Excellency, so grand*
> *Is not a prophet but has a book in hand.*

1
Islamic Discourses: Definitions and Background

To talk of Islam as a monolithic religion with a uniform standard of behaviour throughout, is, to put it mildly, a fallacy.[1] At best it is a misleading proposition overlooking the vast variety of cultures in which Islamic tradition and Muslims have developed throughout history and at worst it is a dangerous assumption risking misunderstanding, misperception and conflict at a local or wider level. Islam, like any other religion, has its varieties expressed through different sects, cultures and interpretations. Any individual or group claiming otherwise has a somewhat shallow or misguided understanding of this faith.

That having been said, the task remains nevertheless of defining what we could term as Islamic, non-Islamic, un-Islamic, or anti-Islamic. To do so we require inevitably a very basic agreement on the essentials of the faith that would apply equally to all divisions within Islam and could provide us with a yardstick to assess and analyse claims made in the name of the religion. Traditionally this would be the task of theologians or religious jurists. This work, however, does not concern itself with either of those. Instead it aims to view Islam through an epistemological prism and assess the approach of Islamic discourses on what we would nowadays consider essential ingredients of humanity. Precepts such as freedom, democracy and human rights have a central position in today's political discourses and an attempt should be made to clarify the position of the last Abrahamic tradition on the authenticity, centrality and applicability of these concepts in human ontology. Without this fundamental appraisal, everything else would only scratch the surface

14

and lack an infra-structural basis upon which arguments could be advanced.

Religion for humankind or humankind for religion

Islam believes in the creation of humankind more or less as described in the Old Testament. The question of prophecy and the philosophical underpinnings of Messengers, outlined in all Abrahamic books, lead to one inevitable conclusion: religion was God-sent to help humanity find the right path, that is, prosperity on earth and salvation hereafter.[2] It is therefore a means to an end and not an end in itself. Islam is no exception. The chronology of creation attests to that. Humans were created and placed in Paradise first and only after their descent to earth did religions come to guide them. They were not created for religion but rather the other way round. Religious sciences such as theology, jurisprudence, exegesis and others are also there to serve humankind.

The ineluctable conclusion from the above is that we can assess the utility of our understanding of religion in terms of its benefits for humanity. Since religion, including Islam, has come to serve and save humankind (and not to serve or save God, who needs neither) we must be prepared to engage in critiquing and re-evaluating our understanding of the text to the benefit of humanity. The spirit of Islam, as a religion, guiding humanity to the right path would not be affected by humanity's inability to understand it properly, that is, Islam is different from any understanding or interpretation of Islam. Whereas Islam is holy, sacrosanct, unchanging and unquestionable, understanding of Islam by humankind is not holy, not sacrosanct, alterable and questionable. This particular point has been deftly dealt with by Soroush in his Theoretical Contraction and Expansion of *shari'a*.[3] Confusing or infusing the two has been the cause of many misguided attempts by Islamic thinkers in the past to try to outline the Islamic response to world developments.

1.1   A question of definition: what is Islam?

When in 610 A.D. Muhammad experienced his first vision few could have predicted his message would form the foundation of a new religion that was to change the course of history. Still less hardly anyone could have foreseen, as recently as only a century ago, that some of his followers would ardently sacrifice their lives and kill innocent others in the belief that they were obeying the command of God. The message of hate and destruction, so feverishly sent out by groups claiming to operate in the name of and for Islam, is now unfortunately associated with the faith, regardless of the fact that the great majority of Muslims have nothing to do with them or that Muslim leaders have in fact condemned such violent and barbaric acts.[4]

There are two main sects in Islam: *Sunni* and *Shi'a*. The Sunnis comprise some 85 per cent of Muslims and all Muslim countries but two subscribe to this sect.[5] Sunnis are divided into four smaller sects: Shafe'i, Hanbali, Hanafi and Maliki. These four groupings are in turn divided into smaller sub-sects. Shi'as, on the other hand, are a minority of 15 per cent among Muslims and are concentrated mainly in Iran, Iraq, Bahrain and Pakistan. They are also divided into smaller groupings. All in all there are over 70 sectarian divisions in Islam.[6] The split, however, between the two main sects, Shi'a and Sunni, was formalised in 1501 when Shah Ismael I established the Safavid Dynasty in Persia and declared Shi'ism as the official religion of the state. Though relations between the two main sects were never easy, it was after 1501 that several military conflicts, rooted in these sectarian divisions, took place between the Shi'a Persia and the Sunni Ottomans.

The main difference between Sunnis and Shi'as goes back to the immediate aftermath of the Prophet's death. For Sunnis the four successive rulers of Muslims after Muhammad, the Rightly Guided Caliphs, Abubakr, Omar, Othman and Ali were all pious men and assumed the leadership of the community in the right order and in a proper manner. The Shi'as, however, dispute that and believe Ali, the fourth successor and the cousin and the son-in-law of Muhammad, should have succeeded the Prophet immediately upon his death. The three intervening caliphs therefore, Shi'as believe, usurped the leadership of the community by depriving Ali of guiding the Muslim community. The division runs deep to the extent that some Muslims, including some Wahhabis in Saudi Arabia and the deposed Taliban in Afghanistan, consider Shi'ism heresy and view Shi'as as infidels.[7]

At the outset it has to be noted that the most important means of influencing followers in Islam is what is referred to as *shari'a*, or religious law. These laws are codified in the religious science of jurisprudence, which provides the followers with a comprehensive list of dos and don'ts. Adherence to a number of them, like *hijab*, the covering by women of their hair and their body, or growing beards by men, can easily be judged by the public. A great number of them, however, relate to the private sphere of life, ranging from ablution after sexual intercourse to dietary regimes.[8] *Shari'a* emerged some two hundred years after the death of the Prophet.[9] As such its validity has now come under scrutiny by certain groups of Islamic thinkers, which shall be alluded to below.

In order to help clarify some of the confusion regarding Islam and its widely varying strands, we have identified three different approaches to the religion which, though not clear-cut and absolute, can nevertheless aid us in a better understanding of what is considered to be Islam. They are what I have termed *establishment Islam* or *institutionalised Islam, political Islam* (a widely used term) and *liberalist Islam*.

The first approach, *establishment Islam*, shares some characteristics with ordered hierarchies of Christianity and Judaism. First and foremost among these is the presence of an official clerical establishment claiming to be the guardian of people's faith and understanding of the true meaning of religion. Whether called rabbis, bishops, or ayatollahs and sheikhs, this class of people performs specific roles and functions in society that have now become indispensable to the institution of religion. They represent obedience to the Divine, presenting a role model for others to follow and as such claim a sanctified status unique to their own class.

In Islam this institution emerged sometime after the death of the Prophet of Islam.[10] The Abbasid Dynasty who, like the Ummayids before them, had changed the practice of early rulers in Islam from *Ijma'*[11] to hereditary rule, sought to secure legitimacy for their privileged position.[12] To this end many Muslim caliphs promoted the emergence of a class of learned religious scholars, closely connected to the court, who in return for privileges granted to them would publicly support the rulers by offering their religious blessing to the government.[13] In consequence the concepts of religiosity and power became entangled in Islam.[14] The word caliph,[15] the subject noun of *caliphate*, used for Muslim rulers after Muhammad, indicates religious representation in the form of a single ruler to whom allegiance must be owed by all Muslims.

The rule of the Abbasids was ended by the Mongolians to be followed by the Ottomans and despite periodic weakening of the centre in the Islamic world, the religious authority of the institution of *caliphate* was never abolished; it lived a long life and was only dissolved after the collapse of the Ottoman Empire in the aftermath of World War I.

Another shared attribute of *establishment Islam* with Abrahamic traditions is the assumption of similar functions by *ulema* (Islamic clerics) in Islam in relation to their counterparts in Christianity and Judaism. Marriages and funerals were conducted by them, religious festivals included a central role for their participation, access to the supernatural became their exclusive domain, close contact with rulers and legitimation of political power underlined their strong social presence, morality fell very much within their almost exclusive area of competence and interpretation of God's commands became their most prominent task. These roles and functions paved the ground for a systematic and all-pervasive influence, if not outright control, of the populace by the official custodians of religion.

Thirdly, institionalised Islam promoted a set of rituals as is practised in the other Abrahamic traditions. In that sense, a Muslim is as obedient to God as he is prepared to display through performing clergy-prescribed rituals in public. Religious festivals are occasions where the sincerity of the followers of the faith to their God and their religion can be measured. Like attending church or synagogue, visiting the mosque is an important yardstick by which to judge the religiosity of individuals. Other public displays of the faith are also thought to be significant in acquiring social status and religious legitimacy for one's deeds. The key to Paradise, in the satirical words of Ali Shari'ati, is to be found for the mass followers of establishment Islam amid the litany of rituals whose meaning and significance (or meaninglessness or insignificance as the case may be) may never be explicated or sought by those who instruct or perform them.[16] This approach provides a doctrine ridden with rituals, which permeates and penetrates almost every aspect of life rendering the Islamic faith more challenging than most other religions.[17]

Fourthly, the class of religious leaders in Islam, as in Christianity and Judaism, have viewed the interests of the faith and the faithful reflected in their own.[18] Since they are the 'true' guardians of the religion, as perceived by them and their followers, it is only right to pursue their own interests. The social foundations on which the interests of the clergy have been based relies on observance of rituals by the public codified by jurisprudence. As stated above, this observance indicates one's devotion to the Almighty and allows the clerical leaders to intervene at every level of social strata and in every aspect of life to ensure true adherence to the word of God: a socio-political influence that emanates from the supernatural but is effective in temporal affairs. Such an instance was the boycott of tobacco decreed by Mirza Hasan Shirazi, the religious leader of the Shi'as, including Iranians, in a nineteenth-century edict, whereby Iranians refused to buy tobacco, causing the reversal of a major economic/political decision by the government.[19]

Lastly, and perhaps most importantly, the question of religious interpretation in establishment Islam falls exclusively into the hands of the religious *ulema*, so much so that anyone outside the clerical hierarchy is either to follow the opinion of the established *ulema* or risk being excommunicated by the religious authorities for any novel interpretation of Islam. The experience of the Middle Ages in Europe, when the Church ruled by decree and the clergy assumed the role of interpreter and executioner of Divine Will, whereby Galileo was put on trial and others made to suffer similar if not worse fate, has now to varying degrees befallen the wide spectrum of Muslim societies where *establishment Islam* pervades. A clear example of this was Ali Sharia'ti, whose radical but novel interpretation of all aspects of religion and in particular Shi'ism led to his being castigated by the clergy in Iran. In the pre-revolutionary Iran of the 1970s Shari'ati found a receptive audience particularly among the young students, whose political goals and aspirations had produced a gap between them and religion. Consequently communism and socialist ideas had gained ground and traditional religious sermons were left for the laity, whose religious ambition centred around life after death and had very little to do with the lot of their fellow human beings on earth. Today Abdolkarim Soroush, Asghar Ali Engineer and others are also engaging in novel interpretations, thereby threatening the exclusive hold of *ulema* on the subject. This will be discussed further in the following pages.

There is, however, one major difference between ecclesiastical establishments in Christianity and Islam. The former has traditionally boasted an ordered and organised hierarchy holding political power at its peak. The complicated organisational development of Christendom, together with the political authority of the pope, was not, however, shared in Islamic historical experience.[20] Though the caliph had the last word on all matters relating to politics as well as religious concerns, there was nevertheless a distinction between him and the group of *ulema*, religious experts. Thus a cleavage of sort had from early days of Islam existed between Islamic and political authority. This despite the fact that legitimation of power, as explained above, had become the task of religion and religious scholars.

To sum up, the main traits of *establishment Islam* can be stated to comprise traditionalism, adherence to jurisprudence and a belief in the ahistoricity of *shari'a*, whereby religious law is immune to socio-political developments and evolution. Separation from politics is also accepted in this approach. The likes of the late Sheikh Shaltut of Al-Azhar in Egypt and the late Grand Ayatollah Boroujerdi in Iran are prime examples.[21] In that regard there is no desire by and large on the part of institutionalised Islam to change the temporal status quo. Pursuing spiritual matters and providing religious services and support for their followers within the accepted bounds of the political environment is considered to be a legitimate and sometimes *the* legitimate religious duty. Violence, in this doctrine, in the pursuit of power by religious authorities, though desired and at times practiced by a few, is generally discouraged and in fact forbidden by many. One instance relates to the tobacco ban edict in Iran by Mirza Hassan Shirazi referred to earlier. When told that as a result of his edict and people's emotions one person had actually been killed in the demonstrations, he is reported to have said that if he thought there was a remote chance of even a nosebleed by someone in consequence of his edict, he would not have issued it in the first place.[22]

The second approach, *political Islam*, has of late been the one that has attracted global attention. The radical tendencies inherent in this interpretation of the faith are thought to be responsible for the promotion of the phenomena commonly referred to as Islamic fundamentalism and Islamist terrorism, the latter allegedly being fed and reinforced by the former. There is much that has been said about this particular politicised version of Islam, yet much has remained unsaid. An attempt shall be made to outline the main traits of this approach to Islam and its various aspects will be discussed throughout the book.

There are essentially two different groups that come to mind when *political Islam* is discussed. Unfortunately the distinction between these two groups is sometimes blurred and somewhat confused. The first group is the Islamic revivalists and the second what I would term Islamist reactionaries.[23] The first group, in the contemporary period, can be traced back to Abdul-Wahhab in Saudi Arabia over two centuries ago, continuing with Asad-Abadi in Iran a hundred years later, as well as Hassan-al-Banna in Egypt, Mohammad Iqbal in Pakistan and Ali Shari'ati in Iran in the twentieth Century.[24] There have of course been others who may not have had any international exposure. Motahhari in Iran is a prime example, whose unfamiliarity with Western languages and lack of travelling may have contributed to his not having gained due international recognition.[25]

The revivalists' discourse emanated from the perceived adverse socio-political environment of their time, both globally and locally, and their firm belief that a return to true Islam would lead to a redistribution of wealth and power in the world and restore Muslim pride and glory. It was perhaps European colonialism that kick-started the revivalist process.[26] As the benefits of technological advances in the West became more tangible and the lot of Muslims deteriorated in comparison, the influence of the rising powers of the West in the increasingly powerless Islamic world began to leave an air of humiliation and despondency that manifested itself in calls for a return to the glorious past. This was deemed a just cause as overt, organised, cruel and successful military campaigns of the West, facilitated by a superior technology, and not its intellectual rigour, led to the gradual submission of what was once a dominant Islamic Empire.[27] The military aspect, according to some, was a significant factor contributing to the decline of Muslim countries. The contemporary Iranian Muslim revivalist, Ali Shari'ati, despite his dislike for the Ottoman Empire, conceded that the defeat of the Ottomans had left the Muslims at the mercy of the West.[28] And of course if glory is lost through military defeat it can be won back through military victory.

However the revivalists were not emphasising the military aspect. In fact their emphasis was more intellectual in nature: to avert the *westoxification* of Muslims and to promote a return to pure and undiluted Islamic values that they believed would rescue Muslims from their plight (a politically subjugated, economically poorer and technologically backward status compared to the West) and allow a re-emergence of true Islam, where Muslims would once again find their true selves and restore the glory of the past. Aware of the allure of Western progress in all fields of science and social science[29] and the consequent rush of Muslim youth to the West, however, concerned the revivalist camp. They feared an extension, both horizontally and vertically, of Western influence on the younger generations of Islamic world through Western-style education that they believed had been tailored to meet the interests of colonialism and imperialism.[30] This challenge, rather than animosity to the West, ran so deep as to cause Iqbal, a leading Muslim philosopher of early-twentieth century, to renounce the influence of ancient Greek philosophers such as Aristotle in Islamic philosophy, an aspect which has always been comfortably acknowledged by Islamic thinkers and seminarians in *establishment Islam*.[31] Equally Shari'ati was adamantly against any Western influence in Islamic societies. He expounded on the concepts of civilisation and modernity, distinguishing the two from one another. In his view the capitalist West had introduced modernity as civility to the Third World, reducing civilisation to consumerism, that is, to be civilised was to be modern and to be modern was to consume new and modern products.

The intellectual aspect of Western influence was also, in fact more so, focused on and attacked, with a zeal that was perhaps more reminiscent of a Cold War warrior than that normally associated with leading intellectual thinkers. Iqbal quoted a passage from the introduction to *The Wretched of the Earth* by Frantz Fanon in which the late French existentialist philosopher Jean-Paul Sartre describes how young students from the Third World, residing in Western cities, were so easily assimilated to Western ways and turned into loudspeakers for the West once they returned to their countries of origin.[32]

Therefore the revivalist camp was primarily concerned with an intellectual counterattack against what they considered the *westoxication* phenomenon in Islamic societies. They did preach *political Islam* and to varying degrees promoted an activist approach in their local settings. Politically they tended to define themselves as anti-Western, sometimes even bordering on socialism. This in turn greatly worried *establishment Islam*, whose main concern had more to do with countering socialist and communist tendencies. Also, the reality of non-clerical figures attempting to preach to people novel religious interpretations meant that cracks in the monopoly of religious understanding by *institutionalised Islam* had appeared. The group of *ulema* were not entirely happy about that either.

Ideological rigour was a prominent feature of revivalist Islam. By stirring passion among the youth, revivalist leaders focused minds on the centrality of Islamic doctrine and the importance of ideologising religion. This in turn meant that the revivalist discourse deprived itself of an enlightening interactive process of self-critique and learning. At best it offered its followers a mandate for deconstruction with no recipe for the necessary reconstruction that would have to follow. Though violence was not preached, violent political protestation by their followers was not condemned outright by their leaders either.

The second group, Islamist reactionaries, are the ones whose violent behaviour has nowadays concerned political leaders throughout the world. They comprise groups who believe that the use of force and the killing of the innocent is justified to advance the cause they stand for. Al-Qaida is the most widely known organisation that belongs to this group of Islamists. The agenda of this group is unclear to many yet it seems to surpass geographical boundaries; the subject matter of their message appears to be based on strong anti-Americanism coupled with a universal declaration to engage Muslims in violent battle with those not sharing their views.

This group does not limit its operation to state boundaries; in fact it tends to reject a state-centric world, at least as far as Muslims are concerned. It is a desperate craving for the Muslim caliph reminiscent of the early days of Islam, united only under the banner of a common faith. The attack on the United States on 11 September 2001 was the single bloodiest act of violence yet carried out by this group. The agenda of the Islamist reactionaries, whatever that may turn out to be, appears to be carried out, given the chance, with little regard to human lives or other concerns.

Though the beginning of this trend may be marked with the Islamic revolution in Iran, what solidified the jihadists' call for holy war against the United States started in Afghanistan during the Soviet occupation era. It was there and then that American policymakers tried to combat the Soviet invasion by fanning the flames of Muslim zealots and offering three billion dollars in aid.[33] The issue of *jihad* in Islam had long been forgotten until it was given a new lease of life in Afghanistan.

The notion of jihad, or holy war, had almost ceased to exist in the Muslim world after the tenth century until it was revived, with American encouragement, to fire a pan-Islamic movement after the Soviet invasion of Afghanistan in 1979.[34]

Among the zealots fighting the Soviet infidels was a tall and wealthy Saudi man named Osama bin Laden. Later he gained notoriety for setting up and leading the most elaborate and deadliest non-state terror organisation that humanity has known. Through bombings and kidnappings his network, known as al-Qaida, has been able to reverse policies of governments such as the Philippines and Spain on their military roles in Iraq. In fact in the latter case the bombings in Madrid led to the defeat of the government at the polls. In terms of impact, therefore, one has to admit that the terror campaign of al-Qaida has not been totally ineffective.

The most important trait of *reactionary Islam* is that it banishes reason from religion and compassion from the faith.[35] In the absence of a clear agenda, there seems little concern in the minds of these groups for the plight of tens or hundreds of millions of impoverished Muslims in India, the Far East, Africa and elsewhere. There are no manifestos or plans addressing problems facing Muslims in the world on how to eradicate poverty or alleviate illiteracy or improve health and hygiene. As an ideological movement it is bent only on destruction with no plans or ideas for reconstruction. Their main preoccupation is to re-create the past in the present, oblivious to the fact that both human and his/her environment have changed. The attempt to re-create the past was vividly tried and tested in Afghanistan by the Taliban. The result could not have been a more fantastic failure of a movement in history, where the historicity of humanity was completely set aside in favour of ideologising rituals and ritualising beliefs. The regime of the Taliban, subscribing to radical politics while practicing conservative Islam, a trait of Sunni fundamentalism, proved beyond the shadow of a doubt that *reactionary Islam* is a befitting name for a movement that can only define itself in adversarial terms.

In their quest to quash the West and their desire to demolish the 'devil', reactionary Islamists exploit religion to the full. For them Islam offers hope where other forces have failed to deliver. The most illustrious example is the Arab–Israeli conflict where pan-Arabism as promoted and propagated by Nasser failed to achieve Palestinian goals. The humiliation felt by Arabs after a series of military defeats by Israel left them desperate to avenge those they felt had offended their pride and honour.[36] The immediate politicisation of religion by *reactionary Islam* in a radical fashion came on the back of *revivalist Islam*, which had already propounded Islam as the way to Muslim emancipation and glory.

Therefore the bastions of reactionary Islam are prepared to, and do, use violence for their cause. Their agenda is vague and offers no concrete solutions to the tangible problems Muslims currently suffer. They appear to define themselves exclusively in terms of 'the other' (the enemy) and seek some kind of change, however abstract and vague, to the status quo. It is unlikely that they can be defeated from without[37] by military means alone; they are not a state and a state-centric world is ill-equipped to fight non-state combatants. In any event ideas cannot be subjugated with bullets but only with counter-ideas. Any effective challenge to them must be launched from within the Islamic world, which turns us to the last group.

Liberalist Islam comes in the aftermath of the spectacular failures of *political Islam*. The disillusionment of many Muslims with the regressive nature of the Taliban in Afghanistan as well as unfulfilled promises of religious authorities in Sudan and Iran resulted in funda-mental re-evaluation of religion and religious doctrine by Islamic thinkers. Unlike the early days of Islam, when a disorganised, tribal and primitive group of Bedouin Arabs managed to build an empire and develop a civilisation, all under the banner of the faith and generally guided by Islamic fervour, the experience of modern Islam demonstrated the opposite. None of the signs of progress so evident then was to emerge in modern settings. This left a bitter taste in the minds of Islamic intellectuals, who searched desperately for the causes of this failure. Then *liberalist Islam* was born.

The essence of *liberalist Islam* relates to the epistemology of religion and religious studies. How we should treat religion and how we should learn from religious guidelines forms the very core that permeates every level of liberalist interpretation of the text. Interesting work in this field has been carried out by Abdolkarim Soroush. His sepa-ration of religion from religious understanding has foundational and far-reaching consequences for Islamic societies. The sanctifica-tion of Divine Message, he believes, does not and should not include the interpretation of the Message. Our understanding changes and newer interpretations may inevitably take hold. This emanates from the relative nature of human understanding. Whereas the Source of the Message is absolute, unchangeable and holy, our understanding is relative, changing and therefore subject to constant scrutiny and doubt. This most important and subtle point has been overlooked by many in the past.[38]

The dyadic relationship of God and human, in the liberalist fashion, belongs to the private domain of the faithful and should not be dictated or directed by fellow human beings. This relationship is sacred and is shaped by traits that define the relationship of a master to a servant. However, in the religious domain of Islam the servant (human being) has the opportunity, the freedom, and the courage to defy the Master – God – if he/she so wishes. The fact that the Master may not be in favour of the act of defiance is a different matter altogether. Adam and Eve and the whole story of Creation as narrated in the Quran would not stand if their act of defiance is overlooked. Therefore, even though there will be punishment by the Almighty for disobedience, the right to disobey and the freedom to defy are very much part and parcel of humanity in Islam. Only the Almighty can interfere in this dyadic relationship and set punishment as He sees fit for His servants.[39] The rules of this relationship are set by the Lord Himself irrespective of a human's relative rationality, for example the daily prayers in Islam. On the other hand, however, the relationship between humans themselves is a temporal discourse impressed by developments in history and guided by rationality. Nowhere in the text are we to see eternal maxims regarding specifics of relationships between humans. Those that relate to rules and regulations on marriage, divorce, inheritance and the like are very clearly prescribed in the context of Arabia fourteen hundred years ago, where and when Islam was born.[40] The gradual evolution of humankind and its ascendance to new heights of knowledge, however, can allow for better relationships among members of the human race without abrogating the essential ethical maxims of the religion. General moral guidelines like the Ten Commandments, shared by Islam, proscribe certain kinds of behaviour and provide a list of obligations. Faith allows us to root our ethical principles in the ontology of man and even in the philosophy of life. Therefore our moral framework remains immune from historicity or relativity of time and place. This is a far cry from trying to interfere in every aspect of life and attempting to muzzle rationality in the name of religion. Beyond the general ethical principles, the faith promotes the application of reason and encourages piety and compassion. That very much is the message of the Quran, liberal Muslims claim.

The liberalists are therefore quite secular in their political outlook. The maxim of rationality is accepted by them as the guiding principle in humankind's temporal affairs and they readily dispense with the idea of *political Islam* as a redundant and essentially misconceived precept. Religion to them has a fluid quality about it and its rigidification through jurisprudence only makes it stagnant and irrelevant. According to them fields such as Islamic economy, Islamic psychology, Islamic politics, and the like are man-made fallacies that emanate from misguided understanding of religion as a whole and have no place in true Islam. By fattening Islam one does not serve the religion, they say. Arduous and painstaking tasks such as trying to extract theories from the Quran and *Hadith* on sociology, education, medicine and other branches of human knowledge reflect a deep misunderstanding of what religion is all about.[41]

The unmistakable significance of human liberty is attested to in the Quran in the story of Creation. Even though God was aware of the sinful quality within man and even though the first two humans had openly disobeyed Him (and although Satan had pledged to deceive humanity until the Day of Judgement, for which Satan had actually asked God, and had been granted, life until the Last Day),[42] the Lord did not rescind their freedom of choice. He exiled them to earth, where they had ample opportunity for sin and disobedience. Such an unassailable position for freedom in the ontology of man as narrated in the Quran cannot be overlooked or denied by the medium of jurisprudential interpretation.

A religious government, in the eyes of liberal Muslims, is concerned with basic provisions for public security, health and hygiene, education, welfare, transportation, science, and so on, just as a secular government would be. After all, empty stomachs do not produce fertile minds for progressive ethics and religion. A poor society, where corruption, poverty and crime are rampant, can hardly heed the calls to spiritual elevation. 'When poverty arrives through the door', it is believed in Islam, 'religion runs out via the back door.'[43] It is only after the material needs of humanity have been met that intellectual and spiritual aspirations can find meaningful and significant expression in individual and public life. Any true religious administration therefore would aspire to successfully manage the temporal aspects of the lives of its citizens thereby providing them with opportunity to engage in contemplation and Gnostic learning. Ritualisation of Islamic values and ideologising ethics is the task carried out under jurisprudential governments, who seek public compliance to the codified religion propagated and disseminated through seminaries and the clerical establishment. They are preoccupied with public presentation and representation of faith through a jurisprudential system, codifying values and ritualising Islam. Growing beards, wearing the veil for women, preventing the socialising of the two groups in the society and similar requirements become compulsory. All traits of true religion such as freedom and rationality are frowned upon as heresy and punished accordingly. Ethics takes the back seat and the religious ideology overtly takes over all aspects of life.

The issue of duties and rights is also perceived differently in *liberalist Islam*. In *establishment Islam*, and more so in *political Islam*, human rights are generally subject and secondary to duties towards God and thus lack authenticity and can only be validated through reference to *shari'a*; authentic rights belong to the Almighty alone and the role of humanity on earth can only de defined and given meaning through the prism of religious learning and interpretation carried out in the seminaries by theologians and religious jurists. Any precept propounded as a human right should only be accepted as one once it has been examined and approved by jurisprudential experts assuring that it does not contradict any of the Islamic dictums. The liberalist camp, however, argues strongly in favour of the independence of human rights from any religious interpretation.[44] In that discourse human rights are God-given and therefore cannot be taken away by humans in any shape or form under any excuse or banner. Freedom, for instance, is a Divine gift bestowed by God on humanity; as such free choice cannot become a negotiating item in the name of or for religion.[45] The same goes for other aspects of human rights. The argument that for every human right there is a corresponding human duty,[46] for example, the right to freedom for one means duty to respect the same freedom for others does not negate the stand of *liberalist Islam* on the issue.

We thus observe that *liberalist Islam* endorses the freedom of humanity and allows for a plurality of interpretation. The hermeneutic approach of liberals in ascending the spiritual/religious discourse is the ineluctable ingredient of their outlook. The God of liberals, in the words of a leading liberal Muslim, is the God of Gnostics and not the God of religious jurists. Religion belongs to all and religious knowledge is not the monopoly of the few. Rationality is acclaimed as a guiding principle in human affairs and the rule of *shari'a* is not given immunity to critical thought and scrutiny. Contextualisation, historicity of man and interpretation, as well as hermeneutics are accepted within the faith allowing an inclusive approach encompassing humanity and discarding any exclusive dogmatic outlook polarising the world and its inhabitants. Human rights are as sacred as human duties as they are God-given and thus irrevocable by humans.

1.2   From Islamic revivalism to fundamentalism: a brief narrative of contemporary leading figures in political Islam

There are many who could be included in the revivalist and the fundamentalist camp in Islam. In this narrative, however, we shall attempt to refer only to those whom we believe have had the greatest impact. As our concern is the contemporary period we shall begin with Abdul-Wahhab of Arabia (today's Saudi Arabia) and end with Osama bin Laden of the same land. In between we shall include Jamal Asadabadi of Iran, Muhammad Abdu of Egypt, Iqbal Lahoori of the Indian subcontinent (today's Pakistan), Hassan al-Banna of Egypt, Ma'dudi of Pakistan, Ali Shari'ati of Iran, Seyyed Qutb of Egypt, Hassan Turabi of Sudan and Ruhollah Khomeini of Iran.

Mohammad Abdul-Wahhab was a religious man who grew up in a traditional family known for their devotion to the Hanbali sect[47] of Islam. Born in the Najd province of Saudi Arabia in 1702 or 1703 (died sometime between 1792 and 1797), he is reported to have memorised the Quran by the age of ten. He learned jurisprudence from his father and moved on to familiarise himself with other branches of Islamic knowledge. His puritanistic approach to religion, whereby he allowed only for the text – the Quran and *Sunnah* (the sayings and the deeds of the Prophet) – was to be the way towards improvement of Muslim life. In particular he subscribed to some of the writings and views of Ibn Taymiyya, a leading Hanbali jurist (1263–1328), who exhorted his followers to take an active role in politics, that is, rise against tyrannical rulers; as a result Ibn Taymiyya spent much of his life in prison.[48] Although some claim Abdul-Wahhab tried to redress the mistreatment of women in Arabia and repudiated cruel and oppressive measures taken against them as well as other errant practices,[49] it remains true that he presented a very dogmatic, rigid and politicised view of Islam; in fact he apparently ruled that it is incumbent on every able male Muslim to participate annually in *jihad*,[50] though his interpretation of *jihad* may not be as clear to all as to some.[51] His rejection of Sufism and equating it with paganism, and his viewing of his time as worse than that in Arabia before the advent of Islam, clearly places Abdul-Wahhab among revivalists bordering on reactionary Islam. One should not forget that his views are the cornerstone of today's Saudi Arabian religious beliefs and that Osama bin Laden, a Saudi Arabian by birth, grew up within that environment.

The second man is Seyyed Jamal-el-din e Assad Abadi – also known as Afghani. Seyyed Jamal was an Iranian but preached pan-Islamic ideas. He travelled widely and could reportedly speak Persian, Arabic, English, French, Russian and possibly Turkish. He was born in Hamadan, Iran, around 1839 and died in 1897. His views went beyond the boundaries of his homeland as he preached pan-Islamic views in his wide and frequent travels. In order to be accepted into the more numerous Sunni communities in Islamic countries he kept his Iranian origins to himself lest he be castigated as a Shi'a and lose the ear of his audience. His main focus of attention was Europe, particularly Britain, as he held the latter responsible for the malaise and the miseries that had befallen Muslims worldwide.[52] One writer notes: 'He was shrewd enough to see Britain as a greater threat to Islamdom than Russia'.[53] In keeping with his hostility to British policies, his periodical called 'Urwat-ol-Wothqa' ('The Strongest Link'), published in Paris in 1884 for four years, attacked Britain strongly. Inside Iran his influence is said to have led to two major developments: the Tobacco Movement of 1891 and the murder of Naser-ed-in Shah in 1896. In the former case, Mirza Hassan e Shirazi, the leading Shi'a religious figure at the time, is believed to have been encouraged by Seyyed Jamal to issue the edict against the use of tobacco, and in the latter case, it was one of his acolytes, Mirza Rezay e Kermani, who killed the corrupt Qajar king.[54] The most significant aspect of Afghani's influence and ideas was his international approach and cosmopolitan outlook. He was clearly a modernist and did not subscribe to *taqlid*,[55] yet his discourse did not limit itself to internal religious semantics or domestic political settings but rather encompassed the role of external factors in the plight of Muslims. In domestic environments he shrewdly recognised the role of social factors and tailored his message to the requirements of his audience. More importantly, he communicated his ideas with respect to the influence of public opinion makers. Thus in Iran he soon realised the significance of some religious leaders (nowadays known as ayatollahs), and established close contacts with them. But in Sunni societies where the influence of religious leaders did not run so deep, he preferred to address the people directly and bypassed the religious hierarchy. His failure was perhaps partly attributable to his death at a relatively young age (he died of cancer of the chin) and that his struggle for greater power for Muslims called for parallel and simultaneous efforts internally and externally. Such a momentous task required a greater international network and called for a more fundamental reinterpretation of the text. Though he was probably suited to the task he set for himself, circumstances failed him and did not allow the completion of his work. He thus died a somewhat disappointed man, but his influence has undoubtedly played a role in the development of Islamic discourse to date.

Asad Abadi's close confidant and follower, Muhammad Abdu of Egypt (1849–1905), was more concerned with intellectual aspects of Islamic revivalism and adopted a less radical approach in his politics. Though his teacher was strongly anti-British, Abdu's rather mild political temperament allowed his being appointed as the Mufti of Egypt by the British authorities that were ruling Egypt at the time. He used rules of the Maliki school in his judgements, though the Ottomans practiced the Hanafi code, which Abdu as the Mufti of Egypt was obliged to follow.[56] Like Asad Abadi he rejected the principle of *taqlid* and instead believed in the application of the principles of *maslaha* (expediency) and *talfiq* (mixture). His opposition to political action against the European rulers emanated from his belief that such actions were futile and only exacerbated the situation to the disadvantage of Muslims. He staunchly advocated the compatibility of revelation with reason, that is, any religious belief that appears unreasonable and goes against rationality cannot by definition be religious and must therefore be false. Although he accompanied Asad Abadi to Paris and helped him in the administration of the periodical (see above), he went back to Egypt in 1888 and, encouraged by his mentor, attempted a reinterpretation of the text that would be to the benefit of Muslims.[57]

Mohammad Iqbal Lahoori of India (1875–1938) was one of the most prominent philosophers of revivalist Islam. In his works he demonstrated the predicament that the Muslims were facing. The ritualisation of religion wherein the spirit and the meaning of religion is lost to the superficial and liturgical expressions of the faith were in Iqbal's view an impediment to the revivalist cause. Very much enticed by the Persian mystic Molavi, known as Rumi, Iqbal wrote poetry in Persian expressing his Gnostic side. Privileged by a traditional as well as a Western education, Iqbal benefitted from mystical ontology and philosophical depth of human discourse. To him the distinction between matter and spirit was not the material-like separation that is usually entertained in the mind; that, he believed, was not only an over-simplification but rather a distortion. 'There are no pleasure-giving and pain-giving acts, only ego-sustaining and ego-dissolving ones. Resurrection is therefore not an external event, but the "consummation of a life process within the ego". Heaven and Hell are states, not localities. ...'[58] Iqbal's views and writings also had a political edge, which reportedly helped the creation of Pakistan after India gained independence. 'The question of artistic responsibility in his discourse is not limited to routine political affairs, but rather he has an expansive and deeply intellectual and humanistic commitment, which necessitates anti-colonialism as one of its definitive and inevitable tools.'[59] Though a multi-dimensional figure in Islamic revivalism, who received tertiary education in leading European institutions, Iqbal viewed Europe as the greatest enemy of moral advancement for humanity.[60] There were very few if any like Iqbal who have a deep and holistic understanding of the plight of Muslims and the contrasting progress achieved in the West. His theme of 'return to oneself' encouraged Muslims to re-evaluate their current situation to come to the understanding that their historical identity and socio-political worth is not defined by the rigid, repetitious, and insignificant rituals prescribed through clerical institutions. By this insight into the past and present, Muslims could reconstruct themselves as a modern but independent and proud people. His impact, though not as wide as certain other revivalists, was more profound among intellectuals and the more educated segments of Islamic community.

Hassan-al-Banna, a schoolteacher and founder of the Muslim Brotherhood in Egypt in 1928, was a more radical version of his fellow Egyptian, Mohammad Abdu. His views were closer to those of Afghani's in that he was a fervent opponent of colonialism and could not see a compromise between Islam (submission to God and God's will and God's rules) and obedience to foreign (non-Muslim) rule. The Islamic code of conduct, *shari'a*, was in his view and the views of his supporters supreme and overrode all other concerns. However, he accepted only the Quran and the most authentic *Hadith* and rejected all else that had dubious origins. The principle of *taqlid*, in his view, was a redundant and in fact regressive concept and was to be dispensed with by all Muslims. His agenda included the transformation of Egyptian society into a true Muslim community, where the evils of sin would all be eradicated. That, he believed, would come via *da'wa*, invitation, where change from within would lead to change in the environment.[61] As such he promoted an athletic programme for youth whereby the minds of the young would be distracted from the appeals of sexual misconduct (sex outside marriage). His disciplinary regime included an assiduous observance of dos and don'ts in *shari'a* refraining from all that was forbidden – *haram*. His political message, however, disturbed the political masters in Egypt at the time with his so-called dissolved organisation accused of the murder of Prime Minister Nuqrashi Pasha in 1948. In February 1949 Banna himself was assassinated. His influence in the revivalist camp throughout the Arab world cannot be overstated. Through his organisation, the Muslim Brotherhood, his ideas were spread to neighbouring countries and in the fluid socio-political setting of the post–World War II period in the Middle East they found a receptive audience. Though his organisation appears to have gone through an uncertain time after Banna's death, it nevertheless managed to survive and through mutation and various political manoeuvring has outlasted its opponents. He was born in 1906 in Mahmoudiya, Egypt, and was assassinated in Cairo in 1949.

Seyyed Qutb, perhaps the most radical and revolutionary Arab
Muslim revivalist of the contemporary period, was born in Egypt
in 1906. An intelligent child who reportedly had memorised the
Quran in early childhood, Qutb went on to become an inspector
in the Ministry of Education. The turning point for Qutb occurred
between 1948 and 1951 when he spent three years in the United
States towards the completion of his master's degree. It was then
that Qutb developed his uncompromising hatred of the West. It is
not certain why he began to harbour such deep hostility and resentment. US support for Zionists and general sexual permissiveness are
cited by him as factors that justified his bitterness, but some feel
there may have been other factors at work. In the insightful words
of Malise Ruthven, 'The puritan is often an inverted sensualist: who
knows what slights or rejections the intelligent and highly educated
but small and dark-skinned Egyptian may have been exposed to
in 1950s America?'[62] The radical ideologue compared the state of
Muslims in the world to those of Arabs before the advent of Islam:
a state of *jahiliya* (ignorance). He went on further to state that even
the *jahiliya* Arabs of pre-Islam were not as ignorant and as misguided
as the current Muslims. Like most ideologues and in keeping with
the nature of many ideological discourses, his views and writings
were clear, firm, and instructive on deconstruction – the dissolution
of the state of *jahiliya* – but they were vague and weak on reconstruction. The true Islamic state he so feverishly coveted was not
described by him in any meaningful way, only that the status quo
had to be abandoned or destroyed before new foundations for an
Islamic community could be laid:

> Today we are in the midst of *jahiliya* similar to or even worse than
> the *jahiliya* that was 'squeezed out' by Islam. Every thing about us
> is *jahiliya*: the concepts (*tasawwurat*) of mankind and their beliefs,
> their customs and traditions, the sources of their culture, their
> arts and literature, and their laws and regulations.[63]

His ideas were in particular more attractive to the youth. They aroused
passion and challenged the status quo. His attempt at ideologising
religion and turning it into a political tool towards the liberation
of his people and Muslims in general were bringing the revivalist
discourse to a climax. Both in social as well as political terms he

preached an anti-establishment view, calling into question even the authority of clerical hierarchies. His weakest point, however, could have been lack of adequate political education. Even though beliefs are the sources from which historical movements are energised, without proper political leadership those movements may go astray and destroy the lives of many, whose hopes and aspirations will have been lost in efforts to realise a dream whose substance was unclear. In the mid-1960s Qutb was hanged in Egypt. His influence, however, clearly outlasted his physical life. The assassination of President Sadat of Egypt in 1980 was committed by an ardent supporter of the radical wing of the Muslim Brotherhood, a wing where Qutb was hailed as a heroic martyr.

Perhaps the least refined character in the Islamic revivalist camp was Abu-l-Ala Maududi from India (later Pakistan). He was mostly familiar with Western thought and one is doubtful about his depth of understanding of original Islamic texts. Most certainly he was no match for his countryman Mohammad Iqbal. But what he may have lacked in philosophical depth, cultural pluralism and mystic ontology he more than made up for in radical conservatism: strict adherence to the most conservative interpretations of Islam. He had no time for those seeking to adapt Islam to modernity. His dogmatic outlook presented Islam as a rigid and ahistorical ideology bereft of spirit and devoid of rationality. Religion was to him a matter of blind obedience to the rules of *shari'a* as laid out and compiled throughout the centuries of ecclesiastical development in Islam. As it usually is the case with jurisprudential Islamists, the world and everything within it are in black and white. Religious deeds of the followers and all temporal affairs of people should be judged by the dichotomised moral standards of Islamic/ist jurists: '...moral gain or loss is much more important than worldly success or failure....'[64] Maududi's political views, all based on and emanating from his understanding of Islam, afforded him a popular status but landed him in prison for a time. His lack of profound understanding of religious philosophy and his unfamiliarity with Western culture and intellectual discourse did not allow Maududi's ideas to generate a social movement; although his works, like some other non-Arabs, have been translated into Arabic, neither his intellectual insight nor the environment he was working in were particularly conducive to that end. Born in 1903, Maududi lived up to 1979, the year that

Islamic revivalism climaxed in the shape of the Islamic revolution in Iran. Maududi could be regarded as the equivalent of Qutb without the latter's intellectual sophistication. The impact of Maududi on Pakistani politics can be summed up as a force, with some success at times, towards Islamicisation of politics in that country.

Ali Shari'ati, born in Mazinan, Iran in 1933, was undoubtedly the most powerful religious intellectual in the country, if not in the entire Islamic world, in pre-revolutionary Iran. The impact of his ideas on the success of the Iranian revolution can hardly be exaggerated. Educated in Iran and in Paris he managed to infuse traditional religious concepts with modern ideas, critiquing in the process the status quo and the clerical establishment. The similarity of his ideas and views to those of Qutb suggests a strong compatibility between the two, perhaps more than has been acknowledged. Yet his powerful lectures and enchanting writing, together with his zeal and passion for a socialist Islam, gave him a unique position in Iran. The intellectual foundations of the Islamic revolution were in large part laid down by him and only his untimely death in 1977 deprived him of witnessing the demise of the political regime he much criticised. Ali Shari'ati was a mystic by nature, an art lover who preferred spiritual ascension to material benefits and worldly glory. But his social commitment to indoctrinate the youth in Iran precluded his devotion to Gnostic affairs. He did not wish that the allure of the beyond would make him overlook or neglect the shade of hunger in the eyes of a child or the bruise of lashes on the back of an innocent prisoner.[65] Though some of his works clearly hint at his mystic moods and state, the great volume of his writings and lectures circled around the revolutionary synthesis that he had brought about with a blend of Islam and socialism. His greatest defect, however, like most other Islamic revivalists, with very few exceptions, was his political naivety and lack of awareness of the very basics of contemporary international relations. Perhaps some of the most enticing of his writings are his prayers, among which there is:

> Lord, Bestow upon me the good fortune of struggle in defeat, patience in disappointment, going without companion, *jihad* without instrument, work without reward, sacrifice in silence, religion without the world, religiosity without people, greatness without fame, goodness without representation, defiance without inexperience, pride without vanity, love without whim,

loneliness amongst the masses and loving without the beloved knowing.[66]

Ayatollah Ruhollah Khomeini epitomised the climax of *political Islam*, representing one of the most fundamentalist interpretations of the faith. Leader of a revolution whereby political Islam for the first time successfully challenged and toppled the state it opposed, he was in the early years of the Iranian revolution a symbol of resistance and triumph to Muslims worldwide. His political life began in 1963 when, following a public denunciation of the government that had led to the suppression and the killings of many by the authorities, he was exiled first to Turkey and then to Najaf in Iraq; an odd choice for a religious exile since the latter hosts the oldest and the most prestigious Shi'a seminary in the world. Khomeini therefore was given access to thousands of young religious students in Najaf, all potential religio-political activists who could in later years prove useful in attempts to successfully overthrow the Shah of Iran. In exile he wrote on Islamic government, propounding the concept of the total guardianship of the religious jurist, *velayat e faghih*. Upon his return to Iran in 1979, he introduced this concept into Iranian revolutionary politics, incorporating it into the new constitution of the country. A man who could influence his fanatic followers and mobilise masses by arousing religious passion, he was unique among senior Iranian clerics in openly infusing religion with politics. All records of his life after assuming the mantle of power in Iran point towards the behaviour of a revolutionary political figure, albeit in the name of and for religion. His difference from other revivalists and fundamentalists, with the exception of Turabi in Sudan, was that he actually held power in his hands and could practice what he preached. The complexities of power politics, however, proved less than fully satisfactory for him as he found himself having to publicly reverse his previous decisions on several occasions. The most important perhaps was accepting the ceasefire with Iraq in 1988 despite earlier rhetoric that the removal of Saddam was a precondition for a truce. Another instance was the dismissal of his deputy, Ayatollah Montazeri, who suddenly after years of being groomed as a successor to Khomeini fell from grace and had to live under house arrest. Such political manoeuvring could not have been easy for the aging Islamic leader.

Khomeini's worldview was not a complicated one. A simple categorisation of people into *mostakber*, the arrogant, and *mostaz'af*, the meek, made his views readily accessible to millions of unpretentious followers. His ability to stand firm in difficult situations and his skill in maintaining support and extending influence, however, rendered him the leader of the Islamic revolution of 1978–1979. What can be said about his religious views, particularly the guardianship of the jurist, is that they were unorthodox, especially in Shi'a Islam. That may have proven advantageous to him however as many non-religious political groups could also identify with some of his views in the earlier part of the revolution. Born in the late nineteenth century, he died in 1989 and was buried just outside Tehran.

Hassan Abdullah Al-Turabi of Kassala, Sudan (1932–) was the second fundamentalist Muslim who actually wielded political power. His legacy was an utter failure to improve the lot of Sudanese who, having broken the yoke of colonialism and having been home to the strongest Communist party in Africa, were now facing another dictatorship. Al-Turabi did not lack egocentrism. He hardly missed any opportunity to downplay the impact his co-fundamentalists had and reserved the highest praise for his own understanding of Islam and his own political programme. He rejected Banna's idea of 'good government out of good society' as foolish.[67] He also dismissed bin Laden, perhaps rightly in this instance, as someone with no vision.[68] Turabi used the levers of power to extend and prolong his rule over the Sudanese. A people whose culture is known for tolerance and boasts a wide diversity of ethnic groups and languages (nearly 500 ethnic groups and over 100 languages) were caught in the grip of a political Islamist who together with his cohorts fanned the flames of ethnic divide and religious separation, contributing to one of the longest and most destructive civil wars in the world.

In the end the net result was the partition of Sudan in 2011 into two separate states, one in the North and another in the South. Turabi has had a rather fluctuating career in politics that has landed him in prison several times. His one-time ally, President Bashir, now wanted for crimes against humanity, has in fact put him behind bars repeatedly.

Osama bin Laden was born on 10 March 1957 in Saudi Arabia and was brought up as a devout Wahhabi, the prevalent sect in the land. Coming from a wealthy family, he had resources at his disposal to commit towards his beliefs and goals. A firm believer in the restoration of *shari'a* as the only saviour of Muslims and a fervent follower of political Islam, he fought the Soviets in Afghanistan, where he allegedly received support from other countries including the United States. Later, however, he turned against the United States, reportedly due to the presence of US bases in Saudi Arabia. He established al-Qaida, an international but reportedly decentralised web of jihadists, who are prepared to commit violence to advance their cause. Al-Qaida is believed to have supported, if not actually designed and executed, the September 11 bombings in New York and Washington as well other bombings around the world.

Bin Laden's difference from other political Islamists, who were also prepared to commit violence, was that although he did not have the mantle of statehood like some others (although he did enjoy the open support of the Taliban in Afghanistan) he managed to use violence (a monopoly of statehood) internationally to such a horrifying degree that it actually caused a shift in the policies of some states. The developments in Spain after the Madrid bombings in 2004 are an example. Yet his allure in the Islamic world, some have suggested, appeared to wane as time passed. On 2 May 2011 he was assassinated by US forces in his hideout in Pakistan.

2
Contextualising Islam or Islamicising Context: Debates on the Role of Islam in Politics

Hearken to this reed forlorn
Breathing ever since 'twas torn
From its rushy bed a strain
Of impassioned love and pain.

Rumi, Masnavi, Book I, lines 1–2

2.1 Islamic Gnosticism and critical theory

Islamic Gnosticism does not consider itself a sect or a religion; it is in a spiritual sense the yearning (*eshtiagh*) of the soul to reunite with its origin. Just like a flute that plays the music of the one who is playing it, the words spoken by Rumi and other mystics are in a way the echo of an inner (and, at the same time, outer) source, hence his likening himself to a reed. It is a discourse of love and knowledge, riches and poverty, mortality and immortality, drunkenness and sobriety, consciousness and unconsciousness, desire, restraint and selflessness, temporality and spirituality, peace and war, detachment and ascension, and, of course, humility and sacrifice. In this discourse there are no schools of thought that claim to offer comprehensive and all-inclusive manifestos for the structuring of human communities, nor does Islamic Gnosticism aspire to assume the political leadership of Muslims or even of its own followers. Yet there are important tenets in this narrative that should be studied and assessed in terms of their utility and applicability in today's egocentric and state-centred international relations. Concepts of love, selflessness, freedom and empowerment are all enshrined and embedded in the Gnostic theology of Islam. This is done in the light of the space opened up for different approaches to IR by the advancement of critical theory. Thus Cox and Falk, among others from the West, are attracting contributions from centuries-old teachings of Muslim Gnostics such as Rumi and Shabestari. This in itself is a fantastic occasion for a meaningful and significant dialogue of cultures and ideas across time and space. As stated by Constantinou, 'Islamic Gnosticism can provide a transgressive politology and a critical theory of international relations'.[1] If critical theory, according to Buck-Morss, can 'provide cognitive experience at a level of reflection ... that has the power to dispel the illusion of the inevitability of events by demonstrating that it is how we conceive them that gives them their aura of fate',[2] then this reflection can be attained at a Gnostic level, where the power and the role of the selfless individual to deconstruct old perceptions and construct new ones would not be diluted in the hands of the state and the international system.

Self and selflessness

> *Contemplate the same grievous war in thyself*
> *Why, then, art thou engaged in warring with others?*
> Rumi, *Masnavi*, Book VI, line 54

As authority seems to be flowing away from states, whether upwards to supranational or multilateral bodies, downwards to regional and local governments, or sideways to private actors – both within nations and transnationally – the focus may gradually shift to the individual. No civilised and sophisticated socio-political system can prosper with uncivilised individuals. Unlike in the past, where civilised individuals lived in uncultured communities, nowadays the reverse appears to be the trend. No system is foolproof in that it can safeguard its members against the consequence of their own deeds. In Gnosticism much attention is focused on the individual in a different way from the individualism that we are familiar with in the West. While in the latter the individual is mostly disempowered in most if not all IR paradigms, in Gnosticism the individual is emphatically enabled to elevate him/herself and thus effect a change in his/her socio-political environment.[3] In Kenneth Waltz's three-image analysis Gnosticism would probably fit in as a first-image perceiver of our environment; therefore Waltz's subscription to the system (third image) perspective is relegated to secondary importance. Some of the new generation of IR scholars also appear to treat the discipline in a more accessible manner than hitherto. The human agent is, in their perspective, empowered to make a difference in spite of the national or international system. Based on a Ghandian approach, for instance, Constantinou seems to describe his holistic homo-diplomacy as an individual act.[4] If wars start in the minds of men (as the UNESCO Charter attests) then it is the minds of men that should be the centre of our attention. Accordingly it would stand to reason to shift the focus of analysis from international structure to the individual and try to find the roots of conflict within human beings before attempting to point the finger in the direction of an international system. The detachment of the individual from the international political environment and the placing of his/her fate in the hands of a supra-human agent called the state, which in turn operates on the basis of signals received from a bigger abstraction called an international system, is as disabling as it is irresponsible and false. We as individuals all bear responsibility for the international political environment we live in and no degree of theorising should thus be allowed to disengage us intellectually or disempower us politically. Gnosticism can be most helpful in this respect. In short, while International Relations focuses more on the external environment and the enemy without, Islamic Gnosticism puts the emphasis on the enemy within:

> *Oh honourable ones, we have slain the external foe,*
> *a more forbidding enemy lurks down below;*
> *Dislodging it, intellect and intelligence would not dare,*
> *the inner lion is not the plaything of a hare;*
> *It is a common lion that breaks the legion's rows,*
> *the true lion is he/she who breaks the inner foes.*[5]

While in the West the individual is allowed (in fact encouraged in some instances) to pursue his/her interest regardless of that of others, as long as the law of the land is not violated,[6] in Gnosticism almost the opposite is preached, that is, to place and advance others' interests before our own; to act in a selfless manner. The advent of the democratic man, whose main preoccupation is the pursuit and enhancement of self-interest, is an illustration of this point. Individuals in Western democracies appear unwilling to forgo their interest for the sake of others, including future generations. As electoral masters (in all forms and factions) of their rulers, their self-centric views are to be heeded by those in power rendering governance a difficult task. Consequently this egoistic trait of the individual unit, which is reflected in sovereign statehood, diminishes the communal spirit of life. It is a selfish man who can create and sustain a selfish state. 'Wheat grows from wheat, barley from barley,' stated Rumi some 700 years ago. The uncaring, loveless and egocentric aspects of sovereign statehood can only mirror the state of human agents in Europe at the time of the Westphalian Treaty in 1648 and not reflect the universal and interminable needs and concerns of humanity.

In contrast, the spiritual and Gnostic dimension of Islamic discourse places much emphasis on the loving and caring aspects of life, the interconnectedness of all and the security and well-being of all members being dependent on the security and prosperity of one another. In effect it propounds a coherent and effective collective security system rooted in the philosophy and ontology of existence, where interests and principles are one and the same. The separation of the latter from the former has caused the marked failure of conventional collective security, where principles have failed, in most cases, to be applied in the face of opposing interests of the state. Sa'di, the Persian philosopher and Gnostic of the thirteenth century, has expressed this beautifully in his poetic language:

> *The human race are members in a body created;*
> *For of a single essence are they all created;*
> *When fortune persecutes with pain one member surely,*
> *The other members of the body cannot stand securely.*
> *O you who from another's troubles turn aside your view*
> *It is not fitting they bestow the name of 'Human' on you.*[7]

This selflessness emanates from a worldview that perceives the creation as one whole universal summed up and reflected in every particular. Noted by Lahiji, 'Every thing is a theophany of one of the Divine Names'.[8] The human agent, the vice-regent of God on earth,[9] is a comprehensive theophany of all Divine Names and qualities, and has been created in the universal Divine form (according to His Image as stated in the Quran).[10] The quintessential human being thus reflects God and His glory in every respect. Shabestari, as reported by Lewisohn, narrates a unity between the 'reality of humanity' or the 'Perfect Man' and the 'Divine Presence' and that these two spiritual degrees are mutually related and absorbed within each other.[11] The everlasting drive (and not cause, reason or rationale) for Creation – love – is thus placed in humanity and, being in conformity with and true to oneself, would uncover the Divine Majesty latent in human form.

If there had not been Love, how should there have been existence?
How should bread have attached itself to you and become (assimilated
to) you?[12]

The selfless dimension of Gnostic discourse in Islam relates to the theology and ontology of life on earth in harmony with the philosophy and truth of existence. Narrated by the prominent Islamic thinker, Ghazzali, everyone's salvation and prosperity lies in that which brings it joy and comfort, and the joy of everything is in that which conforms to its nature, and that which conforms to everything's nature is that for which it has been created; like the joy of lust, which lies in its fulfilment, and the joy of anger in exacting revenge, and the joy of eyes in beautiful faces and the joy of ears in beautiful songs and music. *The same applies to the human soul whose function is to find out the truth of things* (my emphasis).[13]

Finding this truth about oneself, and feeling the infinite richness of Creation, is the key to empowering oneself through self-knowledge and the ensuing liberation that opens the gate to knowing the Creator. 'Anyone knowing their self will know their God', an important philosophical dictum in Islam, according to Shabestari.[14] Therefore, unlike the Marxian and some existentialist views that belief in God weakens and degrades humanity by attributing real power and ultimate choice to a supernatural being, which in turn can be used to justify any status quo, Islamic Gnosticism empowers and prepares the individual for change. The following brief dialogue may be viewed as an illustration of the importance of self-knowledge and self-awareness in Gnosticism, where Shams, the sage of Rumi, states, 'What good is it to say God exists. You must attain existence!'[15] In his only book, *Maghalat*, Shams continues:

> *One said: there is only one God*
> *I said: What is it to you?*
> *For you are in a world of divisions*
> *Hundreds of thousands of particles, each particle scattered in worlds,*
>
> *Sear, and sad*
> *He exists, He is Eternal,*
> *What's it to you? For you don't exist!*
>
> *He is One, but who are you? You are more than six thousand,*
> *You [must] try and become one. Otherwise what is His Oneness to do*
> *with you?*[16]

Against this selfless preaching, the human agent, however, usually seeks to promote the self by whatever ways and means are available to him/her; that is he/she works for the fulfilment of desires and for avoiding aversions as theorised by Hobbes. In the latter case, where self-desires and self-aversions construct a loveless and uncaring world, humanity would turn into a prisoner in the hands of his/herself. Many, both Islamic and Western, have warned against that however. Plato highlights the importance of controlling greed and emphasises self-constraint on coveting material possessions.[17] Ghazzali, in *Kimiaye Sa'adat*, quotes Jesus as saying, 'Seeker of material world is like the drinker of sea water; the more he/she drinks the thirstier he/she becomes; until he/she is destroyed without the thirst having been quenched'.[18] The exile of the first couple from Paradise is itself the direct result of the enhancement of the self. Hafez, the Gnostic Persian poet of the thirteenth century, narrates:

> *Beware that if you heed the temptation of the self prime,*
> *As Adam you will be out of Paradise in no time*[19]

Cox's famous statement that every theory is for someone and for some purpose[20] resonates Shabestari's phrase that 'you theorise about "I" all day and night'.[21] The 'I' is at the very deep centre of all (social science and humanities) theory and the very end purpose of what is theorised. An impartial, unbiased theory, if that were ever possible, would therefore have to be detached from the 'I'. In other words, selflessness (through self-knowledge) is the key to emancipation from all that has conditioned us and all that benefits and promotes the interests of the self, even if this self is represented in the form of state or any other unitary actor(s) established and shaped by the self-seeking human agent. It is very much through this act of liberation that *the other* is deconstructed and unity and uniformity can be established. Constantinou's assertion that 'in homo-diplomacy not only the other but the self become strange, a site to be known or know anew' basically reiterates the very same concept.[22] In an extension of this argument, linking the self (or the selflessness) to the greater temporal environment and beyond, Saraydarian states as the pivotal principle of his new diplomacy, 'Know yourself, and know other people, and know God, and know that all three are one and not separate'.[23] Relating the processes of selfless interaction with others to the ontology of humankind, Wellman concludes that we can thereby find out the truth about ourselves and 'our common Divine origin'.[24] The other, or the stranger, as referred to in mystic terminology, then becomes God or an emissary of God.[25] All this is achieved once the self is cast aside or diluted and the emancipation of humanity from the self is realised. This liberation is itself entwined with love. In the poetry of the Persian Sufi, Hafiz, '... since the time of my having becoming enslaved by your love I have been set free'.[26] And that

> *I say it openly and do so with happy laughter*
> *That I am slave of love and thus free of here and hereafter*[27]

Reason and rationality

> *Hide from the strangers, not friends of the inner ring,*
> *Coats are made for winter, not the bloom of spring.*
> *If reason joins forces with reason seeking delight,*
> *Light shall prevail and the Path will be bright.*
> *Should desire couple with desire and trade,*
> *Darkness will descend and the Path shall fade.*
> Rumi (*Masnavi*, Book II, lines 25–7)[28]

The promotion of the self is linked to rationality, for it is the rational choice theory that depicts the maximisation of self-interest as rational, thus legitimating the pursuit and advancement of self-interest. Closely connected is the discourse propounded by Kant on reason. Many a time reason and rationality are used (mistakenly) interchangeably. The two, however, can convey different meanings and reflect concepts at variance with one another. In the language of Rumi, rationality is referred to as the partial wisdom (*aghl e joz'ee*) as opposed to universal wisdom (*aghl e kol*, which could in a sense be viewed as reason). While the latter can elevate humanity to much higher levels, the former is hugely restricted in its capacity for human development. It is this partial wisdom that pretends to be supreme yet denies humanity the space for love that engenders selflessness.

> *The partial wisdom denies love*
> *Yet it pretends to be a confidant*[29]
>
> *Do not take the partial wisdom as your guide*
> *Make the universal wisdom your guide*[30]

Though it may be difficult to differentiate between the terms of rationality and reason in Western philosophy, the difference has at times been noted. An instance can be observed in the Charter of the University of Vienna drafted in 1365, that while stating the primary purposes of the University, distinguishes reason from rationality.[31] Hobbes describes reason as 'the undoubted word of God'[32] and the 'soul of the law',[33] yet he intimates reason is only a means to an end, that is, to fulfil desires and avoid aversions,[34] in which case of course there can be no authenticity assumed for reason. Kant talks of reason in a more authentic fashion and almost as the differentiating trait of humans from the rest of the animal kingdom.[35] In one essay, however, he uses rationality as synonymous with reason.[36] To notice the difference between the two we can try to replace rationality with reason in the rational choice theory or rational actor model, that is, the *reasonable* actor model or the *reasonable* choice theory. In doing so we instantly compromise the significance of self-gain. The difference between these key concepts lies in that though rationality is solely concerned with pursuit of self-interest, reason appears to encompass something greater than personal gain. In that sense reason accommodates more than just the self and is not predicated to stand in the way of justice; anything reasonable is axiomatically assumed to be fair (there can be differences between fairness and justice though).[37] But rationality is not concerned with justice and is instead preoccupied with maximising self-interest. If states are deemed as rational in International Relations it is because they are supposed to pursue their perceived self (national) interests and not because they are concerned with the pursuit or implementation of justice. Many a time states trample upon the principle of justice in order to enhance their assumed national interests. That does not diminish their rational character at all (in fact it may even enhance it), although it may be against the principle of reason. Therefore states are rational but not necessarily reasonable actors in the international environment.

The term 'justice' referred to above is not derived from the Machiavellian version of state morality but rather is analogous to the authentic, unifying, and all-inclusive morality that does not legitimate building of a palace on the ruins of other people's homes, all in the name of rationality and national interests. The Hobbesian discourse that legitimises injustice in a lawless world[38] (which sounds not dissimilar to anarchical society) that is bereft of authentic morality is challenged in this narrative. One of the most poignant examples illustrating the fallacy of the argument on justice in International Relations can be found in the English School, outlined in this footnote.[39]

The prioritisation of order above justice, as propounded by Bull (see Note 39) misses the point. *Nahj-ol-Balaghe* [The Way of Eloquence], one of the oldest and most respected Islamic texts, defines justice as the 'right and proper order'.[40] If therefore we wish to establish justice (right order) within a wrong order we will be attempting the impossible and will not succeed. Establishing justice in that instance would require the dismantling of the old (wrong) order and replacing it with a new (right) one. Therefore order and justice are not viewed and treated as two disjointed, separate and independent concepts but rather as intertwined and interdependent. Accordingly, to be just one may have to subdue some of what may appear as rational.

In Rumi's exultant parlance, those who have not tasted internal justice and moderation will never appreciate external justice. Those who are not free from internal tyrants shall, at the slightest provocation, sell out the external freedom as well. Those who have not beheaded their own tyrannical desires are unable to recognise the external despots.[41]

As narrated by Rumi:

> *The art of separating the unjust from the just he/she will acquire,*
> *who beheads the inner tyrannical desire.*[42]

It now becomes imperative in normative International Relations discourses to emphasise the difference, and sometimes the conflict, between reason and rationality for much legitimation is sought for rationality in the name of reason. In Islamic discourses, one can use the term *hikma* as different from *aghl*.[43] The former refers to reason while the latter is more concerned with rationality as understood in Western philosophy. *Hakim* (the subject noun of *hikma*) is one who through reasoning has obtained knowledge of things within human tolerance range and has acted according to the expediencies of knowledge; in other words, knowledge per se does not make a researcher a *hakim*.[44] An instance where *hikma* as a Divine quality has been mentioned can be seen in the following lines:

> *The hikma (reason) of God in destiny and in decree,*
> *Made us lovers of one another, joined and free:*
> *Because of that fore-ordainment all particles of the world,*
> *Are paired as mates in love in one fold.*[45]

It is important to note that reasoning does not mean ratiocination, the former suggesting reflection while the latter represents rationality. The two overlap in many instances but there is nevertheless a distinction between them. In Shabestari's categorisation, *estedlal* (ratiocination) or *nazar* (consideration) is a type of reflection. This ratiocination is looked down upon by Rumi who likens people relying on it to those standing on wooden legs.

> *The leg of syllogisers is of wood*
> *And thus not as firm as it otherwise could* [46]

More elevating is the reflection of the heart called *kashf* (unveiling).[47] To Shabestari, reflection is the thought of the heart.[48] Lahiji, a subscriber to Shabestari's discourse, believes that thinking itself (*tafakkor*) is a spiritual voyage.[49] It can be observed that questions of contemplative discourses are not seen entirely in material, non-spiritual terms in Gnostic narratives. Accordingly, reason and thinking assume a lofty rank among Islamic teachings, which can be noted in a *hadith* attributed to Muhammad himself: 'One hour of thinking is better than one year of praying.'[50] The following lines by Shabestari attest to the significance of thinking in Islamic mysticism:

> *In the name of He who has taught the soul*
> *To think and meditate*
> *Who set aglow the heart*
> *With the light of the soul* [51]

Thinking as the bedrock of all mental activity is the path from the outer to the inner, from the surface to the meaning.[52] It is this journey that opens the gates of knowledge to humankind. Whether one goes to thoughts, or whether, as in some cases like the Sufis, thoughts go to one,[53] imagination is the key that gives rise to questions, which function as keys to knowledge.[54] As imagination is achieved in the heart (called reflection), it is through the ordering of these imaginings that the un-understood is rendered understood.[55] Knowledge therefore is in a sense holy. That is why Ghazzali states that the basis of prosperity in this world and hereafter is knowledge.[56] In so saying he is reconfirming the very Divine nature of knowledge and learning. The fragmentation of the world into material and spiritual would in this sense be bizarre for everything is equally holy and spiritual, especially if it emanates from the faculty of reason and reflection. The only unholy thought, word, or deed would be that which goes against reason and is not based on true reflection.

> *O Brother you are your own very thought*
> *The rest is all but flesh and sinew*
> *If your thought is rosy, you too are as a garden*
> *If your thought is thorny, you too are fuel for fire.*[57]
>   Rumi, *Masnavi*, Book II, lines 277–8

On a more practical level, it is painfully clear that sheer rationality per se has failed to bring peace to humanity. The two world wars occurred at the height of rationality and originated on a continent that prides itself with developing the onset of modern rational thinking. As a relative concept, impressed by one's perception of interests, values and other traits, no one can claim to have access to 'absolute rationality', whereby the interests of humanity as a whole can be attained. Both Adolf Hitler and Joseph Stalin considered themselves rational people as have many other tyrants and despots before and after them in history. Though perhaps a necessary condition for human communities, rationality seems hardly sufficient. The weakness of the concept as the only guiding principle in international affairs is therefore self-evident.

2.2   Islam and international relations

A new kind of war, called the war on terror, was proclaimed by former US President George W. Bush in response to the September 2001 terrorist attacks. The new Islamist fundamentalist terrorism[58] and the military response against it has propounded Islam as a serious, if not threatening, political discourse in academic and political circles around the globe. Is Islam inherently violent? Is it intrinsically political? If so, where does it belong on the conventional axis of politics: left, right, or centre? What are its ultimate aims and how does it propose to achieve them? Is radical Islam open to outside influence? Is it willing and able to interact with other political forces within the framework of international relations, norms and practices?

The very birth of International Relations as a discipline has to do with promoting peace and averting armed conflict in the aftermath of World War I. Similarly the story of humankind on this planet according to Islam is associated with conflict and starts with the exile of Adam and Eve to earth, where they were told enmity would reign between them in this abode.[59] Critical theory is also preoccupied with the question of war and peace. As stated by Richard Falk: 'My overriding concern is to foster an abolitionist movement against war and aggression as social institutions'.[60] In the face of conventional non-normative IR theories such as neo-realism, where interstate war is never deemed an international criminal offence, critical theory has now opened up space to move from the descriptive to the prescriptive, attempting to transform armed conflict from the status of indelible fact to erodible symptom in political life. This forms the very essence of an ethical, dialogical and solidarist international environment, where pretensions of 'neutrality' are cast aside and new understandings oriented towards a more egalitarian allocation of wealth and power can come to the fore. After all, as noted earlier, every theory is always for someone and for some purpose.[61] When Cox critiques 'problem-solving theory'[62] it is because he, like many others, has persevered to delegitimise the 'problem' in the first place. The issues that give rise to the *problématique* of war and peace, according to Islamic Gnosticism, all emanate from within (the self) that defines the 'problem' and offers its 'solution'. In that discourse the self, as noted above, is the real problem. Rumi narrates,

> *The wars of the people, like children's fights*
> *All meaningless, empty and vile*
> *The battles fought with wooden swords*
> *All their purposes vain and futile.*[63]
>
> *From a whim springs their war and peace*
> *On a caprice is based their honour and shame.*[64]

Islamism as a discourse can be considered together with critical theory as critiques of modernity in its Western-developed form.[65] Per se, therefore, Islamism does not have to be viewed as terrorism. It is rather the politicisation of Islam in a post-colonial context.[66] It is an interpretation, highlighting specific aspects of Islamic teachings while overlooking important others. Traditionally, it is believed that while the West is concerned with individual liberties, in Islam (and the East in general) priority is given to communal and social justice. The Quran stresses socio-economic justice and essential humanitarian egalitarianism.[67] In order to achieve that justice and establish *madineye fazele* (utopia), Islamism asserts itself as a political doctrine with specific outlines of governance. Governmentality, therefore, is conceived as a way to form and govern perfect human society. More will be said on this in the following pages.

Any system of ideas that aspires to have an impact at the individual, social or political level must inevitably provide an understanding of human nature, its needs, desires, goals, concerns, fears, hopes, weaknesses, strengths, and passions. Islam, too, must invariably offer its followers an account of human nature.

Philosophy of humankind in Islamic discourses

In Islam humankind is gifted with Divine Spirit[68] but is made of the lowest substance, the slime;[69] this combination of a sublime quality and low substance makes for the presence of potential extremes in the unique entity of humankind. 'And inspired the soul with wickedness as well as fear of God', states the Quran.[70] This is subscribed to by Ibn Khaldun, who believes God has put good and evil into the nature of humankind.[71] A human can decide to elevate himself/herself to the highest status or descend to the abject sludge-like levels of existence. The choice rests with the individual. This resembles Sartre's exposition on humanity in the sense that the human being is the only entity we know whose existence precedes his/her essence.[72] Accordingly the similarity between Sartre's existentialism and Islam on human nature rests on the question of choice. The essence of humankind is subject to mutation depending on what choice the individual makes (unlike the rest of beings or entities in nature) and it is this choice that contrary to historical determinism in Marxism or doctrines based on pure *kismet* (fate), empowers humanity to rise above their 'state of nature' and reshape themselves.[73] All humans, however, as stated by Ghazzali, are born with the same nature, and differences relating to religion are due to environmental conditions.[74]

Philosophers have used the 'state of nature' in their discourses on human governance. John Locke and Thomas Hobbes in the West have particularly benefitted from this concept in advancing their arguments. In Islam philosophers such as Ibn Khaldun and Ghazzali have also referred to naked human nature to illustrate their point. In Islamic Gnosticism, Rumi has epitomised the discourse that celebrates the God-given nature of humanity and 'reconditions' the environment based on mystic understanding of human essence, that is, he develops the ruins.[75] Human nature, in that tradition, turns into a shore where the rest of creation has anchored. Objectivity of natural phenomena is diluted in the fluid subjectivity sprung from human nature/interpretation. In other words, mysticism becomes existentialism par excellence and finds common ground with critical theory. As narrated by Linklater, 'Critical theory collapses the subject/object distinction and emphasises the human needs and purposes which determine what counts as valuable knowledge'.[76] The following lines from Rumi attest to the artificiality of this distinction in a profound manner and in a beautiful style:

> *Wine in ferment is a beggar suing for our ferment,*
> *Heaven in revolution is a beggar suing for our consciousness;*
> *Wine became intoxicated with us not we with it,*
> *The body came into being from us, not we from it.*[77]

Here Rumi ascribes the quality of drunkenness to humanity and not to wine. If we were not to get drunk from wine then alcohol would cease to be intoxicating. This is a fantastically powerful and liberating discourse, where humanity is elevated above its surroundings and is in full control, and not the subject, of his environment. In contrast, in Thomas Hobbes desires and aversions appear to define and present a 'quintessential' human being, where rationality and morality are viewed as means towards securing the desire/aversion–driven ends.[78] In that narrative we are all prisoners of the quarrel caused by competition, diffidence and quest for glory.[79] In a life that is infamously 'solitary, poor, nasty, brutish and short',[80] humankind is in a constant state of fear and mistrust of others. It is only to overcome such fears and threats from fellow human beings that a ruler/government becomes necessary.

Interestingly, however, there is one important commonality between Hobbes and Quranic teaching as regards the condition of enmity between human beings on earth. *Then did Satan make them slip from the (Garden) and get them out of the state (of felicity) in which they had been. We said: 'Get ye down all (ye people) with enmity between yourselves. On earth will be your dwelling place and your means of livelihood for a time.'*[81] The state of enmity appears to have been the condition of life on earth for humanity after descent from Paradise, his/her original dwelling. Enmity as a condition of life invokes negative traits such as hatred, cruelty, violence and injustice in human relations. In line with Hobbesian discourse and his cynical view of human nature, Ibn Khaldun, Islamic historian and sociologist of the fifteenth century, believes that 'injustice is a human trait. If you find a moral man, there is a reason why he is not unjust.'[82] Simply put, therefore, there are grounds in Islam also to believe that humankind can by nature be cruel and unjust. *We did indeed offer the Trust to the Heavens and the Earth and the Mountains; but they refused to undertake it, being afraid thereof: but human undertook it; he/she was indeed unjust and foolish*, narrates the Quran.[83]

Locke's 'state of nature', however, is a source of emancipation as he draws three basic rights – life, liberty and property – from it thereby giving those rights authenticity and rendering them inviolable. Unlike the sovereign in Hobbesian discourse, where there is no authentic value to guard but only to prevent the degeneration of society into disarray and chaos (lessening the chance for fulfilment of desire and avoiding aversions) and where the rulers have all the power and the authority to govern as they see fit, in Lockean narrative, the state is, and ought to be, at the service of the individual.[84] It is only to prevent the breach of, and/or to restore, these natural rights that the energising, and not substantive, right of judgement has been deferred to the state.[85] These natural rights can also be traced in an epistemic, and not jurisprudential, interpretation of Islamic teachings. The right to life and liberties, including even the right to defy the Almighty and the right to property are enshrined principles in this interpretation. The first is clearly reflected in the Quran which states that taking the life of an innocent human being is like murdering the whole of humanity, and likewise saving the life of an innocent is tantamount to saving the whole of humanity.[86] On the right to liberty, the freedom of Adam and Eve to disobey the Lord (the right to sin) is common to the Abrahamic traditions, including Islam; and if you can disobey the Almighty directly and still live to commit more sins then both right to liberty and right to life find new sanctity altogether. Also in the verse noted above (see Note 81), God chose the earth as the residence of humankind descended from Paradise, where his/her means of subsistence is provided. The latter point can be used to derive the right to property similar to the way Locke uses Christian theology to authenticate the same.[87]

There is in Islamic Gnosticism, as in other Abrahamic and non-Abrahamic traditions, the concept of *vahdat e vojood* known as pantheism in the West. Perhaps the most celebrated pantheist mystic in Islam, who by some accounts gave his life for his esoteric beliefs, was the Iranian Mansour Hallaj. He lived during the Abbasid rule some one thousand years ago (AD 858–922). Reportedly he used to run in the streets of Baghdad crying out: *ana-al-Haq* (I am God);[88] or 'split this head asunder that has now become defiant for a while'.[89] When he was being executed he was asked, 'What is love?'

His response was 'you shall see, today, tomorrow and the day after tomorrow'. Today they killed him, tomorrow they burnt him and the day after they threw his ashes to the Tigris. However, as noted in the Introduction, there is evidence that Hallaj was advocating the rights of Zanj slaves, brought from Sudan and East Africa to dig in the salt mines of lower Iraq, and was perceived as a threat to the political establishment at the time.[90] Though the Zanj revolt against the Abbasid Caliph Muwaffaq had failed in AD 883, Hallaj supported their cause. In the words of Herbert Mason:

> He demonstrated against the Caliphal authorities on behalf of the Zanj salt field labourers condemned in southern Iraq to subhuman living conditions and slave labour, a position he repeated on behalf of saving Bedouins who stormed Basra and Baghdad desperate for food; and to the end of his life, he raised the outcry to God, the Truth, the Just, on behalf of sufferers from injustice. His life, in this respect, was a consistent line, leading to his trial and execution.[91]

Contrary to the quietism that Sufism has been associated with, detached from worldly affairs, Hallaj as a master Sufi himself believed in the active pursuit of justice. If the Lord is just and His Creation is on that basis,[92] then establishing justice can only be a Divine act.[93] Thus *ana-al-Haq* (I am God) of Hallaj axiomatically translates into I am just and I work for the establishment of justice. Hallaj believed that the outcry of justice is a 'witness to the true Reality of God and the Truth of God's transcendent Uniqueness'.[94] Moreover, the theory of pantheism advances the concept of the unity of existence eroding all separations and manmade zones of exclusion that appear to have hitherto been a condition of human communities. If all are viewed and treated as one essentially, philosophically, and ontologically (the political aspect of which could be found in the theory of collective security), the pains and problems of one become the pains and the problems of all.

> *The souls of wolves and dogs are apart, every one,*
> *United are the souls of the Lions of God, all one*[95]

Thus, for instance, the Rwandan massacre would not just be a matter of international (but ineffective) public sympathy but rather an injustice that hurts the collective body of humanity and thus should have been prevented by the world community. It is appropriate to note the memorable poetry of Sa'di quoted previously:

> *The human race are members in a body created;*
> *For of a single essence are they all created;*
> *When fortune persecutes with pain one member surely,*
> *The other members of the body cannot stand securely.*
> *O you who from another's troubles turn aside your view*
> *It is not fitting they bestow the name of 'Human' on you.*[96]

Pantheism, therefore, in its political dimension could deliver the solidarist and dialogic community that Linklater and others pursue. The mystic and esoteric discourse of Hallaj, and Sufis alike, can thus turn into a liberating narrative seriously challenging the coordinates of wealth and power in human community. Shari'ati's exposition in denouncing Hallaj for lack of political activism is thus innocently ignorant at best or dangerously misleading at worst. The intellectual father of the Iranian revolution of 1979 placed the Prophet's disciple, Abuzar, above the famous mystic and even above the celebrated Iranian Muslim scholar, Avecina. His contention that a hundred Hallaj would render the society a madhouse, but that one Abuzar could change a century,[97] highlights the unawareness of some intellectual leaders including Shari'ati of Gnostic esoteric principles in political discourse. Pantheism, through a philosophical and existential linking of the members of the human race, can be the engine for change in dormant communities, where stagnation of ideas is the protector of the status quo. A pantheist cannot and will not stand indifferent to the plight of his fellow human beings. In that sense one may be able to appreciate the pantheism of Moses, Jesus and Muhammad, all of whom stood for change.

The individual, therefore, in Gnostic Islam, is the fundamental unit of his/her environment, who by knowing him/herself will be able to know their God.[98] The world outside is there for humanity to conquer without, however, being conquered by forces of greed and desire within.[99] The individual's freedom to think, speak and act is inviolable; but it is essential that this freedom emanates first from within and then extends to the world without. As narrated by Shams, 'Your freedom is your purity within you, not in anything without you in which you seek purity'.[100] Higher levels of happiness and ecstasy are not necessarily best achieved, in this discourse, through fulfilment of desires, but rather, as enunciated by Ghazzali, through controlling them.[101] The battle, therefore, first and foremost, is not between the individual and the forces of nature, but rather within him/herself. It is only subsequent to the victory in the internal battle that one may extend it to the outside world.[102] It is reported that Ali, Muhammad's cousin and son-in-law, having defeated an opponent in a one-on-one battle, refused to kill the enemy immediately after he had been spat on. He waited until his anger from the incident had subsided. Rumi narrates the story and the verbal exchanges between Ali and the enemy in the *Masnavi*. Responding to the enemy's question as to why he had desisted from killing him after the spitting, Ali states, 'The sword of my forbearance has smitten the neck of my anger'.[103] This demonstrates that even killing your sworn enemy, who has set out to destroy you physically, should not be committed out of anger but only out of the necessity of defending yourself and saving your life, that is, in the way of God. Anger, greed, lust, competition for resources and glory, desires and fears all should be subject to our control and not vice versa. This is where Gnosticism can be most useful in light of the fact that whatever emanates from the individual in terms of thoughts, words and deeds will have an impact on their environment. An old Zoroastrian maxim states, 'change your thoughts, so that you can change your words; change your words so that you can change your deeds; and change your deeds so that you can change your world'.

It can be seen that the state of nature (expounded by Western philosophers such as Locke and Hobbes) may be viewed in Islamic theology and Gnosticism at two different levels and in two different stages. The first level is the higher level enjoyed in Paradise; it is a stage where the human agent has not yet succumbed to temptation and greed and has not been seduced by Satan. In keeping with this narrative, fulfilment of pleasures and avoiding aversions as propounded by Hobbes are non-factors in human discourse. At this higher level, the subordination of the self to the sublime ordinance of the Almighty is protecting humanity from disobedience and loss of constraint. Peace reigns, harmony flows, beauty abounds, unity stands and love is in supreme command. The human agent stands at the opposite point of the axis of 'solitary, poor, nasty, brutish and short'.[104] The second inferior level begins where and when temptation takes over and greed is in the driving seat. The Word of the Almighty is disregarded, and Satan, through a faith-based seduction,[105] manages to misguide the human agent and lead him to transgress the limit of his self-constraint. Thereafter the abode of humankind is earth, where a lower level of existence is experienced and, as stated unambiguously in the Quran, this new place of residence is where enmity will reign between members of the human race.[106] This view on the second state of nature is the one shared by Hobbes, who suggests the establishment of the sovereign as the necessary institution to save us from ourselves (our enmity towards one another). Accordingly the very institution of a social contract between citizens is a means to averting the evils of enmity among humans. And it is to the question of community in Islamic discourse that we now turn.

Community in Islamic discourse

The Quran starts with 'In the name of God' (In the Name of God, the Merciful, the Compassionate), and ends with 'in the name of the people' (*Naas*). As postulated by Shari'ati, in many a place in the Muslim Scripture, the name of God and the people can be interchanged.[107] Quranic imperatives are usually in plural and rarely, if at all, in singular (e.g. *ayyo-han-naas* [oh people], or *al-lazina* [those]). Islam is basically perceived to locate human beings in the context of the wider community. There is thus commonality between Aristotle and Islamic discourses on the intrinsic sociability of humankind. The following Quranic verse (49:13) attests to this:

> *O mankind! We created you from a single (pair) of a male and a female, and made you into nations and tribes, that ye may know each other (not that ye may despise (each other). Verily the most honoured of you in the sight of Allah is (he/she who is) the most righteous of you. And Allah has full knowledge and is well acquainted (with all things).*

This illustrates the salience of community (as against the individual) in Islamic teachings. In Islamists' interpretation a radicalised version of this communal aspect is promoted. Even the Universal Declaration of Human Rights is viewed as reflecting individual rights, lacking the spirit of social rights altogether.[108] Though reward and punishment will be calculated on an individual basis,[109] salvation is mainly a collective and not an individual affair in Islam. How can one prosper in a backward, undeveloped and poor community? This may be inferred also from Saint Thomas's Gospel, which is not included in the New Testament: 'For this reason I say, if one is whole, one will be filled with light, but if one is divided, one will be filled with darkness.'[110]

There are six broad terms that are used in the Quran, which refer to community of people. They are *Ghabileh*,[111] *Taiefah*,[112] *Ghoem*,[113] *Aal*,[114] *Ummah*,[115] and *Naas*.[116] (References indicate one instance of each usage in the Muslim Scripture but there are many more.) The first four seem to refer to a group of people with similar ways of life and common customs inhabiting a common geography. The last two terms, however, seem to have a much wider domain. Ummah is used in the Quran over 50 times and is the term that is referred to often by the Islamic scholars and theologians as well as Islamist fundamentalists denoting the Islamic community at large as one people. All those working towards God and following His path, as understood and interpreted by any given group of Muslims, belong to the ummah, regardless of creed, language, tradition, geography, history, and so on. In Shari'ati's words: '*Ummah* is a society consisting of those who are one in thoughts, beliefs and religion; their commonality permeates both their thoughts as well as their deeds.'[117] In this interpretation of ummah there is a transnational concept that is central to the formation of an Islamic group. The only criterion for membership is common belief.

The centrality of common belief in ummah signifies, in many Islamist scholars' views, the uniqueness of the Muslim community. Race, history, culture, language, customs, heroes and other commonalities are rendered insignificant in the face of a shared and collective faith and action. 'Thus the finest and holiest relationship that a human being feels towards his/her own kind is bereft of racial, familial, statal, national and biological/physiological elements, but one based on shared belief and shared thinking.'[118] Ummah thus becomes an all-inclusive community, where decision to enter or to exit rests with the individual. It is the leadership of this ummah that has the responsibility to direct those in the group from 'what is' to 'what must be' at almost any cost.[119] Unlike Indian religions where everyone is his/her own saviour in reaching from samsara to nirvana, in Islamic and Islamist discourses the presence of a proper leader is indispensable. The following from one of the great-grandsons of the Prophet is quoted by some to demonstrate the point:

> A human being who has lost his/her imam [leader] resembles a sheep who has lost its shepherd. ... This sheep is wandering ... days and nights ... to reach a herd ... and realising after a while that neither the shepherd nor the herd are its own separates from them and begins searching for its own herd and shepherd in fields and deserts ... wandering and lost, to find yet another strange herd and shepherd ... confounded and wandering in the fields of fright and deserts of disappointment looking for its own herd and shepherd ... until at last it falls prey to the wolf ....[120]

The leadership of the ummah is concerned more with development rather than sheer administration. It seeks to promote values inherent in Islam as it perceives them; in doing so the happiness of the people is not of prime importance. Basing his exposition on the etymology of *politics* and *siasa* [politics in Arabic] Shari'ati explains that unlike politicians in the West, who are concerned with the happiness and contentment of the residents of the polis, Islamic administrators engage in a discourse of development much like a professional rider appears to tame a wild horse (the meaning of the word *siasa*), a process that may well trigger wild reactions and bring about discontent of the animal, at least for a while. So, in the first instance, a Western politician is essentially a *server* of the people, whereas in the Islamic context a politician is primarily a *mosleh* (developer, evolver).[121]

'Humankind is basically a migrant, a passenger; if he/she stops travelling, he/she dies, is no longer human.'[122] Accordingly ummah is a dynamic, migrating and ideal seeking–society.[123] Though democracy may be a value for this group, the higher ideals of the people are not comprised of the ballot box, the discourse claims. The West, while celebrating and practicing certain freedoms for its people, has in effect abandoned true freedom. While 'voting is free, votes themselves are not'.[124] The freedom of the votes has been curbed by many factors emanating from the power of those who enjoy the unequal allocation of wealth and power in the status quo. In the narrative of Shari'ati:

> These atrocities did not take place in the Middle Ages or the era of the royal residents of Versailles; colonization, that meant the massacre of peoples, cultures, history and civilisations as well as the plunder of the wealth of non-Europeans, was created by regimes that were the product of democracy; governments that believed in liberalism. These murders have not been, and are not committed by priests and the Inquisition and not by Caesars, but by the very able hand of Western democracy and liberalism. When? In the Nineteenth and the Twentieth Centuries; that is in the years that liberalism, democracy, search for freedom, humanism and human fraternity, as the only words spoken by Europe, were announced to the world and like a powerful and universalizing surge, overwhelmed modern art, literature, poetry, culture and philosophy and triggered a clamour of joy from the hearts of the intellectuals of the plundered and confounded countries of the East, who were themselves the oppressed, defenceless and unaware victims of these deceptive and mendacious words.[125]

And it is not just the political leaders who are the focus of critical outlook. The liberal project raises many questions that address both the intellectual elite as well as the ordinary citizen in the West. For instance, the condensed labour of the Western worker for Marx is represented in the commodity produced. The latter, however, for an Asian worker, represented condensed murder and plunder.[126] The French massacre of 45,000 people in 1947, or the hundreds of thousands in Algeria a decade later, hardly raised popular objections from the liberal people in France. There is thus a view, in the Islamist fundamentalist discourse, that holds the liberal West, in general, accountable for the decadence and the deprivation that their former colonies are suffering from.

The Islamist discourses would argue that the failure of the liberal project, its exclusionary treatment of parts of humanity, and its reticence against the unequal distribution of global wealth and power, stems from a political ethos that has removed God from the world. For if there is no God, all is permissible and therefore 'when a Divine-based outlook departs human endeavours and faith is denied, then ethics will have no legs to stand on'.[127] The 'civilising mission' and the 'white man's burden' was thus no more than an anti-ethical and shameful disguise to rip the riches from the world. And democracy preached nowadays, Islamists would claim, is worse than open dictatorship, for the latter is known for its poor quality and ugliness, like a poison that is marked accordingly and is forced down the throat. However, a delicious meal offered with much grace by the doctor and not by the killer, but contaminated with poison, will bring the same fate, with the difference that the patient, this time, will be singing its praise while suffering from its crippling and even deadly effects.[128]

In short, to recap, the Islamist would define ummah as a society of those who share a common goal and work towards a common ideal under a common leadership. The bases for ummah are thus: choice, movement, leadership and goal. Despite a forceful underlying drive for ummah as expounded by some Islamist thinkers, there is evidently an absence of specifics in terms of the practicality of governance. *Shari'a* as the only guide has proven less than sufficient to cope with the modalities of social and international life in this day and age. The clear examples of Iran, Sudan and the Taliban in Afghanistan mirror this reality. Though in Iran rationality has been more utilised and the concept of *ijtihad* (interpretative authority) has left room for manoeuvre, the prominence of *fiqh* (jurisprudence) as defined and formulated many centuries ago has narrowed *tariqa* (the inner path) that underlies all that *shari'a* is based on. *Tariqa* is more the discourse of Muslim Gnostics as opposed to *shari'a*, the anchor of Islamist jurists. It would now be apt to critique the Islamist concept of ummah as explicated above.

First and foremost God has not chosen the term ummah for the true community of Muslims and the righteous. This is a fallacy and represents at best ignorance. The term ummah, as clearly stated in the Quran, also describes a group of sinful people and even those going to burn as a way of punishment.[129] This raises the question of why this term has been used by many as a holy Islamic term exclusive to believers. An ummah can be a Muslim, non-Muslim, believer, or non-believer community as attested to by the Quran.

'Any map of the world that does not include Utopia is not worth even glancing at....' said Oscar Wilde.[130] In Islam this concept is much referred to, by Islamists in particular, who contrast it (*madinatol- fazela*) with the Bedouin Arab pre-Islamic era of ignorance (*jahiliyya*). Shari'ati contends that Islam is the only school of thought that has actually been able to realise its utopian dream in the shape of Medina governed by the Prophet of Islam himself in the first years of the Islamic calendar. However, one could perceivably question if the Prophet was content with all aspects of Arabian life when he was in power in Medina and beyond. Were all aspects of Muslims' life perfect in the eyes of Muhammad himself? How about relations with non-Muslims? On close scrutiny, one may be surprised to find out that there was much about the way of life or the conduct of the new Muslims in Medina that was probably not to the liking of the Messenger. Most of the new converts were perhaps still pagans at heart and did not quite believe in the directives of the new religion. How could centuries of tradition (idol worshipping and the ways of the *jahilyya* era) be washed away overnight, particularly when it was all done en masse through the tribal mechanism of *bey'a* and not through individual reasoning and conviction? How could those early converts be ideal Muslims when most of them could hardly read and write? Is that how true Islam envisages its ideal society, ridden with illiterates, some of whom would be ready to sell their soul for cheap material gains? If that was not so, why is it then clearly stated in the Quran, *And among those around you [Muhammad] of the wandering Arabs there are hypocrites, and among the townspeople of Al-Madinah (there are some who) persist in hypocrisy whom thou (O Muhammad) knowest not. We know them, and We shall chastise them twice; then they will be relegated to a painful doom.*[131] And also that *The Arabs are worst in division and apostasy?*[132] Could those Arabs referred to in the Quranic verses be the members of an Islamic utopia in the time of the Prophet? Can a society aspire or claim to be ideal when its members are professed to betray its principles? Believing that Medina at the time of the Prophet was Islamic utopia is an insult to Islam and all Muslims and highly dangerous in terms of setting standards for today's faithful. The same must have been the case as regards relations with non-Muslims. Why else should early Islam have gone to war with the Jewish tribes and expelled them from the city altogether? Was the reported breach of the pact by the Jews of Medina to Muhammad's liking? Would it have been possible to institutionalise certain mechanisms to ensure that such breaches would not take place? And if not – It has to be no because if yes then the Prophet would immediately come under question – was the absence of such safeguards part and parcel of an Islamic doctrine for all time and place? It is clear from the above that Muhammad worked within the constraints of his time and place in relation to the circumstances and the range of possibilities open to him. It is here that the verse in the Quran attesting to the human quality of the Prophet assumes particular significance: *Say, that I am a human being like yourselves*,[133] is the Almighty's instruction to the Messenger of Islam so that people would assess, judge, admire and follow him in human terms and not imagine him as Divine. And as human the Prophet dealt with all matters of governance in relation to the realistic options open to him, many a time far from ideal.

The use of force to reach one's end appears justified in the discourse of Islamist fundamentalists. In fundamentalist Islam, violence as a means to spread the word of God and to implement His Will is accepted.[134] This violence can also be waged against non-combatants if deemed necessary. The terrors of 11 September 2001 and similar carnage in Europe and elsewhere speak for themselves. This can hardly be said to comply with the guidelines in Islam and the Quran though. There are clear and unambiguous verses (*mohkamat*) decrying the murder of the innocent.

For that cause We decreed for the Children of Israel that whosoever killeth a human being ... it shall be as if he had killed all mankind, and whoso saveth the life of one, it shall be as if he had saved the life of all mankind.[135]

It is reported that during the reign of Ali a Jewish woman had an item of jewellery taken from her by force. Ali is reported to have cried on account of the injustice to the woman and to have said that if one were to die from such grief (of the injustice to a fellow human being) it would be justified. However, like many other ideas and religions, Islam also can be exploited for the furtherance of political goals of others. The deeds of the followers of a religion do not necessarily reflect the dictums of that religion. The brutality of the Inquisition and the burning of people at the stake not only did not reflect but in fact betrayed the teachings of Christianity. Security and peace are terms dear to Islam and God swears by them in the Muslim Holy Book. *By the fig and the olive ... and by this land of security.*[136] Therefore the fundamentalists' attempt to associate Islam with terrorism, carnage and killing and attempting to justify their violent hatred of *the other* through Islamic teachings and Quranic imperatives is a monumental fallacy, decontextualising the text of Islam and in effect ignoring and eroding its spirit.

This ummah was governed by the institution of the Caliphate, which started after the death of the Messenger in AD 632 and lasted to the dissolution of the Ottoman Empire after World War I. Nowadays it may be difficult to speak of ummah as an organised cohesive group, however. There are serious rifts within the Islamic world, which have led to violent clashes. The longest war in the twentieth century was between two Muslim countries, Iran and Iraq.

Today, however, the sovereign state is the accepted norm of representation in international life. This form of governance is tied to the concepts of nation and nationalism, both of which are Western in origin. There is much that emphasises the self at the state level. Modern statehood is exclusive, that is, by the virtue of belonging to one nation one is automatically excluded from many, if not all, others. Worse, one's nationality suggests who one's enemies and friends are in the international or even social environment. For instance, Greeks may be less likely to adopt Turks for allies and friends and vice versa. By the same token, Pakistanis and Indians are prone to be adversarial towards one another. Examples are plenty in this regard. The exclusivity of the state system is self-evident. Also, people are divided and fragmented through this exclusionary system. The chance and prospect of solidarity in the world is diminished for as long as competing national interests fight one another and the political ethos of international life legitimises and encourages its members to do so; the individual as the fundamental unit in society is reflected in the shape of the sovereign state in international relations. (To many Muslims, however, who cherish the era of the caliphate and associate Muslims' decline in the world with the import and introduction of modern political concepts of nationhood and statehood, ummah appears a more empowering and thus appealing substitute. And when ummah is represented and led by the caliphate, they believe, the Islamic glory of the past can again resurface and impress and overwhelm the world.)

The five monopolies of statehood (representation, adjudication, taxation, use of violence and demanding allegiance to kill and/or get killed)[137] have rendered this form of representation an outdated form of governance which is no longer able to accommodate the needs and concerns of humanity in this day and age. This holds true irrespective of the nature of the regime in power. 'No matter how democratic the constitution of a state regime, as a sovereign state it is always more than a democracy, and consequently a good deal less.'[138] It is partly the threatening nature of terrorism to these monopolies that has united almost all states in their rightful condemnation of this violent discourse. In claiming and demanding the allegiance of its adherents to engage in killing innocent others Islamist fundamentalism has clearly breached the state monopoly in the use of violence. Furthermore it claims the mantle of representation of all Muslims – though clearly it does not have that. In Pakistan and Afghanistan, sporadic instances of adjudication also take place outside of government control in tandem with the dictates of these groups.[139] Therefore we can see that the state as an institution of governance is under threat by the advance of Islamist fundamentalism. In the words of Susan Buck-Morss,

> ...the national security state that is called into existence with the sovereign pronouncement of a 'state of emergency' and that generates a wild zone of power, barbaric and violent, operating without democratic oversight, in order to combat an 'enemy' that threatens the existence not merely and not mainly of its citizens, but of its sovereignty.[140]

Ironically it is the use of violence that forms the similarity of Islamist fundamentalist discourse with the realist paradigm in International Relations. The following quotation from Samuel Huntington illustrates the point:

> The West won the world not by the superiority of its ideas or values or religion (to which few members of other civilizations were converted) but rather by its superiority in applying organized violence.[141]

If stronger and more organised violence won the world for the West, then the same can be used to win the world back from them, Islamist fundamentalists would argue. If 'the increase in the Prophet's authority and power was partly due to his successful military expeditions', as observed by Montgomery Watt,[142] is held to be true in a generalised and unqualified fashion, then violence appears to hold a pivotal place in the maintaining, and the shift, of power. This emphasis on hard power in Islamist fundamentalist discourse may partly be the result of radical Islam favouring the political concepts of the region of its origin.[143] However, it is debatable if that represents other Islamic traditions. Many in Islam have favoured the utilisation of soft power over hard power. 'The pen of the learned will be above the blood of the martyrs,' said the Prophet of Islam.[144] Knowledge as a means of change and in the conduct of justice is of paramount importance in Islam and is in fact viewed as a value in itself. *Are those who know equal to those who do not?* asks the Quran.[145] Violence to advance or to defend the faith is rejected unless it is deemed necessary to save lives. Abul'ala Ma'arri, a blind Syrian poet living at the peak of Islamic civilisation and power, was a near genius and an atheist who wrote:

> *They all err – Muslim, Christian, Jew and Magian;*
> *Two make humanity's universal sect;*
> *One man intelligent without religion,*
> *And one religion without intellect.*[146]

Yet despite such open anti-religious pronouncements none of his writings were ever confiscated and no violence was committed to suppress his writings or views. This emphasises the importance of tolerating outright opposition in Islamic tradition. One cannot help but draw comparison between the treatment of *The Satanic Verses*, where the author was condemned to death by a contemporary leader of radical Islam, and the liberal approach adopted towards Ma'arri a thousand years ago at the peak of Islamic Empire.

If Tilly's assertion that statehood, both in formation and in development, has followed the requirements of capitalism is correct,[147] then the advent of globalisation must also call for a new form of political community. The desanctification of borders, the universalisation of economic liberalism, and the holistic nature of environmental and criminal dangers facing humanity, all demand an overhaul of the current system, the building block of which is sovereign statehood. The latter has been shared by competing schools in the West and in the Islamic world. Both the former Eastern bloc and their fellow capitalist communities adopted statehood albeit with different system of governance. Among Muslims, communities as far apart as Africa and East Asia, with different histories and cultures, have also adopted (rather have been given) statehood. The sharing of statehood globally, as the organised system of political represen- tation, does not reflect shared history or common heritage among various communities in the world.

Capitalism lies at the centre of critical theory's critique of the international system. The question of underdevelopment is viewed primarily as a by-product of the financial tenets that underpin the world economic system. Frank states, 'Underdevelopment is not the result of not being sufficiently integrated into the global economy but the consequences of being incorporated into the capitalist world system.'[148] The gap between the North and the South therefore should be attributed globally to the world system at large rather than to individual states. He goes on to say, 'Thus in order to understand the process of underdevelopment we must see it as an epiphenom- enal manifestation of capitalism.'[149] Richard Falk shares those views when stating that capitalism is the greatest impediment to reform and that socialism is superior because it seeks to distribute wealth equally.[150] He further claims that participatory democracy cannot by definition be capitalist.[151] Other critical thinkers have also assailed capitalism. In their view, the unequal distribution of wealth and power inevitably carries imbalances in the world that in time mani- fest themselves, sometimes violently. Such violence, called war when committed between states, is an accepted course of action in pursuit of perceived national interests. No a treaty or international cove- nant has ever categorised war as an international criminal offence. Such categorisation would automatically tie the hands of states, including the powerful ones, in waging violence to maintain and/ or to enhance wealth and power. It is very much this emphasis on self-gain, whether at social, statal or international level that renders meaningful, just, lasting and peaceful cooperation an evasive goal in the human community. In pursuit of perceived national interests, described and/or prescribed by conventional paradigms, sometimes violent conflict occurs; to contain this conflict diplomacy and inter- national law are utilised, which means we ourselves question our own rationality when we try to contain its consequences. This in itself constitutes irrationality. How pertinent Rumi's extrapolation on this rationality appears:

> *It behoves me to become ignorant of this worldly intellect,*
> *Clutch at madness, no rationality but neglect;*
> *Flee from whatever you deem profitable to the self,*
> *Drink poison and the water of life you must shelf...*
> *Far-thinking provident wisdom, I have tried,*
> *Madness henceforth, shall be untied.*[152]

Islam is the only world religion to have been founded by a businessman.[153] Accordingly many of the messages in Islamic scriptures have been expressed in business-like language.[154] There is accordingly no intrinsic incompatibility between the faith and free trade. However, the ultimate expansion of capital and its extension to all aspects of life, where financial profit reigns supreme, is also rejected. If capitalism as a social and economic system attempts to subdue all human traits in pursuit of greater profit, Islamic teachings, including Gnostic Islam, would stray from that discourse.

> *Oh son burst thy chains, set yourself free and unfold,*
> *How long wilt thou be bondsman to silver and gold?*
> *If thou pour the sea into a pot,*
> *How much will it hold? One day's lot;*
> *The pot, the eye of the covetous, never fills,*
> *The oyster-shell has pearls that contentment brings.*[155]

Tribalism as an old way of life among Bedouin Arabs was vehemently, albeit unsuccessfully, fought from early days by Islam, which sought to centralise and urbanise. Unlike Christianity and Judaism, Islam developed in relative political success from early on it should, however, be noted that tribalism in the Islamic world is far from over and in fact pervades many Islamic communities). During the Islamic empires of the Umayyids, Abbasids and the Ottomans, many nationalities came under the control of Islamic rule. The rules governing the conduct of the caliphate and those relating to social affairs were gradually put together using some indigenous Arab/Islamic, but mainly Persian and Byzantine, customs.[156] It was not possible to run an empire with regulations and tradition that applied in the Arabian

Bedouin life. Though a system of rules was eventually amassed under the rubric of *shari'a*, it took the new Muslim rulers some two hundred years before they arrived at that.

Thus to sum up, there is perhaps no strict guidelines on how an Islamic community should be formed or governed. What is, however, clear is that there is no room for exclusivity based on race, colour, history, culture, or tradition. The discriminations applied during the Umayyids and the Abbasids against non-Arabs were clearly Arab and not Islamic in origin. Unhindered capitalism as an exclusive and unequal system of resource allocation is also treated with scepticism. In essence the people of faith, in the discourse of Islamic Gnosticism, have been described by Rumi:

> *Love's state is apart*
> *From all religions and faiths;*
> *God is lovers' religion*
> *God is lovers' state.*[157]

2.3   Secular Islam versus politicised Islam

Politicised Islam, or political Islam as it is referred to in the media, is a political discourse that aims to reassert the rule of *shari'a* through whatever means possible including violence. At the theoretical level, their argument is based on the fact the Messenger of Islam was simultaneously a religious and a political leader. Therefore there is no distinction between a political decree and a religious one, they maintain. For if you want to implement the rules of *shari'a* you will need power, that is the domain of politics. Thus religion and politics are infused and inseparable. Just as politics guides us on war and peace, so do Islamic teachings. Just as politics aims to direct people to a better life, so do Islamic rules. But as Islamic rules are the norms set by the Almighty they have priority over any manmade principles. Anyone dissenting from that or resisting the spread of the rule of God, as understood by Islamist fundamentalists, is viewed as an enemy of the Lord and must therefore be exterminated.

At the practical level, however, as outlined in the Introduction and the earlier parts of this chapter, the era of colonisation and the parallel decline of Muslims contributed to the emergence of the Islamist movement. As *westoxification* appeared to overwhelm

Muslim communities, 'the task of reintegrating knowledge and culture imported from the West within the frame of Islamic tradition, or of finding a discourse in which the "eternal message" of Islam could be expressed and understood in terms of contemporary reality, increasingly fell to the religious autodidacts'.[158] In that sense, 'Islamism is not a religious discourse but a political one'.[159] It is a violent reactionary movement against modernity and political settings that have failed to deliver equal progress and prosperity to Muslims as it has to Westerners.

One of the most authoritative guides for Islamist fundamentalists is Ibn Taymiyya, the Islamic jurist of the fourteenth century. An impressive polemicist, he advocated 'unmediated' adherence to the Quran and the *sunna* (the deeds and sayings of the Prophet). Subscriber to the Hanbali sect of Sunni Islam, now prevalent in Saudi Arabia, Ibn Taymiyya, who lived under Mongolian rulers (converts to Islam) declared them infidels and thus set a precedent (in that he sanctioned the overthrow of the Mongolians to be replaced by what he considered true Muslims) that has been followed to this day by radical Islamists. Osama bin Laden was a follower of that school. The following gives a flavour of Ibn Taymiyya's views:

> God has imposed the duty of enjoining the good and forbidding the evil, and that is possible only with the authority of a chief. Similarly, all the other duties which He has ordered, like the jihad, [the administration of] justice, pilgrimage, public prayer, festivals, brotherly help, the application of punishments and so forth can only be observed by means of the power and authority of the leader. It is thus that people say 'the Sultan is the Shadow of God on earth...'.[160]

After the Ottomans' demise, 'once free from traditional institutional arrangements, emptied of political use but dispersed within cultural life, Islam became available for articulations of resistance to post-colonial order'.[161] Here, politics and religion were almost unavoidably blended to offer at once solace and hope to generations of Muslims who felt incapable of locating the enemy (centuries-old traditions that had led to the collapse of the caliphate or modernity that was commonplace in the triumphant West) and thus powerless to do much about their plight. The contrast between the two is well described by Soroush:

A modern person is critical and demanding (not placid and inert), in search of change (not merely of understanding), in favour of revolution (not just reform), active (not passive), at home with scepticism and anxiety (not certitude), interested in clarity and causality (not bewilderment and enchantment), prone to pride and joy (not sorrow of separation), mindful of life (not death), in pursuit of rights (not only duties), sponsor of creative (not imitative) art, oriented to the external (not just the internal) world, a lover (not a despiser) of life, an intervener in (not merely a user of) the world, a user of reason in the service of criticism (not just for understanding). Modern humanity is, in a word, oblivious to its limits and proud of its creative possibilities.[162]

The economic and social backwardness of Muslim communities compared to their Western counterparts provided fuel for Islamist tendencies. *Ikhwan-ol-Muslemin* (the Muslim Brotherhood) in Egypt came to rise against the backdrop of socio-economic problems that modernity, parliamentary system and democracy, in their view, seemed unable to solve.[163] In other contexts, such as pre-revolutionary Iran, the fast pace of reform towards urbanisation and modernity, with little room for a transitionary period, left millions of former, now–urban, peasants wandering in the streets of main cities with pockets full of money but bereft of identity. Devoid of social roles and functions and in the absence of a socialising process, these former peasants turned into a ticking bomb. In search of meaning and significance they turned to religion, a familiar and alluring source offering them security, solace and salvation. This politicised religion also pointed the finger in the direction of modernity and the West as the culprits that had caused them harm and deformed their history, character and religion. Political Islam, as was promised to all, would usher in a new era of unprecedented prosperity. In reality, however, as it turned out, nothing could be further away from the truth.

With the fantastic failure of political Islam in Iran, Sudan and Afghanistan, Muslim thinkers began to revisit some of their long-held beliefs and reflected on some philosophical and epistemological aspects of their religion in the light of the developments that had afflicted their Muslim brothers at home and abroad. A new generation of thinkers approached modernity without the scepticism of their colleagues in the past. Liberalism, for instance, was scrutinised and found to be in tandem with Islamic principles. If one is free to enter a dialogue with God, as inferred from the Quran,[164] and if one is free to disobey God, as narrated in the story of Creation, then how can that freedom be taken away in the name of that same God and that same religion? These scholars did not find freedom in contra-distinction to Islamic discourse but to the contrary very much embedded in it. In the words of a leading Muslim scholar, 'those who shun freedom as the enemy of truth and a possible breeding ground for wrong ideas do not realise that freedom is itself a truth (*haq*).'[165] One of the topics reflected upon by these thinkers was secularism.

In its philosophical sense, secularism is 'nothing but the "scientification" and rationalisation of social and political thought and deliberation'.[166] As religion itself is primarily a matter of faith and not science it may be construed that the above negates religion in all socio-political spheres. That is, however, not the case. Secularism does not translate to either anti-religious governance or a complete separation of religion from politics. In fact many a secular countries in the West have the roots of their laws in the religion of their people. What secularism strongly denotes is the separation of political power and representation from organised religion. Thus, although religion can have political tendencies (for instance few religions, if any, with a belief in God tend to subscribe to communism) and politics can have religious beliefs, religious leaders and representatives should not and cannot assume political roles in a secular establishment.[167]

Gazzali, the renowned Muslim philosopher, believed that politics had four levels:

(1) The highest level, the politics of the prophets; their directives are for both the general public as well as the elite, both for the outward [physical] flow and the inward [non-physical] flow.
(2) The politics of kings and rulers; their directives are for both the general public as well as the elite, but only for the outward and not for the inward flow.
(3) The politics of the learned, who are the inheritors of prophecy; their directives are for the inward flow of the elite only.

(4) The politics of the preachers; their directives are for the inward
flow of the general public.[168]

The above, from one of the most celebrated Islamic figures in history,
clearly demonstrates the division between religion and politics or he
would not have separated the politics of the kings and rulers from
the politics of the preachers. And he stated this at the peak of Islamic
prowess and civilisation and not at its low ebb, like today. It is easy
to infer from the above that Islam, at its most glorious days, when
Baghdad was the global centre of learning and teaching, did not practice politicised Islam as the radical followers of Abdul-Wahhab and
the guru of radical Shi'a Islam, Shari'ati, would have us believe. What
the preachers of politicised Islam advocate amounts to blending the
politics of the preachers with the politics of kings and rulers (noted
above), establishing a new kind of politics that ushers in a dictatorship of *fiqh* (Islamic jurisprudence) and *faqih* (Islamic jurists). It is
that kind of politics that poured tonnes of alcoholic beverages into
the Nile in Sudan (poisoning the fish in the process) in an attempt
to Islamicise the society.[169] It is the same kind of politics that banned
women from studying in Taliban Afghanistan and also forbade them
from visiting male doctors if they fell ill, in effect sentencing them
to death. But if women are never to see and never to be seen, never to
hear and never to be heard, never to speak in public, never to assume
social positions, never to study and thus never to be able to read
and write, never to attract any attention outside the home, never to
judge but always be judged, then they are hardly alive anyway. One
wonders what happened to the *hadith* from the Founder of Islam
stating that 'learning is imperative upon all Muslims'[170] and that
'one must learn from the cradle to the grave'.[171]

In another notable observation, Ghazzali is quoted as saying,
'In matters of reason, I believe in reasoning and in matters of religion I believe in the Quran ... .'[172] He therefore clearly distinguished
the religious realm from worldly affairs. But Gazzali was not the
only Islamic scholar who differentiated politics and religion. Shah
Valiollah Dehlavi, in his *Hojjatollah al-Baleqeh*, distinguishes those
rulings by the Prophet that related to the Medina of 1,400 years ago
from those that stated the eternal rules of the faith.[173] Others also
in the contemporary period have said much the same. Abdullahi
An-Na'im, the Sudanese Islamic reformist, differentiates between

the Meccan verses and those revealed in Medina. To him the latter dealt with the concrete issues of the time and the place whereas the former were meant as eternal rules and guidelines.[174] Other leading liberal Islamic thinkers have made similar statements. Asghar Ali Engineer, Abdolkarim Soroush and Abdulaziz Sachedina, among others, all subscribe to a reformed Islam liberated from the tyrannical dictates of jurisprudence and more in tune with the free spirit of Islamic teachings as understood and reflected by Gnostics such as Rumi. Contrary to the statement made by Lord Cromer that 'Islam reformed is Islam no longer',[175] these emerging and increasing number of scholars believe that the spirit of their faith is all but lost in the intricacies and complexities of a stagnated, outdated and unresponsive jurisprudence that has monopolised religious representation and kept all other aspects of Islamic teachings and knowledge such as philosophy, theology, exegesis, history, literature and Gnosticism under tight restraint lest they leap ahead and question the authority of the jurists, who have spent years of pedagogy in forbidding people to enjoy their God-given freedom and tying the eternal salvation of individuals to obeying their ritualised and static commands of dos and don'ts.

'The fatter you make a religion, the more stagnant it becomes.'[176] By ascribing all facets of life to religion, as political Islam and Islamist fundamentalists do, one does not serve religion or God more profoundly. In fact involving religion in every little detail of life runs the risk of belittling the faith. At times one hears of terms such as Islamic economics, Islamic sciences, Islamic politics, and so on, that reflect the confusion of those who anchor their religious zeal in such concepts. There can only be one physics, one chemistry and one economics. Can we have two sets of physical laws, one Islamic and one non-Islamic? Even in the field of politics, the record of radical Islamists has amounted to nothing more than a strict adherence to 'might is right', which is the linchpin of the realist paradigm in International Relations. Anti-Americanism, the common thread linking all radical Islamists, can hardly suffice in elevating their irrational discourse into a systemic and structured political school. In short, there are no epistemological grounds on which to speak of Islamic politics, Islamic economics, Islamic sociology, and so forth.

The most salient feature of all Islamists is their ideologisation of religion. Religion as an intrinsic need of humanity to accommodate the innate search for the unknown[177] is reduced at the hands of fundamentalists to a dogmatic doctrine that prides itself in the violent destruction of *the other*, with no designs for development. It is therefore not surprising that no Islamist group has thus far appeared to advance a literacy programme for all Muslims, nor is it unexpected that no concrete proposals have been put forward by them to provide Muslim communities with better facilities in medical care, urban development, social welfare, technological advancement, family planning and other facets of life. Instead, schools in some parts of Pakistan teaching small girls are threatened with bombings (sometimes they are actually blown up) if they do not cease to operate. Ideologised Islam 'banishes reason from religion and compassion from the faith'.[178]

One of the most important works on the utter failure of the Islamists is by Olivier Roy. In *The Failure of Political Islam* he ably demonstrates the failings of radical Islamists. In it he states:

> What the Islamists advocate is not the return to an incomparably rich classical age, but the establishment of an empty stage on which the believer strives to realize with each gesture the ethical model of the prophet.[179]

The manifesto for the establishment of this 'empty stage' by ideologised religion is a set of rules called *shari'a*, which has remained static throughout the centuries. Roy continues:

> What will imposition of the sharia mean? Hypocrisy. For, as the true ideologues of Islamism have always said, from Sayyid Qutb to Maududi and Khomeini, imposition of the sharia makes sense only if the society is already Islamic and man finally virtuous. If not, everything is just casuistics, appearance and ruse, the use of which may be perfectly legal ... .[180]

Muslim fundamentalists, it should be noted, are not alone in their violent deeds in the name religion. Other religious fundamentalists do the same. Karen Armstrong points out that there are Christian and Jewish fundamentalists and that 'there are Buddhist, Hindu, and even Confucian fundamentalisms, which also cast aside many of the painfully acquired insights of liberal culture, which fight and kill in the name of religion and strive to bring the sacred into the realm of politics and national struggle'.[181]

An important element that has gone amiss among fundamentalists in Islam, and many conservatives for that matter too, is the difference between religion and religious knowledge. The point is that while religion is sacrosanct and immutable, religious knowledge is not. While the essence of religion remains the same its interpretation varies with time. Just as the laws governing physical nature do not change but our understanding of them alters with time, sometimes negating and refuting previous scientific interpretations, our insight into religious laws should also develop with time. God's words are irrefutable and sacred but the fallible human understanding of them is not. This has been discussed competently in *Theoretical Contraction and Expansion of Shari'a* by Soroush and alluded to in other parts of this work.[182]

Two sets of comparisons between 'rights' and 'duties' and between religious and jurisprudential governments deserve to be noted here. In the West the rebellion of Christian man against an Omnipotent, Omniscient God, who could even trample upon the laws of physics and philosophy (very much unlike Greek gods, who were bound within the limits of rationality and reason), opened up space for the discovery of human rights that could not be breached even by the Lord Himself. Thus humanity found a set of rights that were prior to any duties he/she had. In Islamist fundamentalism, however, there are no human rights that are independent and inviolable. Everything, including such rights, is secondary to Divine Will as understood and expressed by the religious jurist. This profound difference widens the gap substantially between the Islamists and the West.

The second comparison relates to religious and jurisprudential governments. The latter is one which aims to enforce strict adherence to the laws of *shari'a*. Under such governance and in such a system men will have to grow beards, women will have to cover themselves in public, consumption of alcohol is banned, gambling is outlawed, any mixing of the two sexes is not allowed, foreign music is prohibited, scientists and philosophers are not allowed to engage in research that might possibly repudiate the laws of *shari'a*, duties to God as defined by the religious jurists come before any human rights, freedom of speech ceases to exist (though as put by a journalist it is usually freedom after the speech that is missing in such societies), and generally the dictates of the *faqih* (religious jurist) become the law of the land. No one will have the authority or the power to challenge it.

The prime example of such a society was Taliban Afghanistan. But Iran and Sudan are also instances of jurisprudential government. Adherence to the rules of *shari'a* is in fact something they are quite proud of. Newspaper reports also tell the story of a group in Somalia called *shabab*, who in their zeal to enforce *shari'a* have banned the wearing of bras by women lest the shape of their bodies be magnified by such items and possibly become seductive to men. One wonders how they manage to check and verify possible violations.

A religious government, on the other hand, is not concerned, at least not primarily, with the enforcement of the legal codes of religion as defined by *shari'a*. Very much like a secular government, it will aim to improve the lot of the society through proper and rational policies. Thus all aspects of life, such as healthcare, social welfare, education, transportation, communications, economy, housing, agriculture, family planning, employment, industry, tourism, commerce, foreign policy and so on are assessed rationally and within reason and with a view to advance the state of the people. Religious practices will be left by and large to the individual in the secure and prosperous space that their government has provided for them. It is reported that 'if poverty enters the room through the door, religion will run away through the window'.[183] Hungry stomachs will not find much solace in religious dos and don'ts. Thus religious practices in their refined form will only be observed by a people whose material needs are well taken care of. The latter is exactly the job of a religious government, which opens up space for all to engage in loftier and more elevated states of existence. In effect a religious government, unlike a jurisprudential one, respects the freedom of all and through proper administration encourages and promotes intellectual contemplation as well as spiritual meditation of the people.[184]

Two important Quranic verses here may also help. One is *and consult the people in the affairs* (3:157) and another (39:17–18) *Therefore give good tidings (O Muhammad) to those who hear advice and follow the best thereof.* From these verses can be inferred that public participation in temporal affairs and rational and reasonable assessment and deliberation are Divine Commands and virtues. Their message seems to run contrary to those who wish to locate the public behind the walls of complete obedience and render them unable to take active and decisive roles in their own communities.

> *Aid your wisdom with the wisdom of others,*
> *Get to work and consult in their affairs*[185]

Some Islamist radical groups, who appear to disregard rational and reasonable assessment of their deeds and their consequences, reportedly strive for more sophisticated means of violence in order to inflict greater terror. There is in such instances a responsibility upon all to act. In the words of Rumi,

> *Take away the weapons from the madman's hand,*
> *That justice and goodness may be happy with you;*
> *Since he has weapons and no understanding, shackle his hand,*
> *Otherwise he will inflict a hundred injuries, through and through*[186]

The above, to a degree, has elaborated on the misunderstood concept of secularism by Islamists and demonstrated that rationality, reason and freedom are part and parcel of governance in Islam. Politics as a rational human affair should thus not be practiced through the dictates of an ideologised religion that has little regard for one of the most cherished and undisputed values of life: freedom. '...the religious movement begun by Muhammad had no obvious political relevance,' stated Montgomery Watt.[187] Although the concepts of justice and reason should be the basis of political engagement, stagnation of humanity and the rigidity of the socio-political environment was never intended by the faith.

3
The Concepts of War and Peace and Their Comparative Positions in an Islamic Context

The wars of the people, like children's fights
All meaningless, empty and vile
The battles fought with wooden swords
All their purposes vain and futile.

Rumi, *Masnavi*, Book I, lines 3435–6

From a whim springs their war and peace
On a caprice is based their honour and shame.

Rumi, *Masnavi*, Book I, line 71

3.1 What is war and what is peace? A question of definitions, Islamic and Western

No question has preoccupied the minds of IR scholars more than the issue of war and peace. As one of the most cherished goals in human communities, peace has been the ultimate objective of much, if not all, that has been undertaken in research in International Relations. If any particular paradigm appeared to offer a more viable route to global peace and harmony at any given time, as liberalism did in the West in the immediate aftermath of World War I, it duly received more attention and credit. In the Eastern world too, peace was sought after, though perhaps with an equal, if not greater, emphasis on the precept of justice. Humanity could not, it was claimed, simply accept any peace for the sake of it. There are values for which we are all prepared to breach the peace and go to war, it was argued.

The advent of Nazism in Germany and the onset of World War II appeared to legitimise that argument. The peace of Adolf Hitler was imbued with much misery, carnage, racism, massacre, cruelty, oppression and expansionism and could not therefore be tolerated by the rest of the world, including the West. The Quranic verse below appears to narrate this in the context of a wider principle embedded in human discourse:

> *Had God not checked one set of people by means of another, monasteries, churches, synagogues, and mosques, in which the name of God is commemorated in abundant measure, would surely have been destroyed. God will certainly aid those who aid His Cause; verily God is most powerful, Almighty.*[1]

To begin discussing these precepts, however, we need to have a clear understanding of what defines peace in both Islamic and Western traditions. It is only through the knowledge of its constituents and ingredients that peace can become identifiable and thus attainable for us. Accordingly the early part of this chapter deals with the question of definitions.

A question of definitions

Islam in its orientation in human development holds peace in high esteem. Peace was the condition of life in Paradise, the original designated residence of humankind, before it was replaced with enmity and war on earth, the place of exile for humanity[2] after it succumbed to the temptation of defiance initiated by Satan. Clearly, therefore, peace is a Divine condition of existence as experienced in Paradise whilst enmity and war are attributes of earthly affairs as the direct result of satanic deeds. This verse in the Quran is very direct and to the point:... *Satan's plan is* [but] *to excite enmity and hatred between you*....[3] The term 'Islam', meaning submission, also refers to peace. When greeting one another many Muslims use the phrase *salam-ol-alaikum*, which means peace upon you. This peace, however, transcends the silence of the guns and engulfs a more pervasive, all-inclusive and deeper precept that permeates every level of existence. By this outlook individual peace is not separated from social and political peace, and all facets of peace, including the spiritual and political, are viewed as interdependent.

This peace therefore differs from and is wider than the traditional understanding of peace defined as and subjectified in conventional IR paradigms, including liberalism. The more esoteric and ontological aspects in the Islamic mystic discourses view peace as essentially an internal quest within each and every one (the jurisprudential viewpoints will be studied later in this chapter). Until this peace and tranquillity is achieved in the inner psyche of all, the more visible outer peace will be almost impossible to attain. The UNESCO Charter rightly situates the minds of men as the initial battleground where physical inter-community wars take root. If within ourselves we fail to achieve peace and harmony, it would be foolhardy to assume we can do this with others. This peace within also resonates peace with our Maker, peace with the Universal Wisdom, with the entire Creation and with the beauty and the majesty of life in all its varieties. Rumi states:

> *Make peace with this father, abandon defiance so that the world*
> *May appear to thee as a carpet of gold*
> *Then Resurrection will become thy present state*
> *Heaven and earth will be transfigured before thee, so straight*
> *Since I am at peace with this Father, day and night*
> *This world is like Paradise in my sight*
> *At every moment a new form and a new beauty comes my way*
> *So that from seeing the new (visions) ennui dies away.*[4]

One of the main terms in Arabic denoting peace is *solh*, which is the root of the word *islah*, meaning development and improvement. (This in itself propounds an important linkage between peace and development, that is, peace is by nature progressive and must lead to development; otherwise it cannot be peace.) Verse 9 of Sura 49 in the Quran uses the term *solh* to convey the concept of peace. *Moslih*, the subject noun of *solh*, refers to peacemaker; *moslihoon* is the plural. The latter is mentioned in the Quran most favourably when it is used as an antonym to wrongdoers and corruptors: *And when they are told not to commit wrongdoing and corruption on earth they respond, 'but we are only moslihoon* [peacemakers]'.[5] Inferring from that it is noted that in the Quranic discourse corruption and peacemaking stand opposed to each other. Peacemakers are the agents of good engaged in righteous acts whereas the wrongdoers are those who defy and fight the cause of peace. Two more verses plainly illustrate the magnitude and the weight of peace in the Quranic narrative. One postulates: *And your Lord would never destroy towns wrongfully while [as if] their people were moslihoon (peacemakers).*[6] Even more characteristically, another verse openly states: *For their Lord's displeasure is the opposite of peace and tranquillity.*[7] What this demonstrates is the importance attached to the precept of peace in Islamic tradition to the extent that those who promote it engage in a godly act but those who attempt to breach and destroy it do exactly the opposite.

Enmity and hatred, the roots of violence, are the conditions of life on earth after the satanic deception of Adam and Eve and their expulsion from their intended state of existence; thus war and violence are satanic. The very first instance of human violence, an evil act, in the Abrahamic discourses, including Islam, is the murder of Abel by his brother Cain. To restore the original state of humanity and to facilitate a return to the elevated position designated by the Lord, this violence has to be eradicated and peace has to prevail. Peace, therefore, 'is not only a human attempt to regulate human affairs in an orderly fashion in order to escape the scourge of war, but transcendental guidance on how to eradicate the effects of the original sin by rejecting the satanic condition of violence and instead seeking a return to the original and divinely devised condition of peace'.[8]

Peace in some classical Western literature also refers to much more than just the physically non-violent conduct of relations between human communities. Saint Augustine describes peace beautifully as the 'tranquillity of order', order being 'the disposition of equal and unequal things in such a way as to give to each its proper place'.[9] Absent this, frustration builds up leading to violence. The need theory of Burton, where he locates unmet needs as the bedrock of inter-human conflict and violence, also refers to this greater aspect of peace, in effect linking inner and outer peace.[10] Therefore the ideal peace permeates all levels of existence and every tier of representation encompassing the self, the society, the community and the world. Securing peace only partially and not at all levels is fragile and unstable leaving room for violence.

Galtung's definition of violence as 'anything avoidable that impedes human self-realisation'[11] is also remarkably close to the esoteric and mystic interpretation in Islamic discourses. His use of 'structural violence' as impediments to peace openly propounds a direct linkage between justice and peace.[12] Plato's unifying criterion for justice and the very assumption that peace as an ultimate end to all else must itself be just leads us to conclude that peace ought to be a unifying experience.[13] This resonates with the Quranic narrative on peace which states: ... *make peace between them based on justice and equity ... . God loveth just doers.*[14] Justice, as outlined in the Quran, refers to balance and is the foundation upon which Creation stands. Verses 7 to 9 of Sura 55 refer to this point: *And the Firmament has He raised high and He has set up the balance (of justice). In order that ye may not transgress (due) balance. So establish weight with justice and fall not short in balance.* Ali, the son-in-law and cousin of the Prophet, the fourth caliph after the Messenger and the first Imam of the Shi'as, has an incisive definition of justice. He considers justice to be the placement of everything in its proper order.[15] The issues of proportionality and relativeness are thus an indispensable part of justice. Accordingly, peace based on justice would mean a balanced, fair and tranquil state of affairs, where all concerned would enjoy their due rights and protection.

This 'virtuous' commodity – peace – as opposed to a 'virtual one', as termed and elaborated by Richmond,[16] propounds peace in critical thinking as a holistic, inclusive and unifying precept, almost opposite to what liberal peace has achieved at the international level. Kant, in his famous exposition in *Perpetual Peace*, appears to proffer a military-bound concept of peace, that is, a mere suspension of violent hostilities constitutes peace.[17] Both in the Kantian and Hobbesian discourses war is viewed as the 'state of nature' and peace would therefore by definition be an artificial construct;[18] however, it must be noted that even though they appear to share the goal of this artificial peace, they differ widely on how to achieve it.

As peace in the West is usually and axiologically celebrated through a liberal paradigm it is important to study this discourse closely. Three questions on the liberal peace project require attention if we are to look into peace itself in an epistemic way. Addressing these questions would allow us a deeper insight into some of the most important aspects of the liberal peace *problématique* and appraise it in view of Islamic discourses. They are:

(1) Is liberal peace holistic or is it be sought and achieved in a fragmented way?
(2) Is liberal peace a unifying or a divisive project?
(3) Is liberal peace an exclusive or inclusive precept?

A fragmented peace, as addressed by the first question, seeks peace only in separate fields, detached from one another. A holistic peace, however, focuses on a peace that permeates all levels of individual, social and international life. The liberal peace theory appears to link certain socio-political constructs to the establishment and durability of inter-community peace. In that sense it is not concerned, and not impressed, by developments outside its area of focus – the illiberal world. Uncritically it detaches itself from any foreign policy issue between liberal and non-liberal countries. The foreign policy approach of liberal states appears to be irrelevant to the cause of peace between libertarian countries. If, for example, liberal countries happen to be the largest exporters of means of violence and warfare machinery to their illiberal counterparts, little or no effect can transpire from such acts to the state of peace in the liberal world; the liberal peace project does not seem concerned by the devastating and war-generating impact such foreign policy by liberal entities may have on non-liberal communities. This crude detachment of domestic policy structure from foreign policy strategy in the liberal peace discourse, in relation to the liberal and the illiberal worlds, is inconsistent with the link it provides between domestic and foreign policies of liberal countries vis-à-vis themselves.

There appears therefore a philosophical discrepancy of a sort inherent in the liberal peace project. Such fragmented peace can hardly be viewed as the jewel in the crown of human achievement in political discourse. A deeper and non-fragmented approach to peace would begin by enquiring, dealing and engaging with the internal peace within every individual. It would not treat peace only in a certain field – international relations – and between certain actors – liberal states – in a conspicuously disconnected approach from society and the individual. Liberal peace seems to overlook the individual in its assessment of inter-state peace via a fragmented approach. A holistic peace, in contrast, would concern itself with all aspects of behaviour and conduct in domestic as well as foreign policy domains. It would be born out of a tranquil order that pervades all dimensions in life: social, economic, cultural and political, domestically as well as internationally.

The second question asks if liberal peace theory recognises peace outside of the Western discourse and if so how does it actually seek to explain it? If peace is to be achieved and maintained through liberalism, then the illiberal world will inevitably be the scene of war. And as liberal peace does not appear to universalise itself – because liberalism is simply not universal – then, short of introducing or imposing liberalism everywhere, what is to be done in the real world if we are to institutionalise and safeguard peace? Admittedly experience has shown that liberalism as understood and practised in the West is not always the best model for all societies whose differing culture and history may be at a different stage of socio-political development. People's innate love for and appreciation of freedom must not be misunderstood for longing for Western liberalism everywhere, all of the time (note, however, should be taken that this is no prescription or excuse for rulers who seek to justify their tyranny by simply adopting an anti-Western stance). The example of Iraq in the past few years (in spite of outside meddling like that of al-Qaida) points exactly to this important maxim. A tribal society, where sectarianism, religion and collectivism are the norm and where there is no history of freedom (as understood and practised in the West), cannot be expected to respond swiftly, favourably and responsibly to calls for Western democracy (based on individualism, liberalism, secularism and rationalism). This will be studied more closely in Chapter 5.

Explicating, legitimating and accepting only one kind and one version of peace, as the liberal peace project does, disregards the variety of human experience by disallowing and delegitimising the liberty of difference and the factuality of pluralism in human development. That does not sound terribly liberal in itself and may represent yet another inherent inconsistency in the liberal peace discourse. It may be noted that liberal peace concerns itself with people within defined borders and limited in socio-political experience. Just as the supporters of the so-called socialist peace discourse were ill-advised to propound a global kind of socialism, claiming a universalist status for their inter-state 'peace', it would appear equally difficult to suggest the same for the liberal peace theory. In short, liberal peace project advances at best an understanding and an interpretation of the absence of war in the West, within a certain time frame and under specific conditions. That is a far cry from suggesting the only way to make peace globally (and retrospectively in history) is through importing and imposing the Western model, something which it attempts to do (notwithstanding the questions of slavery and colonialism and wars of the colonies on behalf the Western colonial powers). In this regard the categorisation and graduations of the liberal peace project, in particular that of 'victor's peace', serves to highlight the point in question.[19]

The unifying or divisive nature of liberal peace therefore is the core of the second question. Peace as a 'virtuous' commodity, and as opposed to a 'virtual one', is deemed to unify people. As noted earlier, Plato's unifying criterion for justice and the very assumption that peace as an ultimate end is ontologically just leads to the inevitable conclusion that peace ought to in essence be an experience resulting in unity. In other words, true peace brings people together irrespective of their differences, unlike liberal peace that seeks the erosion of socio-political differences before peace can be achieved. A unifying peace does not mean dissolution of varieties in human governance. The disregard for variety in human experiences and tastes inherent in liberal peace theory inevitably leads to classification of people into 'peaceful' and 'non-peaceful'. That is a travesty of justice as true and just peace must be unifying and not divisive.

Derived from the arguments above, the exclusive nature of liberal peace, addressed by the third question, is axiomatic. If one seeks, recognises and legitimises peace only between particular groups and in doing so disunites humanity and categorises human communities into 'incompatible' sections, then an exclusion zone for the few that fit into one's category is automatically established. That is what the liberal peace advocates may inadvertently and unwittingly be promoting. Sovereign statehood, underwriting liberal peace theory, has already rendered much of human population indifferent, if not hostile, to one another. The liberal peace project goes a step further, suggesting that peaceful coexistence is the exclusive monopoly of liberal states. In IR today, liberal peace dictum may appear to lend support to the status – quo, affording moral legitimacy to the underlying structure of global politics.

Therefore, the divisive, fragmented and exclusive aspects of the liberal peace project appear ineluctable. The huge export of arms by the leading liberal countries to the illiberal world casts doubt on the truth and the axiological traits of liberal peace discourse. The post-liberal peace discourse, advanced by critical thinkers, however, appears to proffer a widely different perspective that challenges the claims made by the liberal peace project. This approach finds commonality with the all-inclusive discourse of Islamic Gnosticism.

At its heart liberal peace subscribes to the state and the market and is accordingly framed and shaped by them.[20] Its primary goal in its intervention into the local is actually on an international order between sovereign states.[21] Liberal peace 'validates territorial state sovereignty and a social contract skewed in favour of the state, free markets and the eradication of the indigenous or locally more authentic' traits.[22] In so doing it appears to disengage the local in favour of the universal and by focusing on security (in its classic definition) and institutions it tends to disenfranchise those for whom it purports to build peace. At times it also resorts to the use of force instead of consent to bring about liberalist peace.[23] In the process of all this the everyday care and empathy for the needs of the people are foregone for the sake of the standardised introduction of political rights alone. In many instances, such as Afghanistan, this has been noted to contribute to the division that fuels hostilities inside communities:

> The failure of development actors to ensure that quieter provinces in the north and west receive a tangible peace dividend has played into the latent north–south fault line within Afghanistan.[24]

In the post-liberal peace, however, people are the stakeholders of the process of peace and are the direct recipients of its dividends. In Richmond's words:

> In post-liberal peace people take ownership over structures and institutions, representing their own every day lives rather than

structural attempts at assimilation. Subjects become active citizens and depoliticisation turns into self-government and self-determination.[25]

The Islamic responses to the liberal peace theory can partly be assessed in the light of the nature and the definition of peace in Islam as argued above. An attempt will be made below in this regard.

The term 'Islam' means to surrender. It is by surrendering to the Will of God that one can find peace and tranquillity in life and the afterlife. Accordingly it may be inferred that the state of peace and peacefulness is part and parcel of the faith. The peace propagated and promoted by Islam appears to host elements that stand in opposition to the fragmentedness, divisiveness and exclusion of the liberal peace project as outlined above: *The people are one nation*, reads Verse 213 of Sura 2 of the Quran. A unifying approach to humankind is illustrated in this verse, a salient and indispensible element of the Gnostic discourse in Islam. The peace sought by the youngest Abrahamic tradition embraces the whole of humanity. Although divisions within humankind are acknowledged, no advantage is granted unless based on virtue. *O Humankind! We created you from a single (pair) of a male and a female and made you into communities and tribes that ye may know one another. Verily the most honoured of you in the sight of Allah is the most virtuous of you. And Allah has full knowledge and is well acquainted (with all things).*[26] It is observed that superiority over others is only recognised in virtue. Peace as a praiseworthy quality (see above) cannot be devised in portions segregating humanity into camps, where one system of governance can seemingly delegitimise peace for others. The theology of pluralism in Islam accepts a pluralistic approach to truth and peace.

Rumi narrates the story of Moses overhearing a shepherd talking to God and offering to bring the Lord milk and food and to look after the Lord at all times. Having been reprimanded by Moses for the blasphemous remarks, the shepherd walked off in despair. Subsequently God rebuked Moses:

> *Didst thou come (as a prophet) to unite*
> *Or didst thou come to disunite?*
> *So far as thou canst, do not promote a separate course*
> *Of all things the most hateful to Me is divorce;*

I have bestowed on everyone a (special) way of acting
I have given to everyone a (peculiar) speech for interacting[27]

When awakened to his misdeed by the Lord, Prophet Moses looked for the shepherd and upon finding him said:

Your blasphemy is (the true) religion,'tis the light of the spirit
You are saved and through you a (whole) world inside it[28]

Whether liberal or otherwise, peace is commendable, but in Islamic tradition it is to be based on justice, the quality which is strongly associated with virtue. *O ye who believe! Stand out firmly for Allah as witnesses to fair dealing and let not the hatred of others to make you swerve to wrong and depart from justice. Be just: that is close to virtue: and fear Allah for Allah is well-acquainted with all that ye do.*[29] A just peace, therefore, can be understood as a virtuous peace: a unifying peace, not discriminating among communities, but in fact utilising differences in order to promote contest in good deeds.[30]

The poem of the thirteenth-century Persian Muslim philosopher Sa'adi comes to mind again:

Human beings are members in a body whole related,
From a single essence are they all created.

The above demonstrates the non-fragmented and unifying approach of Islamic discourse with regard to peace. Verse 213 of Sura 2 states the mission of all prophets to be the reconciling of differences between people, that is, making peace throughout the earth. However, this does not limit itself to high politics and the realist approach. If wars start in the minds of men, as the UNESCO Charter attests, then peace is also to be located and constructed within, before it is transported to the outside world. In esoteric Islamic discourses these internal developments, inspired by one's religious faith, are essential underpinnings of externalising the Will of the Almighty. According to Sachedina,

When law and faith merge in an individual's life, they create a sense of security and integrity about the great responsibility of pursuing justice for its own sake. And when this sense of security and integrity is projected to the collective life of the community it conduces to social harmony. Peace, then, is belief translated into action.[31]

This philosophical foundation for internal and external peace, based on justice, has a universal magnitude that does not divide, fragment, or exclude any members of the human community. Submission to the Will of God, in this perspective, is to pursue justice, whereby peace will be attained.

Differences with jurisprudentialised radical Islam, the one based on a stagnant *shari'a* devoid of historicity and thus detached from contemporary needs, concerns and desires of humanity, and instead immersed in a discourse of hatred that delivers carnage and promises nothing but misery and retrogression, are most striking on the question of violence. Verse 32 of Sura 5 in the Quran (belonging to the category of *mohkamat* – unambiguous and clear) reads: *if anyone slew a person it would be as if he slew the whole of mankind; and if he saved a life, it would be as if he saved the whole of mankind.* Its relevance, therefore, to the concept of peace and the practice of peace-making is uncompromising. As no Muslim is sanctioned to engage in violence against the innocent, the end does not justify the means if the latter breaches the former (aims and principles). If the goal is to spread peace, harmony and tranquillity on earth (Sura 2:213 states the mission of all Messengers is to reconcile differences in human community), one cannot commit acts of senseless violence against the innocent, cause chaos and wage war in order to achieve it. That would clearly defeat the object of the exercise. In the language of a Western scholar:

> If Islamic rules were followed today, much of modern warfare would be impossible, and terrorism would be unthinkable. There would be no attacks on civilians, no retaliation against innocent parties, no taking hostages of non-combatants, no incendiary devices.[32]

3.2   Universalism in Islam and the West and the narrated history

All IR schools have devised theories and paradigms based on their understanding of the 'world', as if the world is an objective reality out there to be discovered and understood by 'humans' presumed to be objective assessors of that 'world'. Both 'humans' and the 'world', however, are relative entities, and thus by definition subjective. Realism and liberalism for instance may both seem appropriate in the world they see through their prism and the reality they interpret through their very subjective, relative mediation. This point is axiomatic and those opposing it are themselves attesting to its validity through their opposition. Gnosticism has alluded to this point in its discourse.

In a parable Rumi talks of a group of villagers who had never seen an elephant and arranged for one to be brought to them; alas, the elephant arrived at night and the villagers, unable to see, could only touch the animal. The morning after, when exchanging notes on their experience of the elephant, each villager gave an account of his/her own. The ones who had touched the trunk differed in their account with the ones who had felt the tusk; likewise those who had touched the legs had a different experience from those who had felt the main body of the animal; and so on. They all seemed to differ in what an elephant actually looked like and disagreed with one another on the shape of the animal. Rumi narrates:

If there had been a candle in each one's hand,
Their differences in words would all but disband…
The eye of the Sea [holistic] *is one thing, and the foam* [phenomenon]
another:
Leave the foam and look with the eye of the Sea, ye brother.[33]

Accordingly IR paradigms may each, in their own right, strike a chord with an aspect of human inter-community relations but may fall short of offering a general, universal and all-encompassing discursive outline of all inter-community affairs.

What is universalism?

Defining the term 'universalism' may appear superfluous as the meaning seems all too clear. It would nevertheless serve the purpose of this work to outline those features that give rise to the universality of any system of ideas, concepts, religions, or schools of thought. The holistic and all-encompassing aspect of any universalist claim is primary among such traits. All universalist beliefs, including religious ones, consider humanity as their audience and domain.

Though there may perceivably appear to be differences and divisions within humankind as to the applicability of such ideas and beliefs, acknowledged by the subscribers to such systems, there is no recognised conceivable merit, in the view of those believing in them, in limiting the geographic and demographic influence of those systems. Accordingly, though Leninism and Maoism were devised to cope with the necessary adjustments to enable Marxism to explain and operate in the Russian (Soviet) and Chinese contexts, such deficiencies do not appear to discredit communism in the eyes of its supporters; nor does the *un-event* of the final and victorious proletariat revolution as predicted by Marx himself. Marxism may still be held by them to delineate the course of a materialist history with iron necessity.

The second feature of universalist claims is the fairly *absolutist* nature of their outlook on the world and their subjects, the human community. As they consider their beliefs fit to apply in all geographies, all circumstances, and all of the time, there is little that can be allowed for the kind of *relativism* that defines and narrates historicity in human development. While historicity sketches a rather *fluid* humanity and narrates his/her discourse by and through *relativism*, *universalism* appears to ground itself in *solid absolutist* assumptions defying relativism in almost all ontological, axiological and philosophical respects. To construct such an absolutist and universal outlook and worldview there is a corresponding need (for universalists) to define humankind and history in universal terms; in cases of supernatural systems of beliefs a universal theology is also included to link the *absolute* temporal here and now to an *absolute* eternity. This absolutist trait may arise from the 'meta-narrative' quality of universalist systems, which is looked down upon by many postmodernists, including Lyotard.[34] It is the incredulity toward such meta-narratives that is (in an oversimplified manner) the defining feature of postmodernity.[35] The pre-modern and the modern, however, appear to accept, or at least concede, space to the viability of all-encompassing schools though they may radically differ with one another as to the contents of such systems. Medieval Christianity, for instance, may have believed in the absolutism of Christian faith, whereas the modern era has shifted that emphasis to the concept of human rights.[36]

Universal history is an indispensable part of universal discourse. The origins and the development of humanity and even the beginning of life are all celebrated in universal narratives with universal explanations. Thus in Marxism all conflict in human communities stems necessarily from the haves and the have-nots and all human societies go through the same stages of development. In universal religions (Christianity and Islam are meant here) all humans are subject to the Will of the Almighty and history as the arena of a universal battle between the Good and the Bad embedded in human nature will inevitably end in the Day of Judgement. And of course there is universal guidance for all to find salvation. As the Christian and Islamic accounts of history 'makes clear, an "end of history" is implicit in the writing of all Universal Histories. The particular events of history can become meaningful only with respect to some larger end or goal, the achievement of which necessarily brings the historical process to a close. This final end of man is what makes all particular events potentially intelligible.'[37]

Last but not least, universalism seems to claim a monopoly on the truth. Whether secular or religious, universalist doctrines usually tend to disregard other interpretations and view their knowledge and understanding of the truth as the only way that yields results. Accordingly, in Marxism there would be no authenticity for other factors, material and non-material, instigating meaningful change in society other than those relating to the process of production. In Christianity and Islam, too, salvation can only be achieved through one way, by following the teachings of Christ and Muhammad respectively. The absolute and all-encompassing Truth, in its totality and unadulterated form, remains the monopoly of these religions, they each claim. Those who disagree with such views are chided as misguided at best and infidels at worst. In consequence systems representing universalist beliefs tend to standardise behaviour in a manner compliant with their interpretation of *right* and *wrong*, at times closing the door to difference of views and expression. Rumi, in his pluralist language, however, narrates a different message when he writes:

> *Every prophet and every saint hath a path to run*
> *As each leads to God, they are all but one*[38]

The contrast could perhaps not be greater. Mysticism celebrates difference and variety in the world as varied expressions of the Same One God and humanity taking different routes to get to the same Truth. The Quran states: *Had Allah willed He could have made you (all) into one* [non-differentiated] *nation.*[39] However, the differences between communities emanate more from modes of expression than from substance according to Rumi:

> *The disparity in humanity is caused by names*
> *Peace ensues if substance reigns*[40]

Therefore the three traits of holisticism, absolutism and monopoly of the truth can be viewed as features of universalism under study here. We shall now turn to the question of universalism in the West and in Islam.

The West and universalism

For the purpose of this study two instances of universalism in the West shall be referred to: Christianity and liberalism. Perceivably there may have been other such instances in Western history but we shall limit ourselves to these two and deal with them in chronological order.

Christianity and universalism

The starting point of a universalist Christian faith can perhaps be traced back to the First Crusade in 1099 and the attack on Jerusalem. The Roman Empire had already adopted Christianity in the fourth century and Christians were continually trying to convert others to their religion. The following was a clear guideline to all Christians to universalise their faith:

> *Go ye therefore, and teach all nations, baptizing them in the name of the Father, and of the Son, and of the Holy Ghost. Teaching them to observe all things whatsoever I have commanded you: and, lo, I am with you always, even unto the end of the world. Amen.*[41]

However, no notably aggressive Christian universalist advance had taken place until the decree by Pope Urban II to march to the Holy Land against the 'wicked race'. In that respect universalism in

Christianity, as in some interpretations of Islam, was in many ways irredentist; to ensure Christian superiority over its rival universalist faith, Islam, acquiring territory, particularly the Holy Land, seemed as natural as it was indispensable.[42] Inevitably this territorial expansionism required hard tangible power, without which the word of the Lord could not be spread. Thus force became part and parcel of religious doctrine in Christianity and waging violence against non-Christians was encouraged and legitimised in the name of holy war.

This irredentism was later carried out by non-religious representatives in the West, called sovereign states, ostensibly for temporal gains under the rubric of colonialism. Though the 'white man's burden' and the 'civilising mission' were noted as the moral responsibility of the colonisers towards their 'inferior' brutally colonised people, religious fervour and Christian themes did not appear among the prime motives of the Western colonial rulers. Still, the universalist aspect of Christianity played its part in the unjust and cruel subjugation of the colonies; this in turn contributed to the development of its antithesis, liberation theology, started in Christian churches in South America. According to Philip Berryman, Central America is 'based on an act of conquest and domination, with thousands of Indians being killed.... In this conquest the church was a key factor. Missionaries were the only force denouncing the cruelties and attempting to moderate the effects of the conquest. Despite heroic exceptions, however, the church normally acted as an integral element of the overall enterprise of conquest and domination.'[43]

The importance of proselytising non-Christians lay in erosion of religious differences that in turn could have weakened resistance by the local population to exploitation and colonisation by the European powers. If conversion was successful then colonial masters could be introduced and viewed as religious brothers and not as foreign occupiers. Also as an inroad into the indigenous culture of the new colonies and the manipulation of the minds of their inhabitants, religious teaching and preaching played an important part. If one could instil the fear of God into the hearts and minds of people, and if one was accepted by the people to represent that God, then any resistance to colonial masters could be presented and punished as an act of defiance against the Will of the Almighty. In effect a universalised Christianity could aid universal colonisation by the West.

As once noted by Ali Shari'ati, no religion has probably spoken more of peace than Christianity, yet ironically no religion has caused more bloodshed than Christianity.[44] Neither during the Crusades that lasted for two centuries nor later in the colonial phase of Western history, not to mention the Spanish Inquisition, can one overlook the role of Christian universalism in claiming the ultimate representation of the truth. This marks a notable trait of religious universalism shared between Christianity and Islam; that is the use of force in universalising their respective belief systems and attempting to institutionalise manners in which the hierarchy of power in their organised religions were preserved. In Islam, however, comparatively speaking, this occurred more expeditiously than in Christianity. More shall be said on that later.

Liberalism and universalism

Western supremacy in today's world has naturally given rise to the idea that Western culture must intrinsically carry elements that have contributed to and sustained that supremacy. Arguably the most salient feature of Western culture is liberalism. Western philosophers such as Voltaire, Locke and Montesquieu have placed certain critical human rights at the centre of their philosophical outlook, all of which circle around the precept of freedom. The right to life and the right to free speech, among others, are celebrated achievements of the West, culminating in the distinctly anti-religious French and the anti-colonial American revolutions.

The liberal tradition focuses on the dignity of humankind and promotes the rights of the individual to partake in the political process and maximise his/her enjoyment of life through participation in a free/liberal market. Liberalism, theoretically at least, blends the free market of Adam Smith with the political philosophy of John Locke, offering a secure space for all to have a role in their political and economic lives. Accordingly liberalism is the emancipated outcome of the struggle against the excesses of religion in today's Europe where rationality, and not religious beliefs or dictums, run the affairs of the community.

Unlike religious universalism, liberalism is (at least in name) secular and non-irredentist. Its influence lies in its soft power of ideas and not the dictates of brute force. Other Western schools that stand opposed to liberalism and view it in the service of capitalism to the detriment of the masses, such as Marxism, have proven poor competitors in political and economic fields. That was demonstrated clearly in the collapse of the former Soviet Union and the Eastern bloc and the gradual shift of Communist China to free-market practices. Extreme right-wing tendencies that also disagreed with liberal principles were exemplified in Nazi Germany, Fascist Italy and in Spain (ruled by Franco) of the twentieth century. However, those too were short-lived. The early 1990s was a euphoric period for liberals, who believed history had in fact traversed its path and reached its conclusion in the triumph of liberalism over all other discourses.[45] That, too, proved a short-sighted view. The events of 11 September 2001 heralded a new era, where an Islamist fundamentalist challenge to liberalism was violently declared.

Basically there are two problems with universal liberalism. First it appears that the freedom and the public participation in political life that the Western world cherishes at home is not the goal of the West in its international relations. Many dictatorial regimes are either openly or covertly aided by the Western powers (in their quest to further their perceived national interests) to the detriment of the people who live under such dictatorships. In other words, liberalist countries seem happy to pursue non-liberal imperialist policies outside their borders. Galtung has demonstrated this in his writings through the depiction of 'centre' and the 'periphery' and how the centres inside the states work for harmony of interests, and that ultimately the periphery in the leading states are better off than their counterparts in the weaker states.[46] (Long before him, however, Ibn Khaldun had propounded the same concepts in his monumental work, *The Muqaddimah*.)[47] In short, liberalism in the West appears to have worked against its own universalisation. A liberal developing world may be more difficult to manipulate and control in terms of the *national interests* of the liberal world than dictatorial regimes. In IR terms, *realist* foreign policies of liberal states stand against international *liberal* precepts and practices.

Secondly, as will be pointed out later in this work when examining the case of Iraq, Western traditions in liberalism are based on certain pillars that may be lacking in other parts of the world. Pillars such as rationalism, nationalism, secularism and individualism are not present in many Muslim countries. Expecting those societies to adopt a Western-style democracy with little or no regard to local traditions and culture may be more harmful than advantageous, at least in the short to medium term. Freedom as the quintessential trait of humanity can be expressed via other mechanisms more tailor-made to the needs of the communities in question. There is seemingly a philosophical barrier to the universalisation of liberalism. That, however, should not be taken to support autocratic regimes, aplenty in the developing world, who stand opposed to human freedom and dignity.

Islam and universalism

Islam was the only Abrahamic religion that grew in political success from its infancy. The unification of Arabian tribes and the subsequent defeat of the Persian Empire and other conquests were all legitimised by the belief that God meant Islam to be the universal religion even by the use of force if necessary. In view of many Muslim jurists and theologians, Islam is for all humankind and as the last of the Abrahamic traditions supersedes Judaism and Christianity. The use of the term *naas* (people) in the Quran is cited by this group to validate their claim of the universality of the Islamic message. There is a body of evidence, mainly in the shape of *hadith* (reported sayings of the Prophet) that attest to the same. The letters, reportedly written by Muhammad himself to the leaders of Persia, Ethiopia and Rome at the time to accept Islam, are among the most crucial pieces of evidence by those advancing the universality of Islamic faith.

The political success of Islam in its early days and the ensuing civilisation that came about by blending Persian, Byzantine and Greek traditions supported the claim of those who staunchly pursued universalism in Islam. If the Bedouin Arabs, who were living a tribal life at the time, could overrun empires such as Persia in such a short time and establish centres of power that attracted and encouraged science and knowledge, it was thought Islam obviously had an enlightening and empowering quality that rendered it fit to embrace the entire world.

There are, however, a group of Islamologists, some of them Western but also prominent scholars from Muslim countries, who cast doubt on the religious nature of the universal claims made by the Arabs in the name of Islam. In their view, there is hardly any evidence that can link the irredentism of early Arabs to Islamic teachings either in the Quran or in the *hadith*.[48] To substantiate that, they refer to several Quranic verses in which it is clearly stated, they claim, that Islam was meant for the people of Arabia. Some of those verses are cited below. *For We assuredly sent amongst every People an apostle* (16:36); *We sent not an apostle except (to teach) in the language of his (own) people, in order to make (things) clear to them* (14:4). Verses 14:9, 13:7, 32:23, 5:46–7, 11:36–7, 11:52–60, 11:61–2, 11:84–91 also attest to the principle that the Lord has sent different, they claim, messengers to different people.

Other Quranic verses point in a similar direction stating why Arabic has been chosen as the language of Islam's Holy Book: *And thus We have inspired in thee a Lecture in Arabic, that thou mayst warn the mother-town and those around it, and mayst warn of a day of assembling whereof there is no doubt* (42:7); *And* [bethink you of] *the day when We raise in every nation a witness against them of their own folk, and We bring thee (Muhammad) as a witness against these* (16:89). Similar verses can be found in 9:28, 62:2, 10:20 and 32:3. The advocates of universalist Islam, however, reject those claims.

The irredentist and the violent aspects of Christian universalism also appear in Islamic history. The non-Arab converts to Islam in its early days came from the vanquished societies, who found advantages in adopting the new faith. The egalitarian aspects of the new religion in treating all people equally that had been promoted from the outset were almost non-existent from the start. Arabs were given priority in all matters and considered themselves the chosen race by the Almighty.[49] Marriage of Arabs to non-Arabs, for instance, was derided. The verse, *The dearest of you in the sight of God is the most virtuous amongst you*,[50] had vanished all but in name. In many cases, non-converts, who preferred to keep to their traditional beliefs, were openly humiliated and persecuted. The verse, *There is no compulsion in religion*,[51] seemed to have lost its substance and appeal among the victorious Bedouin Arabs.

Fundamentalist Islam and universalism

> *Hard-headedness and prejudice is immaturity,*
> *For an embryo, blood-sucking is security.*
>
> Rumi, *Masnavi*, Book III, line 1297

Today fundamentalist Islam pursues universalism by violence. To fully appreciate the claim advanced by the fundamentalist Islamist movements a brief outline of their most basic tenets may be helpful.

The argument that lies at the heart of fundamentalists' discourse relates to the concepts of *rights* and *duties*. Basically the relationship between these two represents the true essence of the Western world's approach to religion. All human beings are viewed, at least in theory, to be equally entitled to certain rights as defined and outlined in the Universal Declaration of Human Rights (UDHR). These rights are basically the product of Western liberalism that has been accepted, at least in theory, by the majority of countries in the world. The UDHR followed the defeat of an omnipotent, omniscient tyrannical God in the Christian West, who had for centuries dictated the affairs of humanity there through the rulings of the Church. Even though the Church itself was the inheritor of the Roman and Greek traditions, it nonetheless turned its back on that heritage by invalidating and excommunicating rationality and reason as the guiding and organising principle of life. The Christian God in the Dark Ages could trample upon all rationality and physical as well as philosophical laws. Nothing could stand in the way of the Almighty, who had placed duties on His servants on earth to worship Him in ways described and prescribed by the Church. Humans were thus duty-bound to perform rituals and pay homage to the Church. Their *duties* in complying with the wishes of God's representative on earth outweighed any possible *rights* they may have had. *Rights* were at best of secondary importance and significance, textualised only in the context of *duties*. The Western rebellion against that God paved the way for the discovery of human rights as understood in the West today. They are not privileges, that is, they are axiomatic and come before any duties including those towards the Almighty. Even the Lord Him/Herself can/would not interfere with those rights. Therefore in the modern liberal era in the West human *rights* come before any human *duties*.

In the Islamist fundamentalist narrative, however, we are still bound by duties to our Maker, and any *rights* can only be considered in the light of such responsibilities; the most important of which is the universalisation of the faith as seen and understood by the fundamentalists themselves. Very clearly such an interpretation stands in the way of any normal diplomatic relations with other states as practised today. The doctrine of Abdul-Wahhab, the founder of the Wahhabi sect in Saudi Arabia, itself an offshoot of the Hanbali School of Sunni Islam, for instance, requires annual participation of Muslims in *jihad* as interpreted by his sect. Other figures like him, as described in Chapter 1, all appear to prioritise duties over rights. This relationship between these two precepts is one of the distinguishing traits of Islamist fundamentalism.

Implied in the violent campaign of Islamist fundamentalists is that humanity, or those members of human society that consciously refuse to convert to Islam, deserve to be outcasts or in certain cases even killed. And such killings can take the form of mass murder like the killings on 11 September 2001. The innocent, who may also lose lives, can be considered martyrs. It resonates with the exhortation by an Orthodox bishop during the Albigensian crusades that you must 'kill all and let God sort out the innocent'.[52] Here the commonality of fundamentalist thinking, particularly in its universalist religious manner, is clearly visible. In a one-to-one encounter of the author with a leading Muslim fundamentalist jurist, the latter openly stated, 'If I were living in the West I would have directed all Muslim drivers to go through red traffic lights', against which I responded, 'But what if Muslims get killed as a result of accidents arising from such disobedience?' He replied, 'Then in order to secure and preserve the lives of Muslims one must contemplate ways and means necessary.'[53] Such an approach to religion is rejected in mysticism as narrated by Rumi in the beginning of this section. Rigidity can also be a sign of arrogance that can impede development. Humility, shown in the tolerance of *the other*, can foster progress and advancement. Rumi writes:

> *How should a rock be covered with verdure in Spring?*
> *Become earth so that flowers of many a hue you may bring*[54]

3.3   Hermeneutics, Islam and the West and the dialogue of civilisations

> *O (thou who art the) kernel of Existence, it is the place (object) of view,*
> *That gives rise to the difference between the true believer, the Zoroastrian and the Jew.*
>
> Rumi, *Masnavi*, Book III, line 1258

Christianity and Islam are both universalistic in their teachings, that is, they proclaim a universal mission to convert the whole of humanity to their organised and ritualised approach in worshipping God and complying with His/Her perceived wishes. In the words of John Esposito, they compete for the soul of mankind.[55] This has been the source of legitimacy for jurisprudence in both religions, staking their claim on the uniqueness of their message in their righteousness and the invalidity of all others. Though jurisprudence in Islam may have acquired greater dimension and breadth than in Judaism and Christianity, that has not detracted from the weight of the claim in the latter. At the heart of this perceived obligation to proselytise everyone is the belief that the truth lies only in one message and one faith. Religious pluralism runs against that claim, however, and views all expressions of faith as valid within certain and very basic parameters.

If the view that God has guided all humanity and has not selected one section over others in Divine guidance through messengers is held to be true (as attested to in the Quran),[56] and that humanity in its diversity and variety shares the common element of reason, then universalism of Christianity and Islam faces serious challenges. For the immediate question to address is why, despite Divine guidance for all and in spite of shared reason, humanity remains divided in religious affiliation after thousands of years of debate and discussion. Did the Lord Him/Herself intend/will variety in expressions of faith? If not, then there is a pressing need for an explanation/theory that would account for the plurality of religions in the world. All factors such as enmity with the truth, distortion, personal interests, prejudice, and so forth, advanced by any one group of believers of one denomination against other/s, fail to provide a convincing explanation for they would be equally applicable to the beliefs of the one/s, who advance them.

Why have Christian and Muslim thinkers and scholars not been able to convince one another of the unique and monopolistic position they hold with regard to the truth? The debate between them is over a thousand years old and yet there are no major shifts in the wake of their intellectual encounters. Just as Immanuel Kant cited *sufficiency of reason* as the factor for the inconclusiveness in the debate over the nature of the universe (whether it is eternal or created),[57] the same could be said to hold true for the discussion between various religious believers. On the eternal or created nature of the cosmos both sides have raised all rational arguments they possibly could and yet neither has appeared able to overwhelm the other sufficiently so as to cause a major shift in the belief system of the other. Similarly no religious paradigm, whether in organised Christianity or in organised Islam, has been able to philosophically subdue the other.

The need here for an understanding that would at once explain pluralism in religious beliefs and not invalidate anyone's access to truth at the same time has been addressed and accommodated by hermeneutics, an approach that allows for variety in access to truth. This approach provides for plurality in religious faith without adding weight to or invalidating any one denomination. In the words of Thiselton,

> Hermeneutics seeks to establish bridges between opposing viewpoints. This does not necessitate giving ground to the other view, but sympathetically to understand the diverse motivations and journeys that have led in the first place to teach respective view or argument.[58]

Hermeneutics is 'the art of understanding.'[59] It explores the *conditions and criteria* that operate to try to ensure responsible, valid, fruitful, or appropriate interpretation. 'This shows why, once again hermeneutics has to call on various academic disciplines. It shows why we draw on philosophical questions about how we understand; psychological, social, and critical questions about selfhood, *self-interest, and self-deception* (my emphasis).'[60] That is why hermeneutics is essentially a multidisciplinary approach.[61] It goes beyond simple explanation and engages in genuine understanding. This requires that 'one be able to step out of one's own frame of mind into that of the author'.[62] Accordingly empathy and mutual understanding are said to stand at the very heart of hermeneutics, which in turn promotes tolerance, mutual respect, and reflexive dialogue with patience and integrity.[63]

Another aspect of hermeneutics relates to the evolution of interpretation and its non-objectivity. Even though the text may remain the same, as the Bible or the Quran do, our understanding of the text continually evolves in line with the advancement of human intellect in all branches of knowledge. Physicists, chemists, physiologists, biologists and other specialists have evolved their understanding of how we and the world around us function. The progress made in these fields is not due to changing conditions in the subjects of study but rather in our understanding of those subjects. The epistemology of science necessitates a constant critical review of established scientific beliefs so that no specific interpretation can be held sacred and immutable. 'There are no right theories, only theories that have not been proven wrong,' said Karl Popper.[64] There are no limits to the advancement of our understanding and how we can better interpret the world. Why should we therefore place any limits on our understanding of holy texts? As we develop and learn more, should our new knowledge not aid us in a better interpretation of our religious beliefs? Why should religious knowledge be immune to development and evolution? The epistemology of knowledge should apply equally to all branches of human understanding, including religious learning. That is not to desanctify the text, which is held holy and sacrosanct, but rather to improve our own fallible interpretation, which is not holy and prone to mistakes. Holy text does not mean holy interpretation; the text comes from God but interpretation from humans. The former is eternal, absolute and infallible whereas the latter is mortal, relative and fallible. To hold the two equal is in itself improper and sacrilege. According to Abdolkarim Soroush, religious knowledge is the sum of all right and wrong interpretations of religion, as observed from our point of view:

> But of course in this judgement we confront one interpretation with another interpretation of religion and not the religion itself. And basically wherever there is a dispute, it is between various understanding of religion and not a dispute between religion and interpretation of religion. And this last point, is a key to many problems in epistemology of religions.[65]

In not treating humanity as a monolithic entity Islam alludes to this very point. The faith respects the differences that are the product of nature or even culture. Accordingly Muhammad, the Founder and the Prophet of Islam, and the Master Gnostic, is reported to have remarked that, 'Differences within my people are a blessing'.[66] Such differences give rise to social and intellectual interaction, which in turn inspires probing, seeking and searching, debating and evolving understanding of the religion itself. The differences become a source of movement of ideas and the elevation of human intellect.

At another level, however, these different interpretations between and within religious beliefs, including Islam and Christianity, may give the impression of doubt and the absence of certainty among believers of the faith. Promoting such an image would not be welcome by fundamentalists, who may feel compelled to react so as to project the certainty of their beliefs. The pursuant intellectual and even physical battles, however, according to Gnosticism, emanate from overlooking the substance and heeding the form instead. A Master Sufi, Hafez, attributes the disputes between various sects of Islam to their misguided followers:

> *Set aside seventy-two sects and their fray*
> *For they failed to see the truth and thus went astray*

Mysticism adheres to an overarching approach that nowadays hermeneutics appears to subscribe to. *Haq-ol-yaqin* (the righteousness of certitude) is the gift bestowed upon those who have achieved the lofty heights of Gnosticism and have sunk deep into Sufi states.

> *Sea-spotting eye has the one, who drowned*
> *Otherwise all on the shore can spot the waves.*[67]

Such states afford a degree of certainty that transcends the previous levels of *Elm-ol-yaqin* (the knowledge of certitude) and *Eyn-ol-yaqin* (the eye of certitude) and move the Gnostic to the state of *Haq-ol-yaqin* (the righteousness of certitude). These can be exemplified by the state of one seeing smoke from behind a wall by the virtue of which he/she concludes there must be fire causing the smoke (the knowledge of certitude). The second state is when he/she goes behind the wall and actually sees the fire (the eye of certitude). The last stage, however, is when he/she goes closer and feels the warmth of the fire on his/her body (the righteousness of certitude). Those states elevate humanity to new dimensions, where differences and enmities melt away in the unity of existence; peace and security embrace the Gnostic keeping him/her immune from all dangers. This is a stage of selflessness. In a majestic narrative Rumi describes the state of a mystic sage, Ba Yazid Bastami, who, at his own request, was attacked by his disciples when making esoteric pronouncement:

> *The disciples thus in a frenzy*
> *Began stabbing their sage, so crazy...*
> *Everyone who plunged a dagger into the sage*
> *Was wounding himself in reverse*
> *Not a single mark on that Sage of sciences*
> *But the disciples drowned in their own blood and senses*
> *Whoever aimed to slash his throat*
> *Had his own throat cut and died thereof...*
> *O you who stab the selfless ones with the sword*
> *You are stabbing yourself, heed the word*
> *For the selfless has passed away in God and is safe*
> *And dwelling forever in safety, immune from strife*
> *His image has passed away and he has become a mirror*
> *There is naught there but the image of other/s*
> *If you spit, you spit on your own face*
> *If you strike at the mirror, you strike at yourself*
> *And if you see an ugly face, it's you*
> *And if you see Jesus and Mary, it's you*
> *He is neither this nor that, only simple and pure*
> *And has placed your own image before you...* [68]

In another of his parables Rumi describes the state of four people, a Persian, an Arab, a Turk and a Greek, whose different words for grape drive them to quarrel. Each, eager to spend their one *derham*[69] on buying the fruit, uses his/her own language. Thus whilst the Persian asks for *anghoor*, the Arab refutes him/her by seeking *a'nab*; the Turk disputes both wanting to use the money for *ozom* and the Greek going against the three of them asking for *stafili*. A dispute ensues where the four throw punches at one another until a wise man appears and informs them that he/she can fulfil all their four wishes with the same one *derham*. He/she told them:

> *Your individual talks will bring you disunity*
> *My talk will harness unanimity and unity*[70]

Many differences, as narrated by Rumi, are the result of verbiage and the lack of spiritual insight into substance. A more holistic and a more elevated outlook and a deeper insight may, however, eradicate the source of such differences and conflicts. The differences in appearance should not misguide us into the disconcerting and dislocating dogmatic path that speaks of spiritual and fundamental divisions. It may seem ironic that Rumi and his sage, Shams, belonged to two different sects in Islam; Shams was a Shafe'i while Rumi belonged to the Hanafi sect. The followers of these two sects spilled one another's blood at every opportunity at the time;[71] yet those two formed one of the most celebrated spiritual relationships in mystic history. Molavi narrates:

> *Believe in this truth that not all speak the truth*
> *Nor are all beguiled and perverted in finding the truth*
> *The claim that all are right is foolishness*
> *And the one saying all are wrong, thoughtlessness*[72]

Clerical Christianity and Islam, however, do not lend themselves to that approach. For them the truth lies with them and their professed faith alone giving them a monopoly on salvation here and hereafter.[73] Such branding of the other/s as the 'misguided', 'wicked', 'infidel', and so forth, has been the linchpin of most, if not all, violence and bloodshed committed and carried out in the name of God by these two universalistic, clerical and organised religions either between themselves or with others throughout history. The Crusades was perhaps an illustration of this most poignantly distressing religious discourse. To the contrary, non-jurisprudential approaches, more akin to mysticism, display a remarkable degree of similarity between the two religions and a considerable overlap of spirituality.[74] As reported by Lewisohn on the Iranian Muslim mystic, Shabestari, 'nearly all *his* technical terminology, style of expression and views on the ineffability of the mystical apprehension were to be echoed in identical terms some two centuries later in Spain by St. John of the Cross (my emphasis)'.[75]

In many cases of course they were just instances where religion was instrumentalised to maintain or further political power. The brutalities and savagery of some of the Islamic caliphs, all in the name of religion, provides ample proof for that assertion.

Dialogue of civilisations

The publication by the late Samuel Huntington on the clash of civilisations and the subsequent shift in what appears to be religious–fundamentalist–inspired violence, both qualitatively and quantitatively, has been an issue that has concerned both politicians and academicians alike. A possible inter-civilisational clash between Islam and the West, as stated by Huntington, could usher in an era of total devastation for all. The unanimous decision of the General Assembly, at the behest of the former Iranian President, Mohammad Khatami, to declare the year 2001 as the Year of Dialogue among Civilisations, indicated the importance that the world attached to this issue. Nowadays the United Nations has formed the Alliance of Civilisations headed by two states, Spain and Turkey, to continue working on this important project.

However, there are some observations to be made. First, while the clash of civilisations was a view projected and articulated in a scholarly fashion, where the author produced a book elaborating on his idea, no equally substantive work appears to have been produced in opposition to seriously challenge the central thesis of Samuel Huntington. Khatami's rhetorical approach to this issue, though important in kick-starting the process, was hardly sufficient to see it through. Even today, those officially engaging in this process appear to have achieved little in the way of bringing fundamentalist Islam and the West closer to a dialogue. Though procedural formalities are important in themselves they can be no substitute for substance. There is a conspicuous lack of meaningful work being carried out to address the challenge posed by the onset of the clash of civilisations. This leads to the second point.

Many spoke and wrote against the thesis propounded by Huntington. Among them, Amartya Sen, Paul Bernam, Seizaburo Sato, Edward Said, Abdolkarim Soroush, and Fouad Ajami cast doubt on the validity of his paradigm. Said's post-colonial critical approach views the theory as legitimising a certain kind of politics. Soroush elaborates on the ambiguity and the imprecise nature of civilisation itself, which if theorised into paradigms, he states, can at best lead to vague conclusions and at worst mislead to antagonistic scenarios. There is no inevitability associated with the clash of civilisations, Soroush has argued. After all, such theories are usually self-negating and suicidal, like the final revolution predicted by Marx, which failed to materialise, Soroush states, precisely because its publication alerted certain forces to work against it and prevent it from happening. Clash of civilisations could follow a similar path.[76] Ajami's critical view of Huntington's thesis, however, is more political revolving around the state-centric nature of our world. States, and not civilisations, formulate and execute policies, Ajami writes. They do so based on their perceived national interests, on occasion despite civilisational or religious bonds. One instance, Ajami states, is the Islamist government of Iran, which in the Azerbaijan–Armenia dispute over Nagorno-Karabak appears to have sided more with Christian Armenia than Muslim Azerbaijan. Berman, Sato and Sen advance similar arguments. Thus, in the absence of any clear indication for the departure of state-centrism from international relations, it would seem groundless to propound, and difficult to locate, a world ridden by civilisational politics.[77]

However, to counter-argue, one could point out that the violence committed in the United States, Spain and the United Kingdom, in 2001, 2004 and 2005 respectively, to mention only the most poignant instances in the West, is best explained by a civilisational paradigm. No nationalist, ideological, or even religious doctrine can per se account for those atrocities. A close look at the perpetrators and the circumstances pertaining to their act attests to the relevance of the clash of civilisations thesis. Admittedly there may be over-simplifications by Huntington in places[78] and some rather arbitrary grouping of civilisations by him, but those do not invalidate his central argument altogether. He has identified a possible source of international conflict and in a well-articulated argument has contributed to our understanding of global affairs.

If civilisations, as the largest grouping of human community, or cultures, as the software of the mind and the media through which we conduct a socio-political life, are to engage in a meaningful intellectual intercourse, the state is hardly a fit institution to carry out that momentous task. Civilisations and cultures are bigger than states; they define, shape and influence communities, including states. While civilisation is an imprecise term with no outward external reality, imbued with vagueness and riddled with inconsistencies (the Western civilisation, for instance, has given birth to liberalism as well as Nazism and Fascism. It has produced capitalism as well as Communism. Islamic civilisation also has produced inconsistencies such as the *Mo'tazele* school as well as the *Asha'ere* school),[79] states are territorially well-defined entities with a population and a concrete degree of control. The vagueness and the relative arbitrariness that is inherent in civilisations, whether territorially or otherwise, would be anathema to states. Furthermore states are established to pursue perceived national interests, usually defined in terms of power. They were not conceived to advance cultural or civilisational interests particularly if the two (national interests and civilisational interests) came into conflict with one another. In other words, the first aim of any state involved in any civilisational dialogue would be to look after its own interests and only subsequent to that boost cultural and civilisational projects. To expect the state to commit to a course it was not made for, like supporting civilisational understanding, would at best be foolhardy and futile and at worst dangerously irresponsible.

Finally, can dialogue between civilisations proceed meaningfully when dialogue within civilisations is actively discouraged or, worse, forbidden? In order to better critique the *other*, you must first be able to view the *self* critically. Many an Islamic government, however, may not allow the free flow of ideas that may ultimately undermine its hold on power. Therefore it would seem rather odd to expect Muslim scholars to participate in free, critical dialogue outside of their home countries but revert to a quietist, non-engaging mode when back at home, for dialogue outside the country will encourage dialogue inside. And that may not be a welcome scenario for some states. Therefore those engaging in dialogue must be given space to roam the intellectual terrain freely and without fear for their safety or the safety of their loved ones. These points may not have been addressed adequately by those wishing to strengthen the dialogue.

The above is not to take away from the work that is being done by the United Nations. However, responsible scholarship dictates that the truth be told even at the risk of appearing politically incorrect. Some may argue that discussing this thesis in itself may add more fuel to a civilisational clash. As against that one could counter-argue that the discussion and further analysis of it may actually prevent such an outcome despite certain forces pushing us in that direction. And in any event a critical review of the theory and the efforts under way by the international community to address this challenge can only serve the cause of better and deeper understanding between civilisations. In an effort to further encourage debate and discussion on the issue and to address core civilisational issues of relevance to international peace a number of questions, summarising some of the points made above, are outlined below with regard to the United Nations Alliance of Civilisations:[80]

- What is the current status of the Dialogue among Civilisations, including achievements, failures, missed opportunities, and so forth?
- To what extent has the process been exclusive, focusing primarily on dialogue among big/global civilisations at the expense of smaller/less global civilisations, but also hybrid and syncretistic cultures?
- Even within the established parameters, how far has the process of participation been democratic (who has been invited, excluded and why)?
- Can inter-civilisational dialogue succeed without intra-civilisational dialogue and, if not, has the latter been addressed sufficiently?
- How far has the Dialogue among Civilisations been delegated to or appropriated by the state and other power institutions and consequently co-opted by their priorities and agendas?
- To what extent has the 'dialogue' managed to move beyond mutual monologues and into reflexive discourse, bringing about new understandings of the *other* but also of the *self*?
- Can the Alliance of Civilisations be a credible and viable mechanism to address current challenges?

To conclude this section the following may seem appropriate:

Dealing with civilisational themes is by nature vague[81] and very much subject to interpretation. In that sense one can neither announce the defeat nor celebrate the victory of any civilisational project; at least not in the short or medium terms. That having been said, international developments in the last decade or so appear to have swung more in the manner described by Huntington than Khatami. This is taking place on the back of increasing violence, or the threat of its use, in a polarised fashion around the globe. The vociferous minority amongst Muslims, who preach and promote violence, have monopolised the global Islamic platform. That must change through a more representative system in the Muslim communities requiring first and foremost some reviews and revision by Islamic scholars themselves. Failure to do so can prove catastrophic for the future of our world, for nicely wrapped-up phrases cannot hide conflicting realities beneath indefinitely. There was and remains a wide gap in political philosophy between the West and the Islamist doctrine.[82]

4
The Question of *Jihad*

4.1 The definition of the term *jihad*

The term *jihad* comes from the word *jahd*, meaning to struggle and to strive. Its derivatives, but never the term *jihad* itself, have been mentioned about 40 times in the Quran, the holy book of Muslims. The terms *mojahedoon* and *mujahedeen* are the subject nouns of *jihad*, which have also been used in the contemporary world in Afghanistan and other places. There is, now, clearly a distinct military slant to *jihad*. Islamist fundamentalism appears to preach *jihad* as an armed struggle against those it considers the enemies of Islam.[1] To be clear, there are two aspects to the concept of *jihad*: lesser (outward) *jihad* and greater (inner) *jihad*. Though they are interrelated, it is important to bear in mind the distinction between the two. The lesser *jihad* is defined by the Prophet himself.[2] It reports on the material and physical activities that are directed towards a Godly cause. External battles, whether military or otherwise, fall into this category. The Ottoman Sultan's proclamation of *jihad* against Britain, France and the Allies in World War I, was an instance of military/lesser *jihad*. The exhortation was a religio-political statement deriving its authority ultimately from *shari'a*, the legal code of Islam, which has traditionally been the exclusive domain of jurisprudence. The political and military impact of lesser *jihad* is derived from its religious orientation, though the religious value of *jihad* is somewhat independent of its political weight. This may indicate the predominance of jurisprudence in Islamic sciences in recent history in this respect.

The greater *jihad*, however, refers to self-purification and it is thus an internal challenge. It recounts the journey towards God starting within before it can be stretched and extended without. The discourse of faith for a believer is initiated first and foremost at the spiritual/Gnostic level in the mind and heart prior to any physical expression of the faith in the outside world. The UNESCO Charter begins by locating the origins of violent inter-human conflict in the minds of men. Similarly Muhammad appears to have identified internal journey for purity as the prelude to outbound struggle to serve God. Without the greater *jihad* the foundational steps of the religious discourse would therefore be missing.

At the outset one general observation regarding *jihad* is noteworthy. One verse in the Quran narrates: *There is no compulsion in religion. The way of development has now been distinguished from error.*[3] The inference is that violence cannot and should not be used for converting others to Islam. Peace is preferable to war and military campaign unless there is no alternative. Violence is the last resort. Tariq Ramadan states that 'the essence of *jihad* is the quest for peace, and *qital* [one Quranic term for war] is, at times the necessary path to peace'.[4] It is generally accepted that not every peace is suitable and that some kind of war is preferable to certain kinds of peace. That is why the world fought the Nazi-imposed peace that rested on racism. Ramadan continues to say that all forms of *jihad* are linked to the notion of resistance.[5] Another Islamic scholar, Khadduri, also believes that the ultimate goal of *jihad* is peace.[6] A Quranic verse cited in this regard is 4:91, where the faithful are exhorted to fight those who do not offer peace.

The lesser *jihad* will now be focused on before moving on to greater *jihad*.

Lesser *jihad*

The lesser *jihad* or the physical aspects of the concept can be divided into two categories: violent and non-violent (the term violence is not used axiologically here). Violent *jihad* can be subdivided into military and non-military. The non-military refers to circumstances where and when, for a perceived greater good, an individual or a group of individuals resort to violence without necessarily having planned or coordinated the violence in advance. The military aspect, however, describes situations where the presumed greater good is perceivably better served through coordinated violence with all the possible advantages and risks assessed beforehand. The keywords in both cases are 'greater good'. Who and what determines the greater good? Understanding the telos of *jihad* would better aid us comprehend the notion of 'greater good'.

Jihad can be understood both through *ta'vil* (interpretive conjecture of the Quran) and *tafsir* (substantive interpretation of the Quran) interpreted by many to be applicable only in a defensive context.[7] The terms used in the Quran for violent skirmishes and/or war consist of *qital* and *harb*. Their distinction from *jihad* must not be overlooked. The former appears to allude to what is commonly referred to as war, whereas the latter describes a much wider precept, only one of the components of which points in the direction of violence. At this point the link between the two aspects of *jihad* is noteworthy. The more salient and Gnostic component (inner greater *jihad*) teaches contemplation and spiritual purification as the path to tranquillity and peace and the prelude to outward lesser *jihad*. In view of this the classical concept of peace in International Relations, describing only the absence of war, may thus fall short of a basic requirement when referring to the Gnostic discourse in Islam or critical theory.[8] They seem to locate peace within the individual that can lead up to intra-communal and/or inter-communal peace. The telos of *jihad*, therefore, is peace and any activity under its banner must ultimately and inevitably serve the cause of peace. Much of the work of greater (internal) *jihad* is directed to that end.

The non-violent lesser *jihad* can be any activity that is carried out with the aim of serving God and people. (In some verses in the Quran the terms God and people can be used interchangeably.[9] For instance, in Sura 59, Verse 8, there is talk of those who assist God; but God does not require assistance and therefore inference is made by some to the interchangeability of the term *God* with the term *people* in some verses.) Accordingly the migration of early Muslims from Mecca to Medina around 622 to 623, seen as one of the most significant developments in the spread of Islam, can also be viewed as *jihad*. The revolutionary Islamic regime in Iran, set up in 1979, declared a *jihad* in development. Similarly a *jihad* in agriculture was proclaimed and an organisation was established to carry out its mandate.[10] Interestingly some Islamic scholars have even stated that 'defense of humanity and humanity's rights is the holiest form of *jihad*'.[11] Correspondingly Ziad Abu Ghanima of Jordan observes that 'democracy is a form of *jihad*'.[12] This expounds the struggle for justice and a more humane world.

This lesser *jihad* has been understood by the general public to be *jihad* proper – and not as only one aspect of it – and has been the concern of many around the world. The bold, non-state-centric and indiscriminate nature of the violence associated with Islamist militants such as al-Qaida has perhaps justifiably raised alarm particularly in the West about the discourse of this seemingly Islamic precept. All contemporary Islamist radicals such as Abdul-Wahhab, referred to in Chapter 1, appear to condone, sanction and even prescribe violence (what he refers to as *jihad*) once a year for every Muslim to promote a world based on their understanding of Islamic teachings.[13] Ali Shari'ati, another Islamic revivalist, who had the unfailing appeal of an inspiring writer and speaker, and infused the faith with socialist principles, wrote that *jihad* was a maxim and imperative to all Muslims against oppressors, throughout the ages, exhorting them to 'kill if they can, and get killed if they cannot'.[14] This radical, violent and forceful interpretation is/was shared by many Islamist militants around the world, most notably bin Laden, who owed much of his religious learning to the Wahhabi/Hanbali school of thought in Islam and derived his religio-political zeal from the jurisprudential dictates of Ibn Taymima, the Islamic jurist of the fourteenth century, whose views are not shared by all Muslims. One example is the Creed of Abu Zur'a and Abu Hatim Muhammad ibn Idris, who are in the main opposed to rebellion against their rulers.[15]

Islamic jurists have divided the world into *dar-ol-Islam* (world of Islam) and *dar-ol-harb* (world of war). This division, as viewed by Montgomery Watt, is closely associated with *jihad* and is particularly important in the theorisation of the expansionist aspirations of some Muslims.[16] This may also give credence to those Islamists who claim that war should be pursued with non-Muslims until and unless they convert or are governed by the rules of *shari'a*. In this outlook there is no room for neutrality. All land is either Islamic or a land of war to be conquered by Muslims and thus be taken out of its state of war. Diplomacy can have little role to play unless in the manner of trying to prepare the ground for the final conquest of the world by Islam. It is, in a way, a zero-sum portrayal of the world and there is no win-win scenario, where perceivably a positive-sum interpretation of international relations can also come into play (Islamists would of course claim that conversion of non-Muslims to Islam [their brand] is a victory for all, including non-Muslims). This polarisation by religious jurists was also in tandem with the Iranian revolutionary leader, Ayatollah Khomeini, who viewed the globe consisting of either *mostakberin* (the arrogant) or *mostaz'afin* (the meek). Usually for ideologies, including ideologised religions, black and white are typologies more readily adopted than perspectives that accommodate many different varieties and shades in between. The discourse of violence, and religious violence in particular, sees little, if any, use for finesse and nuances that may weaken its grip on the sword that is to behead all those who question its absolute authority. That is why calls by people like Khadduri stating a third ground as *dar-ol-solh* (world of peace) – neither abode of Islam nor abode of war – may not appeal to radical Islamists.[17]

Therefore, *jihad* as a war prescribed by the Almighty in order to advance the cause of justice, is in general a precept that can impact inter-human affairs. But who can declare *jihad*, against whom, and who should or can participate in it? These questions as addressed by jurisprudence in Islam are briefly discussed below.

Four kinds of *jihad* can take place according to religious jurists: by tongue, heart, hands and the sword.[18] These can be used for either greater or lesser *jihad*. In this interpretation, *jihad* is not a centrally authorised and authoritatively proclaimed policy of clerical hierarchy to wage war against the infidel but rather the process of continuous and systemic adherence to the will of the Almighty in every aspect of life. Accordingly, an agricultural engineer, who is more familiar and more akin to the laws of nature governing the soil and plants, and therefore more aware of the Will of God (laws of nature), can better serve the cause of *jihad* in harvest (lesser non-violent *jihad*) than can an untrained gardener. In the case of lesser violent *jihad*, sermons preached by radical clerics inciting hatred could, according to radical Islamists, also be cited as examples. Alternatively, words spoken by moderate Muslims advancing the cause of peaceful coexistence could be categorised as *jihad* – by liberal and non-violent conservative Muslims. Clearly what makes the difference is how one defines and understands the cause of God and justice. Generally, jurisprudence claims a monopoly of understanding, which is impervious to interpretations of Islamic philosophy, theology, exegesis and other branches of Islamic teaching. Soroush states that past revivalists wondered why religious law had closed up space for inner substance and essence and 'why fiqh [jurisprudence] was so unkind to ethics'.[19] In the case of military *jihad* therefore the question can be posed as to why jurisprudence should be treated as the sole source of understanding as regards this very important precept.

Military *jihad* can be waged against four kinds of people: polytheists, apostates, scriptuaries (people of the Book), and dissenter rebels.[20] But what are the circumstances where and when such *jihad* could be waged? There are many Quranic verses that can be interpreted in favour of military *jihad* describing those circumstances. One verse is 4:91, where permission to fight those who do not offer peace is granted. Other verses, 22:39–40, appear less lenient on the enemies of Muslims and provide less stringent conditions to wage war.[21] However, to generalise inferences from these and similar verses would first require decontextualisation of the Quran that would detach it from the specificity of its application in Arabia 1,400 years ago, a quality common among Islamist militants.[22] Such decontextualisation renders Islam and the text of Islam ahistorical. An argument raised by Islamist zealots and clerics in favour of the applicability of *shari'a* is that just as mathematical and geometrical laws, like the Pythagorean theorem, are universally and eternally applicable, the rules and laws of Islam are equally suited for all places and all time. That is why, they claim, Islamic civilisation came about and if applied again *shari'a* would revive that civilisation.

The above assessment disregards the important role of foreign cultures and civilisations in the melting pot of Islamic polity at the time. It also overlooks the fact that mathematical and geometrical laws determine the qualities only of fixtures such as lines and angles. Those fixtures have perceivably remained constant without any change and will perceivably remain so for eternity. Therefore laws on their interaction will accordingly remain the same. Can we, however, possibly talk of humanity as the embodiment of fixed qualities like a constant? Nothing could sound further from the truth. The only constant feature of humanity is change that has given rise to such voluminous history. The only historical species known to humankind is him/herself exactly because he/she can learn, be original and advance. In consequence rules governing the behaviour of this species should advance with him/her. Can we seriously suggest that the laws of even only a century ago would be suitable for today's needs and requirements? This would appear regressive and obscene. Claiming eternal relevance and application for rules devised fourteen centuries ago in the dry desert of Arabia regarding various and detailed aspects of human behaviour defies rationality, a quality that both the Quran and the Prophet have repeatedly emphasised.[23] It is as strange as comparing someone in Sweden today, for instance, with the Bedouin Arab in Arabia in AD 630 and concluding that they are identical in behaviour, in motivation, in their sense of justice, in desires, ambitions, hopes, fears and aversion, outlook on life and the afterlife, in governance, trade, art, culture, in military establishment, security matters, technology, in education, in science, respect for others, human rights, relations with others, family...and ultimately in their views on God. If ever such an analogy and conclusion could stand and be accepted then the applicability of laws devised one and a half millennia ago could be equally acceptable today. In short, lines and points do not change but humans do and so should laws governing them.

The above does not aim to question the validity of ethical maxims such as the Ten Commandments (or other such ethical principles), which are shared by the Abrahamic traditions. General moral guidelines for humanity are one thing, a legal system governing their behaviour in every aspect of life quite another. Though legal systems and codes could be based on moral guidelines, they are usually formulated with regard to the needs and circumstances of the people they are meant for. In other words, ethics could provide the basis for the law of the land but that does not mean jurisprudence could actually codify that law. The two are quite separate.

The requirements for *jihad* are said to relate to defending religious freedom (Quran 22:39–41), in self-defence (Quran 2:190), and those who are oppressed: men, women and children, who cry for help (Quran 4:75). This provides a vague basis upon which claim for *jihad* could be made and its imprecise nature renders the precept open to abuse. An instance was Saddam Hussein's call to *jihad* against the American forces in 2003 when he felt he was losing power. His call, however, was not recognised as valid by any of the leading religious hierarchies in the Muslim world.

Military *jihad* must usually be called for by the highest religious authorities. The only exception is if Muslims are under attack and

have to defend themselves.[24] Once declared, those eligible to participate have to either do so *en masse* without exception (*einee*). In other
instances, where only a group of Muslims can achieve the objectives
of *jihad*, not all are obligated to participate (*kafayee*).[25] Those participating in *jihad* must fulfil the following requirements: (a) they must
be firm believers in the faith; (b) they must be of mature and sound
mind; (c) they must be of male gender; (d) they must be able-bodied
physically; (e) they must be independent economically; (f) they must
proceed to action with good intentions; (g) and they must go by a
certain code of conduct during the *jihad*, such as obedience to the
commander, no mutilation, no retreat or desertion unless the enemy
is too powerful.[26] Moreover, according to Haleem, proportionality
and discrimination in *jihad* must be observed.[27]

Jihad, as noted before, can be waged by different means against
certain groups of people. These dicta, however, may be subject to
other conditions usually referred to as *maslaha* (expediency). That
is to say they are not absolute and their application may vary from
phase to phase. Muhammad himself fought pagan Arabs at times but
opted to conclude peace treaties with them at certain other times.
The Jews of Medina, for instance, were protected under the constitution of Medina written soon after the arrival of the Messenger of
Islam into the city, but that protection was waived when it was determined that there had been a breach of its terms by some members of
the Jewish community in Medina.

An important observation on violent lesser *jihad* may be found
in the *Kimiaye Sa'adat* (Elixir of Salvation) by Mohammad Ghazzali,
whose importance in the Islamic world can hardly be overstated. In
this book that professes to have been written for the general and
not the expert reader, all aspects of a prosperous life are expounded,
sometimes in great detail. For example there is much emphasis on the
question of piety and self-purification (greater *jihad*) and there are
many pages on friendship and other temporal and religious facets.
Yet there are no headings at all on the question of religious fighting
(lesser *jihad*) in this important book.[28] Inevitably this must pose a
question on the relevance of military *jihad* to prosperity as understood and narrated by Ghazzali; the contrast with Abdul-Wahhab
and the latter's exhortation that every Muslim is duty-bound to
engage in military *jihad* at least once a year could not be greater.
The difference between the two readings tells us of a great variety of

interpretations that can be found on this very contentious precept within Islamic tradition and literature.[29]

Military *jihad* has often been invoked and abused by many a ruler in order to justify offensive and irredentist policies in distant lands or to suppress dissent within their domain.[30] Even after the death of the Prophet of Islam the Arab expeditions into the Persian and Byzantine lands, conducted in the name of *jihad*, had, in some scholars' opinion, probably little if anything to do with the spread of the faith.[31] What was probably taking place was *razzia* and not *jihad*, the primary aim of which was booty for most participants.[32] According to Montgomery Watt, the military expeditions of early Islam could be linked more to the Arab custom of raid, which could not be stopped all at once. Muhammad himself might have noticed this as early as AD 626.[33] Even later Islamic rulers abused the precept of *jihad* when it suited their perceived interests.[34] When in the Battle of Tours early Muslims did not acquire much booty, their zeal for more combat to conquer France, according to some, was somewhat diminished.[35]

Haleem states that Muhammad and his companions fought for three reasons: one was when there was persistent breach of agreements; another when hostilities were initiated by others against Muslims or people were barred from conversion to Islam; and lastly when Muslims were expelled from the Holy Mosque or from their homes.[36] An important observation on the brinksmanship of the Messenger of Islam must be made here. When deciding to go to war, Muhammad made all the preparations necessary for an armed confrontation. Based on religious maxims he made every human effort to maximise the chances of victory for Muslims even though they lost in some of the battles. Understanding Muhammad's policies, therefore, would require a human study of his thoughts and deeds as a human (however elevated he must have been). Portrayals of him as a super-human (of a different kind), however, tend to make such studies difficult. Conventional religious narratives of Muhammad's life and sayings appear to overlook his very humanity, his experiences, his rationality, his brinksmanship, his taste, his courage, his free choice, his likes and dislikes, his input and ultimately his character as a human being; after all it is the very verse of the Quran that clearly states: 'Tell [ay Muhammad] that I am a human being like you'.[37] The near-complete disregard of Muhammad's human nature and its replacement by an almost-divine nature ascribed to him, to his life and sayings has made him inaccessible to Muslims and his followers. Only humans can be role models for humans. When studying the wars of the Prophet, inevitably we have to delve into the circumstances wherein he made the decision to go to war. However, if we are to assume that every decision made by the Messenger was divinely ordained how can we possibly examine, assess, or even learn from them? If the source of all his post-prophetic life and decisions was the Divine, then, since we have no access to that source, we cannot relate and thus cannot learn from them. This divinisation of Muhammad, in itself contrary to Quranic teachings, renders the study of Islam a distant and rather detached affair.

A recent article by Abdolkarim Soroush, where he acknowledges space for mediation of Divine inspiration through and in the shape of the person of the Messenger of Islam, therefore recognising the significance and the impact of the particular conditions and specific circumstances pertaining to the character of the Prophet, is noteworthy.[38] Contrary to the conventional beliefs of many Muslims, it is the very human nature of Muhammad that renders him supreme in the eyes of Islam; it is his free choice and his opting to only serve God amidst all the tribulations, limitations, hesitations, contemplation, conflicts, thoughts and after-thoughts, hopes and despair, joys and pains, friendship and enmities, loyalty and betrayal, forgiveness and revenge and all other facets, all part and parcel of social life, that makes his elevation to the prophetic Gnostic level all the more astounding and admirable. God does not choose just anyone to be His Messenger.

Another instance of lesser *jihad*, according to Islamic jurisprudence, is that of *ribat*: the defence of Islamic state borders.[39] If attacked, all Muslims are obligated to fight a *jihad* defending the borders of the Islamic state without necessarily waiting for a call to *jihad* from religious authorities.[40] Four types of relationship between a Muslim and warring neighbouring countries have been identified by Haleem: (a) defensive war; (b) peace treaty; (c) state of truce; (d) a situation where enemy envoys can travel safely in the Muslim land.[41] In the first instance the defensive war may constitute *jihad*, though one definition of a defensive war may vary substantially from another.[42] The reader should note a distinction between an Islamic and a Muslim country. While the latter refers only to the faith of the majority population, the former describes a system whereby the rules of conduct in politics, society, economics and other facets of life claim to correspond to *shari'a*. I do not wish to say much on the paradox of 'Islamic state' at this stage as an inherently conflictual entity since sovereign statehood, established and developed along Western interests, rests on certain secular and nationalist pillars that are at best alien to political Islam and at worst stand in stark contrast to Islamist politics.

Greater *jihad*

The importance attached to inner strength and development through which spiritual elevation can be achieved lies at the heart of greater *jihad*. It is an attempt to control the excesses of greed (*nafse ammareh*) that drive us to do our utmost to fulfil our desires. Muhammad is reported to have stated, 'True wealth does not lie in the riches you possess. True wealth is the wealth of your soul.'[43] There is a report by mystics that a rich and generous man once addressing a poor Sufi living in desolate conditions asked why the poor man had not asked for help and charity from him. In response the Sufi said how could he have possibly asked the man, who was a slave of the poor man's slave, for help. That response appeared arrogant and angered the rich man, who irately asked the Sufi to explain himself. The Sufi calmly pointed out that while he was in control of anger, anger seemed to be in control of the rich man. Reportedly the man felt embarrassed by the deep Gnostic response. Another *hadith* from Muhammad refers to much the same: 'A strong man is not a man who overcomes his enemy. A strong man is a man who controls himself when he is angry.'[44]

It is also interesting to note greater *jihad* in comparison with Western philosophy. Inner strength to control greed is also an important moral dictum propounded by Plato,[45] whose works as well as those of other Greek philosophers were read and found in tandem with Islamic philosophy.[46] Unlike Hobbes, who appears either oblivious to higher qualities in humanity or opts to disregard them altogether, greater *jihad* aims to foster inner strength to resist material attraction and the desire to 'take' and instead to promote the joy of 'giving'. In neo-realist terms in IR, greater *jihad* emphasises the first image analysis in the Waltzian outlook. Though other images are not denied, the role of the individual as the ultimate agent of change in the world is highlighted. The disempowerment of the individual unit in the Waltzian discourse (a third-image analysis), where the underlying cause of war is the international structure, and that of the liberal peace tradition (a second-image analysis), where the national and societal structure is the major determinant of peace and/or war, the greater *jihad* reenergises the much-overlooked first image analysis. If 'wars start in the minds of men' (individuals), then so should peace. The construction of a peaceful communal and global structure by a violent human agent is a philosophical paradox and a contradiction in terms. It is the selfish man who constructs a selfish state, and a selfish state that lays the foundation for an exclusive and divisive international structure. All three, at all three levels, reinforce and feed one another.

This much neglected aspect of social life in the West, when one's duties are basically summed up in compliance with the laws of the land and where one's functional existence in his/her environment is driven by excessive individualism to enhance self-benefit and accumulate wealth, even at the expense of others, has reduced 'the meaning of life in existence to the amount of money in the bank account'.[47] The discourse of greater *jihad* entails processes of reflection that involve the loss of ego-consciousness to varying degrees.[48] This reflection is not another attempt at ratiocination in the much celebrated discourse of rationality where self-interest is the prime motive and mover; rather it is a process whereby one's knowledge is enhanced, aiding the individual to transcend beyond the self and approach, in relative terms, the state of selflessness. This is preached by Gnostics through the remembrance of God (*zikr*) and proper reflection. Muhammad himself is reported to have stated that one hour of reflection is greater than 60 years of prayers.[49] As noted by William Blake,

Reason, or the ratio of all we have already known... is not the same that it shall be when we know more... He who sees the infinite in all things, sees God. He who sees the ratio only, sees himself only.[50]

A man who has lost God in his ego is lamentable according to Shabestari, the famous Iranian mystic of the thirteenth and fourteenth centuries.[51] This reflection on the self aims at controlling the egocentrism that is within each and every one of us. 'But better not to know this "self" – "self"-ignorance is best!' says Shabestari in his celebrated *Garden of Mystery*.[52] Rumi has also stressed repeatedly the importance of controlling this 'self'.

> *O kings, we have slain the outward enemy,*
> *(but) there remains within (us) a worse enemy than he;*
> *To slay this (enemy) is greater than intelligence could care,*
> *The inward lion is not subdued by the hare;*
> *This carnal self (nafs) is Hell, and Hell is a dragon of desire*
> *Its fire undiminished by oceans, it will not retire*
> *It would drink up the water of the Seven Seas,*
> *Yet the blazing of that consumer of creatures would not cease*[53]

In an allegory highlighting the temerity and ignorance of mankind, Rumi narrates the story of a man, who in search of a large snake found a seemingly dead dragon in winter amid snow and dragged the beast back to Baghdad to amaze the people. During the show, where thousands had gathered, the dragon was revived by the heat of the sun and sent shivers up the spines of all spectators, who rushed to flee the scene. Alas, thousands were killed by the beast, including the snake-catcher himself.

> *The snake-catcher stood there, frozen.*
> *'What have I brought out of the mountains? What have I chosen?'*
> *Against a post the snake braced*
> *It crushed the man and consumed him in haste*
> *The dragon is your animal-soul [nafse ammare]*
> *Don't take it for a warming stroll*
> *Warmed by the hot air of desires, wealth and power*
> *The dragon will all in its way devour.*[54]

The above is adopted here to illustrate the significance of the 'self' in the conduct of individual/s and how important it is, in the Islamic Gnostic doctrine, to subjugate it and not heed its call. Without this chief imperative the lesser *jihad* may be of short-term consequence at best. The point here is the removal of the distinction between within and without and the disbanding of the detachment between the inner truth and the outer reality. Selfishness in the outside world is clearly a manifestation and function of selfishness within. One contemporary Islamic thinker, Ali Shari'ati, more renowned for his revolutionary ideas, however, has the following listed among his prayers: 'O Lord, do eliminate selfishness in me so decisively, or purge me from it so resolutely that I would not feel the selfishness of others and thus would not suffer from it'.[55]

In another prayer, Shari'ati pleads: 'O Lord, against all that, which leads to the depravation of humanity, strengthen me with "not having" and "not wanting"'.[56] These and other such reflections attest to the point heeded in greater *jihad* to develop oneself against the limitless traits in human beings such as greed, jealousy, arrogance, hypocrisy, cruelty, lying, egocentrism and the like. The fundamental agent of human community, the individual, is thus empowered to effect change in his/her environment through an act of self-reflection. More was said on this in Chapter 1.

4.2   The issue of just war and *jihad*

Just war as a Western concept comes from the Latin phrase *jus ad bellum* (justice of war). It is distinguished from *jus in bello* (justice in war), which refers to the conduct of warfare. Accordingly a just war may be fought unjustly (through unjust means such as lack of proportionality) or acceptable conduct of warfare may be applied in an unjust war. It is generally agreed that the requirements for just war consist of the following:

- The war is used as the last resort after all other peaceful alternatives have been convincingly exhausted.
- The war must be waged by a legitimate authority (this usually means the state).
- The war must be in response to a wrong committed, for example, aggression and it is carried out only to redress the injury and with the right intention throughout.
- There must be a reasonable chance of success for the war to start.
- Peace, as the ultimate objective of the war, must be superior to the peace that prevailed before the war.

- There must be proportionality in the conduct of the war. All unnecessary deaths, injuries and suffering, outside the remit of the objective of the war, must be avoided.
- The war should discriminate between combatants and non-combatants, particularly civilians.[57]

Unjust aggression therefore, like violating the territorial integrity of another state out of irredentism, as Iraq did with regard to Kuwait in 1990, is generally viewed as the criminal policy of a government and not as the policy of a criminal government – let alone a criminal system of government.[58] This absolves the institution of the state from criminality and considers criminality only as an optional policy. The pursuit of perceived national interests, and all that it may entail including conflict with other states, is, however, a distinct quality of a sovereign state. It is therefore questionable to what degree criminality can be viewed as detached from the essence of the institution of state and only located outside of the state as a voluntary inclusion.

The concept of just war may also hint at the notion of holy war in Christendom, reminiscent of the Crusades. The term 'holy war' does not exist in Islam and any insinuation to the contrary may be an uninformed juxtaposition of a Christian concept into Islam. *Jihad* is not holy war. As stated by one scholar:

> Another term which is misunderstood and misrepresented is *jihad*. This does not mean 'Holy War'. 'Holy War' does not exist as a term in Arabic, and its translation into Arabic sounds quite alien. The term which is specifically used in the Qur'an for fighting is qital.[59]

Ibn Khaldun believes that war is a natural condition of life for humanity and that no part of the human race can be free from it.[60] Its origins, according to him, lay in the desire for revenge, jealousy, zeal on behalf of royal authority and zeal for God and religion.[61] He puts war into two main categories, just and unjust. Each of them in turn are divided into two sub-categories:

Unjust Wars:

- Between neighbouring tribes or competing families
- Caused by hostility and usually among savage nations

Just Wars:

- Holy war[62] [lesser *jihad*] as described by the religious law
- Dynastic war against those who disobey[63]

The emphasis on religious law as noted above by Ibn Khaldun, however, seems to present a paradox when considered along with another important observation made by the same author. There is an important argument by Ibn Khaldun on the negative impact of law on people's fortitude. In his own words:

> When laws are (enforced) by means of punishment, they completely destroy fortitude, because the use of punishment against someone who cannot defend himself generates in that person a feeling of humiliation that, no doubt, must break his fortitude.[64]

He later states, 'Clearly, then, governmental and educational laws destroy fortitude, because their restraining influence is something that comes from outside'.[65] He thus appears to attach great importance to the inner potency of people to observe the dos and don'ts that would strengthen their fortitude rather than to an outside intervention by agencies that would force compliance or serve punishment. Therefore he appears to highlight the significance and magnitude of greater (inner) *jihad*. In other words, everyone should police themselves and their own behaviour and should observe the rules and regulations agreed upon, which would reflect and empower them to elevate to higher levels with greater fortitude. According to Rumi:

> *Fools venerate the mosque in appearance only*
> *And are cruel to the men of heart, surely*
> *That is a metaphor, this is the truth, ay you the berated*
> *There is no mosque unless in the heart of the spiritually elevated*[66]

Therefore Ibn Khaldun appears to subscribe to greater *jihad* as a means of orderly life in human communities or else the fortitude of the members of the community will have to be compromised. The real restraint in humans should come from within themselves. That is why, he believes, religious law does not, unlike government laws decrease fortitude. In his view, 'The religious laws, on the other hand, do not destroy fortitude, because their restraining influence is something inherent'.[67]

There are two observations to be made here. One is that not everyone in Muslim communities will necessarily have been elevated to such spiritual heights as to have the inner strength to police themselves, which somewhat brings under question the 'inherent' aspect that gives rise to Ibn Khaldun's argument. Whether in the past or nowadays, from the time of the Ummayids to Abbassidas, from the Mongols and the Ottomans right through to today's Muslim states, the spiritually elevated have not formed the majority of the Muslim community. This is not just the case in the history of Islam but also other religions. The elevated, spiritually and intellectually, have usually been in the minority. That being the case, Ibn Khaldun's reference to religious law authorising the lesser *jihad*, referred to above, must inevitably (based on his own argument) diminish the fortitude of Muslims, unless we believe that he meant all members of Muslim communities are always spiritually elevated and fully understand and follow the rules of the faith, which they have internalised. That would, however, sound rather exaggerated. Therefore, his reference to religious law must inexorably take account of his own argument on fortitude, which leaves us wondering how Ibn Khaldun can categorise a war as just, when the waging of that war would lead to the destruction of fortitude of at least some of the Muslim warriors.

The second observation relates to his separation of government and religious laws. This was noted in the quotes given above. One inference could be that for Ibn Khaldun, in a general sense of the word, religion is separate from politics or he would not have made such a clear distinction between governmental laws and religious laws. That inference, however, seems at odds with other passages in the *Muqaddimah*. For example:

In the Muslim community, the holy war [lesser *jihad*] is a religious duty, because of the universalism of the Muslim mission and (the obligation to) convert every body to Islam either by persuasion or by force. Therefore, caliphate and royal authority are united in Islam, so that the person in charge can devote the available strength to both of them at the same time.[68]

The above suggests very directly the amalgamation of religion and politics for it places the most important issue in politics – conflict (at least certain aspects of it) – within the domain of religious duty. This, very clearly, indicates a belief in political Islam, which is at variance with the distinction of governmental laws from religious laws as noted before. It may be concluded that there is a certain degree of inconsistency in Ibn Khaldun's writings on this point.

Is lesser military *jihad* the same as just war referred to in the West? The answer is seemingly affirmative, at least inasmuch as the cause of the war relates to justice. *Jihad* is only proper because it complies with justice; for justice is the basis upon which all else is based. War or peace, kindness or harshness, forgiveness or punishment, giving or taking and all other facets of life can be given meaning only in the context of justice. The ultimate authenticity, at least in temporal affairs of human community, must inevitably belong to this under-lying and overriding precept. The following verses from the Quran attest to the same:

> And the Firmament has He raised high, and He has set up the Balance (of Justice), in order that ye may not transgress (due) balance. So establish weight with justice and fall not short in the balance.[69]

> We sent Our Messengers with clear evidence, and sent with them the Book and the Balance so that people would maintain justice ...[70]

Even the exile of Adam and Eve from Paradise onto earth is presented as the result of the injustice that the two did to themselves:

> And We said: O Adam! Dwell you and your wife in the garden and eat from it a plenteous (food) wherever you wish and do not approach this tree, for then you will be of the unjust.[71]

Therefore, there seems to exist much common ground between *jihad* and just war. However, though axiologically similar, the religious nature of the former is the main distinguishing feature from the latter. That can make much difference due to the criteria that determines the justice of any particular cause. A Muslim scholar has narrated this point with the added reference to the abuse of this precept by those seeking to exploit it for personal and political gain:

> Islam, it will be recalled, abolished all kinds of warfare except the *jihad*. Only a war which has an ultimate religious purpose, that is to enforce God's law or to check transgression against it, is a just war... Throughout the history of Islam, however, fighting between Muslim rulers and contending parties was as continuous as between Islam and its external enemies.[72]

An attempted abuse of the precept of *jihad* was when Saddam Hussein found himself facing defeat in March 2003:

> We say to all sons of *Jihad* and supporters, to our nation, our people, wherever they are, that whoever is able to march and reach Iraq, Baghdad, Najaf, and blow himself up in this American invasion... This is the climax of *Jihad* and climax of martyrdom.[73]

In *jihad*, as a just war conducted for the cause of God, some conditions apply. Specifically four main principles must be carefully observed:

- Righteous intention. By this it is meant one must make sure that one's personal desires and feelings are not driving one to the conflict but only, and only as, sanctioned by God (this of course has been open to much abuse throughout Islamic history).[74]
- Discrimination. Non-combatants must be spared and no harm must come to them, at least not intentionally. If the process endangers the lives of non-combatants, then many Muslim scholars/ jurists would not sanction the conflict in the first place.
- Proportionality. This principle states that the degree of harm inflicted upon the adversary must be in proportion to the degree of harm received from them.
- Transgression avoidance. This is explained by Haleem in the following words:

> Transgression has been interpreted by Qur'anic exegetes as meaning initiation of fighting, fighting those with whom a treaty has been concluded, surprising the enemy without first inviting

them to make peace, destroying crops or killing those who should be protected.[75]

The points on *jihad* noted above and those on just war in the beginning of this section are extremely similar. In fact, according to Khadduri, in Islam no war is allowed except that which is just (in the way of God and thus a military *jihad*).[76] The same author considers the ultimate goal of Islam to be peace,[77] which would in turn render the ultimate goal of *jihad* peace too.

4.3   *Jihad*: political violence and/or religious piety?

The concept of lesser military *jihad* can at times be utilised in the service of the foreign policy of the Muslim community as perceived by their leaders. An instance was when the Ottomans supported Germany in World War I. The latter was training Ottoman officers and was engaged in building railways from Istanbul to Baghdad. The Germans also offered two warships to the Ottomans, who were eager to get Egypt back from Britain and the Caucusus mountains from Russia. People in the Ottoman Empire supported Germany and the Sultan, in defence and aid of Germany's policies declared *jihad* against Britain, France and Russia.[78] The precept of *jihad* can also reinforce militancy as it did for the original Turks for whom raiding settled people was a favourite occupation.[79] It has also legitimised raids for booty, wherein spread of the faith had very little role to play, for that would have meant sharing the booty.[80] In short, many rulers abused the practice of *jihad*, instrumentalising a precept whose main function was self-purification before anything else.[81]

The violence embodied in lesser military *jihad* is taken by some scholars to have emanated from the very origins of Islam. '...few if any world religions besides Islam were founded by a person who led his armies in more than twenty-five battles (only two of which were in defence of Medina, the Muslim capital at the time) and ordered his armies to fight more than 30 additional battles during his lifetime'.[82] To be more accurate, Muhammad, in his ten years of rule in Medina, fought 65 battles with his adversaries, out of which he led and participated in 27 and 38 were led by those appointed by him. Other sources put the figure of battles where the Messenger participated at 48, and the total number of battles at 75.[83]

An important observation on the history of early Islam and the battles fought therein, is that fundamentalists who preach and practice violence are more than willing and ready to overlook the context within which that violence was conducted. Decontextualisation is one of the most common qualities among all radical Islamists, who take pride in eternalising a specific act that may have been tailored to suit a particular occasion. When there are, however, Quranic and *hadith* injunctions that appear to defy extremism and preach moderation, generalisations are deliberately avoided by Islamists. Some of these are:

> God does not forbid you from being kind and equitable to those who have neither made war on you on account of your religion nor driven you from your homes. Lo! God loveth those who are equitable.[84]
>
> Fight in the way of God against those who fight against you, but begin not hostilities. Lo! God loveth not aggressors.[85]

According to one Muslim writer, 'no precept is to be found in the Kuran, which, taken with the context, can justify unprovoked war'.[86] Tariq Ramadan also reports a *hadith* from Muhammad, which speaks against radicalism:

> Moderation, Moderation! For only with moderation will you succeed.[87]

That appears in harmony with the Quranic verse, *We ordained you a people of moderation (between extremes).*[88] The merit of moderation is also alluded to in mystic discourses. While reporting a parable Rumi says:

> *The Sheikh turned to the poor darvish and said*
> *In every case take the middle course instead*
> *It comes in Tradition that the best comes between extremes*
> *Humours are beneficial only in balance, as it seems*[89]

The call for *jihad* can come in the shape of a fatwa, which, contrary to popular belief, is not an edict but merely a legal opinion.[90] On lesser military *jihad* as well as on other issues, however, opinions may vary between various jurists. An instance was the fatwa issued by Ayatollah Khomeini on Salman Rushdie in 1989 effectively issuing a death sentence for him. At the same time religious authorities in Saudi Arabia and the Sheikhs of Alazhar in Cairo, prominent figures in Sunni Islamic jurisprudence, as well as all but one member of the Islamic Conference in March 1989, considered that fatwa un-Islamic.[91] A more recent difference of opinion with radical Islamists can be noted in the opinion of the leading Islamic jurist in the United Kingdom, Sheikh Tahir ul-Qadri, who stated unequivocally in 2010 that suicide bombings were un-Islamic. His fatwa has been expressed in 600 pages of text that take account of the Quran and other Islamic writings.[92]

An important observation is that lesser *jihad* should be the subject and function of greater *jihad*. 'The perpetual inner and greater *jihad* will guide the conduct of lesser *jihad* in both its objectives and its conduct.'[93] While lesser military *jihad* may teach how to die for God, greater inner *jihad* explains and describes how to live for God. As life precedes death it is the importance of how to live that can guide one into the manner of his/her death. In one of his prayers, Shari'ati writes:

> *O, Lord, Teach me how to live; I myself shall learn how die. Let me choose that myself but the way you like it.*[94]

In order to internalise *shari'a* (if one accepts the authenticity of *shari'a* in its present form)[95] one must first understand *tariqa* (path), which is the inner mystery of *shari'a*.[96] *Tariqa* is an internal journey of self-discovery. Ghazzali stresses the importance of inner *jihad* in the following words:

> The fruits of meditation [*fekrat*], then, consists of varieties of knowledge, states and actions. The fruit specific of each, however, is nothing other than a form of knowledge. When knowledge is acquired within the heart, the state of the heart is altered. When the heart's state changes, the actions of the bodily members change. Thus action follows spiritual state, state follows knowledge, and knowledge follows meditation [*fekrat*]. Meditation [*fekrat*] is thus the beginning of and key to all action.[97]

And that is the focus of greater *jihad*. The path to outside starts within, where all the journeys commence; even the discovery of God begins with self-discovery. Quoted by Ghazzali, the narrative reads: 'O Humankind, acquire self-knowledge so you may know thy Lord'.[98] Such an outlook on religion and *jihad*, where self-discovery, contemplation and meditation is the prelude to outward behaviour in society and all temporal affairs, agrees with the Gnostic reading of human nature and his/her environment:

> *Behold the surging armies of my 'states',*
> *Each at war and strife with another*
> *Contemplate the same grievous war in thyself*
> *Why then art though engaged in warring with others?*[99]

No doubt the advent of Islamist fundamentalism is one of the greatest challenges that is now facing not only the West but also the majority of Muslims, who have no desire to engage in violent conflict and would much rather pursue their interests via more peaceful means. However, the West would also be well advised to rethink some of its conventional practices and perhaps attempt to redefine its interests in the wake of challenges it is facing from the increasing number of radical Islamists who are falling prey to a discourse of hatred and violence. Every effort must be made to disengage those who wish to embark upon a new Cold War. In the words of Pat Buchanan:

> To some Americans, searching for a new enemy against whom to test our mettle and power, after the death of Communism, Islam is the preferred antagonist. But to declare Islam as an enemy of the United Sates is to declare a Second Cold War that is unlikely to end in the same resounding victory as the first.[100]

This view is echoed by Buck-Morss, who believes that the biggest threat to US national security is the disappearance of an enemy from the scene.[101] That kind of political outlook, which reflects more realpolitik than the demands of this day and age, should give way to a more dialogic perspective that would not shy away from tackling some of the fundamental shortfalls of the current international system. Critical theory, much like mysticism in Islam, opens the way for dialogue and debate, creating space for self-awareness and eleva-tion. Whether in the corridors of power in the White House or in Whitehall, or sleeping in the shadowy maze of Tora Bora caves in eastern Afghanistan, we must all first begin to look within before attempting to manipulate the world without. In a world where the underprivileged know what they are missing, and are probably aware that their fair share has unjustly been taken away from them, and where the dispossessed and the victims of injustice and brutality have access to the means of destruction, global politics will probably continue to suffer from unseemly developments such as radicalism in political Islam. International Relations should continue to encourage and welcome contributions from critical studies that would encom-pass all disciplines, including Islamic Gnosticism.

5
Current Conflicts and Muslim and Islamist States: Two Contemporary Cases

5.1 War and peace in Iraq: political philosophy versus organised violence

The terrorist attacks of September 2001 in the United States by Islamist suicide bombers prompted a massive US-led military operation that ousted the radical government of the Taliban from power in Afghanistan and led to the fleeing of the leaders of the al-Qaida organisation, the primary sponsor of the 2001 attacks.[1] The neo-conservative US administration at the time declared a War on Terror, whereby it reserved the right of preventive strikes against those it considered potential terrorist threats against the United States.[2] Attention was thereafter focused on the dictatorship in Iraq, where for decades the tyrannical government of Saddam Hussein had resulted in a brutal suppression of the Iraqi people and caused two major wars, one with Iran and another with Kuwait.

The Ba'ath party, to which Saddam Hussein belonged, was, however, a secular socialist political organisation.[3] Its northern neighbour, Syria, was also affiliated with the same party, though that had not led to particularly warm relations between the two countries. Iraqi politics, therefore, was a discourse of totalitarianism pursued through socialist principles with zero tolerance for dissent. There were no strong religious contributions, officially or unofficially, into a system that was willing to gas its neighbours as well as its own population.[4] Therefore, as contemptible a dictator as he was, Saddam was far from an Islamist fundamentalist. To date no hard evidence has been presented to the world to show a credible link between the former Iraqi ruler and Islamist radicalism.

In its international dimension the expansionist designs of Saddam had already started a war with Iran in 1980 that had lasted for seven years and had consequently earned the unceremonious title of the longest war of the twentieth century. Later in 1990 the Iraqi leader had invaded and occupied Kuwait declaring it the nineteenth province of Iraq.[5] That had led to the most successful ever application of *collective security* in human history, whereby a united world assembled its forces and resources, led by the United States, to reverse the invasion and force the aggressors out of Kuwait.

Moreover, there were talks by US high officials, including former Secretary of State Condoleezza Rice, that a new US policy would be centred on fostering stability in the Middle East based on democratic governance:

> The 'freedom deficit' in the broader Middle East provides fertile ground for the growth of an ideology of hatred so vicious and virulent that it leads people to strap suicide bombs to their bodies and fly airplanes into buildings. When the citizens of this region cannot advance their interests and redress their grievances through an open political process, they retreat hopelessly into the shadows to be preyed upon by evil men with violent designs.[6]

This new approach seemed to promote a *greater Middle East* that boasted freedom of speech and democratic governance. Freedom of the people, it was believed, expressed in libertarian fashion, could be the key to solving the phenomenon of arbitrary killings preached and practised by Islamist radicals.

It was against the backdrop of these factors (a brutal dictator in Baghdad, who was also an aggressive adventurer abroad, the new terrorist threat posed by radical Islamists against the West in general and the United States in particular and the perceived remedy, to purge the Middle East of dictators) that the plans to invade and occupy Iraq in 2003 were put into effect.[7] Despite opposition by many countries, including Russia, France and Germany, the US-led forces, backed by the United Kingdom and Spain among others, managed to topple the Iraqi regime in a relatively short period of time, sending Saddam into hiding. The 'major combat' phase of the military operation in Iraq, as declared by President Bush, came to end on 1 May 2003, about 40 days after it had started on 20 March of the same year. There was perhaps little doubt on the military outcome of the conflict, even though according to some, unlike the war in Afghanistan a couple of years earlier, it had failed to secure the full and unequivocal support of the United Nations.

The road to rebuilding Iraq as a country and institutionalising democracy, however, was fraught with hurdles right from the beginning. The military victory over Saddam was not easily translated into winning the peace in the country. The war had been won but peace had not been secured. This baffled US policymakers, who wondered why peace was proving so elusive to them in Iraq. After all, if freedom and democracy were the foundations of peace and stability, why then despite the new-found democracy in the country, the streets of Baghdad and other cities in Iraq were the scenes of carnage and violence? What were the missing ingredients in Iraq for peace and stability to be secured?

The first observation to be made was that while war is a military project, peace is generally a political discourse. That had been witnessed in Afghanistan only very recently, where the process of peace-building was still under way.[8] Therefore, though the amount and quality of military hardware may be a deciding factor in war, they do not seem to have a comparable impact on the peace process. Perhaps this point eluded policymakers in Washington at the time. The second observation relates to the very question that was being asked. The question 'Why had peace not been won in Iraq?' should perhaps be rephrased to: 'Why had the liberal peace not been won in the non-liberal post-conflict polity of Iraq?' That rephrased question could conceivably have better guided attention to the elements that have possibly contributed to the impasse in that country. As Arabs say, 'a good question is half the answer'.

Three possible sets of answers could be identified in response to that question:

- External factors, both state and non-state actors. This would include regional and non-regional countries as well as organisations such as al-Qaida.
- Conspiracy theory, which would view the violence in Iraq as planned in order to divide the country along the sectarian lines of Kurds, Sunnis and Shi'as.[9]

- The non-compatibility of the liberal mechanism applied in post-conflict non-liberal Iraqi society, which caused disharmony and discord.

The first set of factors would cover a wide range of countries. Many a powerful state was against the US-led invasion of Iraq to begin with. One instance was former president of France, Jacque Chirac, who had openly stated his opposition to military action against Iraq and had threatened to veto any resolution in the UN Security Council that sought to authorise such action. That led to open and hostile postures between Washington and Paris that involved other countries also. The political resentment found its way into the language of leaders rebuffing one another, newspaper headlines and even French fries being renamed freedom fries in the United States.[10] The question remains if the hostility of these countries to the invasion and the occupation of Iraq, emanating from perceived national interests, had diminished after the war started.[11]

Regional countries were also unsure about US designs on Iraq. Would the ousting of Saddam not have consequences for their own countries? Iran and Kuwait, both subjects of the Iraqi dictator's aggression in the past, must have felt relieved at the prospect of removing Saddam from power. However, in the case of Iran, policy-makers in Tehran must have wondered if they were not next on the list to come under military attack from Washington. It was perhaps this concern that prompted Tehran to temporarily halt its nuclear activities in 2003 in fear of crippling military reprisals from the United States.[12] Saudi Arabia and other regional states, including the littoral countries of the Persian Gulf, also had mixed feelings about the US-led invasion of Iraq. If democracy was to replace the totalitarian regime in Iraq, would that not act as a catalyst for democratic change in their own countries?[13] These and other concerns produced a murky picture, wherein it was difficult to locate the exact perceived interests of each state in regard to the military defeat of Saddam's regime. Accordingly, it may be argued that a host of countries may have not been so eager for a successful outcome of the US-led invasion of Iraq.

The second scenario portrays the much loved, and subscribed to, conspiracy theory in the Middle East. In this instance, the conspiracy narrates the designs of the big powers to divide up Iraq along sectarian lines. The grounds for such a policy are twofold. First, experience has shown that dealing with smaller states is much easier than dealing with bigger ones. Larger countries are by definition more powerful, particularly if they possess oil or other such important sources of energy. Accordingly three different smaller states within Iraq, carved up along sectarian lines, would be less likely to threaten their neighbours or be a menace to international peace and security than one central large Iraqi state. Secondly, as Iraq is basically the amalgamation of three different millet systems of the dissolved Ottoman Empire, put together by Britain, there may be little that binds the three different ethnic groups within the country to form a nation. The gap between them is so large that it works against the formation of a cohesive community. There may in fact, in certain respects, be antipathy and deep-rooted hostility between them.[14] Long-term peace within the country may accordingly be only guaranteed by separating these sects in order to facilitate self-determination for each. It may be noted that these sectarian groups never lived together as one country under a democracy. It was always the use of force that coerced them to live together in peace.

There are, on the other hand, grounds that can negate conspiracy theorists on designs to break-up Iraq along sectarian lines. First, any serious prospect of statehood to the Kurds, let alone the act itself, could potentially trigger unrest and demands for secession among the Kurdish population in neighbouring countries, most probably Turkey. There is little doubt, in such a case, of the military response of Turkey and possibly Iran and Syria. The region would then be embroiled in a long-term conflict that could threaten regional stability. Therefore the outcome of the break-up of Iraq could in fact have adverse consequences for peace and security. Secondly, the establishment of an independent Shi'a state in the south could place it under the strong influence of Shi'a Iran, rendering it little more than a satellite state, a prospect hardly to be cherished by Washington either.

The third answer, which deals with the non-compatibility of Iraqi society as a whole with the principles of Western-style democracy, is the focus of this section. Without intending either to endorse or to dismiss the previous two sets of factors, the attention here is on this last option. At the outset we have to be clear what is meant by liberalism and liberal peace. There are no canonical definitions of the term liberalism,[15] but for the purpose of this work four correlates of this precept will be taken into consideration. They are: (a) nationalism; (b) rationalism; (c) secularism; and (d) individualism.

To begin with the first correlate, one must define the term 'nation'. Is there an Iraqi nation and what can one make of Iraqi nationalism? Despite various sets of commonalities introduced as criteria for nationhood, such as history, religion, language, customs, race, and so forth, it may be safe to assume that there is no universally agreeable set of conditions that would enable a single definition of this term. In Europe, for instance, race plays a more prominent part in nationhood compared to the United States. Shari'ati's ideological claim that common pains, rather than anything else, give rise to a nation is yet another variation on this precept.[16] Thus the question turns into 'What set of criteria should we adopt if we are to talk of an Iraqi nation?' Close examination reveals that the commonalities between various sects of the Iraqi people may be less than one may expect. The three components of the Iraqi population, the Shi'as, the Sunnis and the Kurds, were all separate under the Ottoman Empire and amalgamated into one country by the United Kingdom in the wake of the dissolution of the Ottoman Empire and the establishment of the mandate system authorised by the League of Nations. It was accordingly a country formed out of political convenience rather than the imposing realities of history and tradition.[17] That is why Al-Wardi talks of 'the disjointed nature of Iraqi society held together by geographical imperatives of coexistence in the same space rather than a common sense of shared history and purpose'.[18] He continues: 'The people of Iraq are divided among themselves and their sectarian, ethnic and tribal struggles exceed those of any other Arab people'.[19]

One of the striking differences between the three different groups in Iraq is that despite the main common religion of Islam and the shared language of Arabic, there are very few, if any, common heroes that would transcend sectarian divides. The national hero of one sect may in fact be seen in an adversarial terms by other sects. For example, Mostafa Barzani, a national hero in the eyes of the Kurds of Iraq, is looked down on by Sunni-populated central Iraq. Equally, Saddam Hussein, a hero for some Iraqi Sunnis, was a demonic figure for the majority of Iraqis comprised of almost all Shi'as and Kurds. The lack of bond among the various sects in Iraq had perhaps hampered the establishment of a truly national Iraqi institution with the possible exception of the Iraqi army, which ironically was disbanded by the United States after the fall of Saddam.

Therefore, notwithstanding the relative unity of Iraqis during its eight-year war with Iran, Iraqi nationalism may not be as compelling a precept as experienced in some more cohesive communities. This has also been evident since 2003, when the dictates of a heavily centralised military command structure forcing compliance and suppressing divisions was replaced with a new-found freedom by the indigenous people to openly locate communal gaps and express differences. These divisions have contributed to the violence that has gripped the country to varying degrees ever since. In short, there may be strong intra-communal bonds among the various Iraqi sects working against any inter-communal cohesion that could be the source of Iraqi nationalism.

The second correlate points to the rational nature of the liberal discourse in the West. In very general terms, rationalism could in the context of this work be interpreted as the prevalence of rationally defined ways and means, goals and interests over other dicta such as ideology, that is, ideology would be subjected to rationality and not vice versa. In its extreme version, subscribed to by Hobbes and hard-core realists, it is rationality that makes up (and not discovers) morality as a means to fulfil desires and avoid aversions.[20] Authenticity, therefore, in this discourse rests with desires and aversions. Morality takes the back seat and when opportunity presents itself for political action to further interests at a cost to morality, there is little that can be expected in terms of moral observance. The main political actor in International Relations, the sovereign state, follows the same path and its rational character, an accepted norm in international life, is the driving force in pursuit of perceived national interests even at the cost to the perceived interests of other political communities. In liberalism in the West, therefore, interests reign supreme in politics, which may explain why the newly revolutionary liberal government in France in the late eighteenth century commissioned one of its top generals to invade and occupy a country as far as Egypt with plans to go further towards India. How were such military actions consistent with the liberal nature of France? The answer lies in the rational character of Western liberal discourse, which renders Western liberalism indifferent and even adversarial to moral principles in its foreign relations if they appear in conflict with their perceived interests.

Secularism, the third correlate of the liberal discourse as noted above, refers to the separation of religious establishment from the institutions of the state and not, as commonly and mistakenly feared by some religious zealots in the Muslim World, the separation of religion from politics. In the secular West, religious leaders are revered by the society and can express their political views but in the main do not enter politics.[21] Secularism, therefore, is not an anti-religious principle that aims to stifle the faith of the people out of existence, but rather a maxim that opens up space for rationality, another principle of the liberal discourse, to guide the temporal business of the society. In today's international relations, the affairs of the state, at least in the liberal West, are dictated by rationality that since the time of the French Revolution, if not before, has managed to legitimise a formal separation of political machinery of the community from organised religion. The secular tradition in the West, therefore, sanctions the utilisation of rationality.

In a deeper insight, the secular and rational traits of liberalism are the cornerstones of some of the most basic human rights. It is a secular and rational appreciation of equal personhood of all human beings that gives rise to the right of life and liberty.[22] Otherwise, such rights can be subsumed by religious beliefs projected and codified in the rules of jurisprudence. To be rational, thus, one has to be secular first, and in order to attain secularism, there must inevitably be a separation of political establishment from religious hierarchies.

The last correlate of liberalism to be discussed here is individualism. This refers to the very basic rights of the individual as distinct and opposed to those of the state. It denotes the good of the individual in terms of its moral weight against the good of the state or the nation.[23] John Locke's views, much heeded by the founding fathers of the American Constitution, are noteworthy in this regard. As narrated by McClelland:

> As a mechanism, the state [in Locke's view], like any other mechanism, is there for a purpose, and the position of men in the State of Nature can easily tell us what that purpose is. Men in the State of Nature expect to enjoy the exercise of their Natural Rights, and men come into Civil Society to enjoy them more securely.

It is part of God's purpose for men that they should enjoy these rights, and so no Natural Right can be permanently alienated. Government exists to protect Natural Rights and should confine itself to that function. It follows that any government which threatens the Natural Rights to life, liberty and estate (Locke's word for property) is a government in the process of forfeiting its title to govern.[24]

In his elaboration on liberalism, Michael Doyle outlines three sets of rights for individuals that would form 'the foundation of an ideal version of Liberalism.'[25] They are 'positive freedoms', 'negative freedoms' and the right for democratic participation and representation. The first set refers to such social rights as equality of opportunity in education and economic rights such as health care and employment, which are 'necessary for effective self-expression and participation'. 'Negative freedoms' refer to freedom from arbitrary authority, and include free press and free speech,[26] equality before the law, right to property, freedom of conscience and the like. The last set of rights, according to Doyle, is necessary to guarantee the other two. He writes: 'To ensure that morally autonomous individuals remain free in those areas of social action where public authority is needed, public legislation has to express the will of the citizens making laws for their own community.'[27]

In the individualist outlook of the liberal discourse in the West, there is priority of 'rights' over 'duties', where no degree of authority by religious authorities or the state can trample upon or withdraw such rights from the individual. They would include all basic human rights as enshrined in the Universal Declaration of Human Rights. This can be observed even in Hobbes' *Leviathan*, which was an attempt to guarantee the most possible satisfaction of desires; in that sense Hobbes was a radical individualist and an extreme modernist, where individuals are rational egoists at least in that they rationally calculate the satisfaction of their passions and desires. All individuals' social responsibility is codified in the law of the land, beyond which he/she bears no duty towards the community.

Therefore these four traits of nationalism, rationalism, secularism and individualism stand as strong pillars upon which Western liberal discourse is founded. To introduce liberal democracy may accordingly require the presence of these important precepts beforehand.

The question now is to what extent did Iraqi socio-political tradition embody these characteristics for Western-style democracy to have a reasonable chance of success there? To answer that question we shall outline two of the most prominent aspects of the Iraqi polity and assess their in/compatibility with the pillars of Western liberalism.

The first trait is tribalism, where people are socially grouped into different communities, called tribes, with certain rules and norms governing their conduct. The tribal leader, called sheikh, has traditionally been the most powerful and the most prestigious man in his tribe.[28] In tribal Arabia, as in many tribes in Iraq, loyalty to the tribe was part of the Arab code of virtue called *murawwah*.[29] The significance of tribal loyalty can be noted in Saddam preferring, political intrigue permitting, to have his closest aides from his home clan of Tikrit.[30] In the 1990s, Saddam Hussein, a dictator renowned for concentration of power in his own hands (but eager to secure tribal support), gave up two of the important monopolies of the state, adjudication and control of means of violence, to tribal leaders, thus reflecting the importance of tribalism in Iraq and rewarding the tradition in the process. This led in some instances to townsmen, removed from the countryside for generations, seeking to rediscover old, or even forge new, tribal identities.[31] One scholar notes:

> On a more general level across Iraq, these tactics reflected the favour shown by Saddam Husain to the hierarchies of tribal sheikhs, inducing them to cooperate with the regime and to 'deliver' the loyalty or at least the acquiescence of their fellow tribesmen to the head of state. Officially, this led to edicts in the 1990s which recognised the authority of tribal sheikhs to settle disputes and to regulate affairs amongst their tribesmen and with other tribes, bringing back a form of separate jurisdiction for the 'tribal areas' (situated in many cases within the towns of Iraq) that recalled the days of the monarchy. Unofficially, Saddam Husain favoured the most co-operative of the tribal sheikhs, granting them land rights, promoting their tribesmen and allowing them to arm their followers.[32]

The traditional code of *murawwah*, referred to above, was somewhat represented in the tribal system in Iraq. 'Bravery in battle, patience in misfortune, persistence in revenge (the only justice possible at a time when no government existed – in pre-Islamic Arabia), protection of the weak, defiance towards the strong, hospitality to the visitor (even a total stranger), generosity to the poor, loyalty to the tribe, and fidelity in keeping promises' formed the core of *murawwah*.[33] Traditionally the tribal system in Iraq also valued certain similar norms: possession of land by force, authority by instilling fear, which, paradoxically, brought respect, honour, loyalty and lineage.[34] Most, if not all, of those precepts are unmodern or even anti-modern. State, itself, as a modern formation of community, was to the tribal man a usurper and exploiter and as the defining feature of advancing civilisation stood in contrast to tribal solidarity as an organising principle.[35] This conflict was most evident when tribal claims to land were disregarded unless supported by title deeds issued by state authorities. There was thus a battle between modernity and tribalism without a clear winner. Iraq was an imperfectly modernised country, where, according to Ali Al-Wardi, the pervasive dichotomy between the city with urban civilised values and the steppes representing the prevalence of nomadic tribal norms was evident.[36] The same author believes that under circumstances of invasion, Iraq would shed its civilised veneer and resort to tribal nomadic values.[37] All this makes the tribal system a shadow state in Iraq.

Perhaps the instance of *bey'a* and its analogy with modern voting systems would serve to exemplify the conflict between tribal traditions and modernity. The concept of *bey'a* refers to the consent of all tribal members with their leader, usually through a handshake, which would indicate allegiance to the person of the leader and not his/her ideas. Therefore in *bey'a* people identify with personalities rather than with policies. That was the main reason for the wars known as *ridda* that took place after the death of Muhammad between his successor Abubakr and some tribes who saw no grounds for continuing their fidelity to Islam. For many of them, it was the person of Muhammad, whose leadership they had consented to through *bey'a*, that gave meaning and substance to their loyalty, and not a system of ideas and beliefs called Islam. The contrast with the modern practice of voting is twofold. First, there is usually, but not always, the personal contact (the handshake) in *bey'a* that consummates the consent of the ruled; in Western-style democracy personal contact is unnecessary, impractical and insignificant. Second, and more importantly, comes the identification with personalities and not policies. In *bey'a* a change in policies of the leader would not necessarily constitute grounds for a breach of loyalty by the members of the community, whereas change of leadership, however identical their policies with previous leaders, would. In liberal democracy it is almost the opposite. As long as policies remain the same the support of followers can usually be counted on even if leaders change; accordingly leaders who change course of policies are likely to lose their following too. This difference in social behaviour, identification with personalities or policies, is an instance of the cultural gap that may separate Western liberal society from communities with other traditions.

The tribal nature of Iraqi society was perhaps one factor contributing to the military rule that had gripped the country up to 2003. In the absence of what one could in modern terms label as a nation, dictatorship was perceivably an easier (but, as ever, despicable) method of governance. This was perhaps the lesson to be drawn by some from the uprising of the Iraqis against Britain in 1920; however, that 'could not withstand the withering contempt from the messianic advocates of full-blown democracy as a precondition for the broader changes to be effected in Iraq and the rest of the Middle East.'[38] In 2003, before the invasion began, Iraqi society was divisive, vengeful, had deeply felt grievances and bottled-up ethnic and sectarian passions.[39]

The second important trait of Iraqi society, in this regard, is religiosity. The latter refers to ideologised and/or ritualised religion, where almost all aspects of life come under the influence of religion. This is strongest among the Shi'as in the south of the country and weakest (almost nonexistent in some cases) among the Kurds of Iraq living in the north. The Shi'as in the south are also believed to be less tribal than in some other parts of the country, like the northwest.[40] Even though Iran is the only country in the world that espouses Shi'a Islam as the state religion, it is Iraq that hosts the oldest and most prestigious seminary (*hawza*) in Shi'ism in Najaf (one thousand years old). Moreover, Iraq is home to the shrine of many Shi'a saints, including Imam Hossein, the anniversary of whose martyrdom in Karbala, Iraq, in AD 680, marks the largest annual religious occasion in Shi'ism. This religiosity is, however, not immune to the sectarian divide in the country either. On the anniversary of *A'shoura*, the martyrdom of Imam Hossein, there have in the past few years been attacks by Sunni fundamentalists against those participating in the religious festivals. Sunni radicals have been exhorted to kill 'satanic *Ayatollahs*' (referring to Shi'a religious leaders).[41] Religiosity, therefore, appears to be an exacerbating factor in sectarian divisions in Iraq.

In order to illustrate the power of the institution of Shi'ism, the denomination of the majority in Iraq, the occasion of the tobacco boycott would serve well. In 1890, the feeble Qajar dynasty in Iran granted all rights for the production, sale and export of tobacco, for 50 years, to Major G. F. Talbot of Great Britain. In protest, the leading Shi'a cleric at the time, the Chancellor of the Najaf seminary in Iraq, Mirza Hassan Shirazi,[42] issued a religious fatwa declaring the use of tobacco *haram* (forbidden). Reportedly even the then queen of Persia refused to smoke tobacco after the fatwa, admonishing her husband, the king, with the statement that 'the same man who had wed them (legitimized their relationship) had now delegitimized smoking tobacco'. Under huge public pressure and the prospect of the near collapse of the industry the king withdrew the concession in 1892.[43] Thus for the first time the institution of religion in Shi'ism successfully competed with the state and forced its retreat. 'The State, supposed to have no equal internally and no superior externally, found, to its dismay, that the Shi'a institution was more than its equal in the country.'[44]

The political impact of Shi'ism can perhaps be traced back to 1501, the year of the establishment of the Safavid Empire in Iran when the sect became the official religion of the state. Ever since, with some exceptions, the role of religion in the state and the influence of *ulema* (clerics) have been evident. This has been achieved partly through the ritualisation of religion:

> Perhaps the greatest asset for the institution of Shi'ism has been its ability to ritualize most, if not all, aspects of faith thus allowing a greater impact upon and deeper influence on its followers. Islamic lunar calendar abounds in religious festivals for Shi'as where the faithful are regularly reminded and called to perform rituals associated with them. The elaborate network of mosques...often provides the focal point for the gathering of the zealots during these festivals, where the clergy can communicate socio-political messages normally mediated through a sentimental and powerful narration of Shi'a grievances in the earlier part of Islamic history (*rozeh*).[45]

In Iraq, specifically, the chancellor of the Najaf seminary has traditionally been the highest source of emulation and the most revered cleric in Shi'ism throughout the world. Today, in 2011, this belongs to Grand Ayatollah Sistani, an Iranian ethnically, who has demon-strated his influence time and again in developments in Iraq.[46] Moqtada Sadr, the young seminarian student, though politically and financially supported by others, stands poor in comparison. It ought to be noted that Ayatollah Sistani does not subscribe to political Islam even though Shi'a fundamentalists have continually tried to promote radicalism among the Shi'as of Iraq.[47]

Taking on board the influence of religion in Iraq, one is hard-pressed to find any foundational basis upon which secularism, a prerequisite to other traits of a liberal discourse, could stand. Together with tribalism, religiosity is a barrier to the foundational pillars of Western liberalism: nationalism, rationalism, secularism and individualism. Accordingly, attempting to introduce a Western-style democracy into Iraq with little or no regard to the traditions of the country meant at best wasting resources on a project that was near impossible and at worst risking cultural disharmony with devastating consequences.

Does the above mean that the people of Iraq are not ready for freedom? Do the arguments advanced in these pages indicate that Iraqis are not mature enough to freely elect their own government and run their own country? What can we learn from the points noted and what do they tell us about Western liberal discourse in communities emancipated from dictatorships?

In response to these questions the most important observation is that freedom as one of the most fundamental traits of humanity, theo-logically attested to in Islam as narrated in the story of the Creation of Adam and Eve, is the inalienable right of all human beings. No degree of philosophising and no amount of trying to interject arguments on cultural relativism can detract from the important and pivotal role that freedom does and ought to play in the life of humankind. Stifling freedom in the name of religion, the state, or anything else must be condemned unequivocally and without qualification wherever, when-ever and however it occurs. Accordingly nothing in this work should be interpreted as a justification for dictatorship and totalitarianism.

Having said the above, what ought to be noted in this regard is the not openly claimed monopoly of liberal discourse on peace in global politics and International Relations.[48] Richmond observes:

> Interpreted through an understanding of peace, since the end of the Cold War, these debates have effectively concurred that

the liberal peace, as defined by democratization, the rule of law, human rights, development, in a globalised economic setting, guided by liberal hegemons, satisfies the core concerns of these theoretical debates [in International Relations].[49]

Conclusively, what has to be conceded is twofold: first is full public political participation and a representative and accountable government in liberated post-conflict communities; second, and equally important, however, is respect for local traditions and culture that are the means through which the new-found freedom has to be articulated and institutionalised. That means that Western-style democracy representing people with specific history and culture and suited to particular ways of expression in the West would not necessarily work the same way in all settings for all peoples. No doubt the substance of the liberal discourse, the quest for freedom, is a common value to all humanity regardless of variations in culture, history and religion. But the manner in which freedom is practiced in communities can vary in accordance and with respect to local settings. Just as blood, which is a necessary component of physical life for all, varies in type between people and those receiving blood must ensure it is compatible with their own, freedom can have different styles of expression. Essential to intellectual and spiritual survival, expression of freedom varies in type and this difference ought to be respected and not taken to mean that freedom itself is less desired or less appreciated by any group or community.

Accordingly, due regard for political philosophy in the case of Iraq could have possibly contributed to a reduced level of violence in that country in the post-2003 era.

5.2   Iran: cold peace versus hot war, conflict in transition

An ongoing challenge after 33 years of revolution, the Islamic Republic of Iran continues to grab international headlines in gestures of defiance regarding, among other things, its continued enrichment of uranium and its alleged intention to develop weapons of mass destruction. With a long and rich history that predates Islam, over 70 million people, some of the largest oil and gas reserves in the world, and a geo-strategic position that overlooks the Persian Gulf and the Strait of Hormuz (through which the majority of oil from the Middle

East flows) Iran's value in international politics is obvious. Its foreign policy, however, driven by Islamist principles since the revolution of 1979, chiefly defined in anti-American and anti-Israeli stands, has of late troubled more than just Washington and Tel Aviv. Now European powers as well as Russia appear concerned about Tehran's unremitting pursuit of nuclear enrichment and its possible military implications. The United States may still be outside the range of Iran's ballistic capabilities but Russia and Europe, not to mention Israel, are certainly not. A nuclear Iran, thus, in case of a conflict, may be less of a direct threat to the United States than to Europe and Russia.

Brief historical background

A brief background delineating major landmarks in the contemporary history of Iran may be a useful tool in better understanding the current developments surrounding the international efforts to foil Iranian attempts at nuclearisation. An instance of such efforts is the infiltration by the computer virus, Stuxnet, into the Iranian nuclear network, which appears to have substantially slowed down, if not damaged, uranium enrichment in Iran.[50]

Four major events have shaped, or hugely influenced, political developments in Iran for the past hundred years or so. First among these was the Constitutional Revolution of 1906–1909, where Iranians, mainly *bazaris* (traditional traders), together with a group of *ulema* (clerical leaders) and the middle classes, forced the establishment of parliament on the tyrannical Qajar regime. For the dictatorial yet feeble Qajar king at the time ruling Persia, Mohammad Ali Shah, this was an unpleasant outcome and he tried to force its closure by dissolving it and shelling the parliament building one year after its opening. The clergy was also divided on this. Some were for and some were against parliament. Ayatollah Mohammad Hossein Na'eeni for instance was a renowned supporter of the move for greater public participation whereas Sheikh Fazlollah Noori was a famous cleric against change.[51] The latter was later hanged upon the victory of the Constitutional Revolution.

Though Iran has never been a colony, during the ineffectual tenure of the Qajar dynasty (1797–1925)[52] both Britain and Russia managed to influence organs of the state at many levels. This influence at times found iniquitous dimensions. For instance, towards the end of the rule of the dynasty, British and Russian embassies in

Tehran were issuing letters of immunity from prosecution to their proxy Iranian nationals inside Iran. Such acts openly disregarded the sovereignty of the country and outraged nationalists, who were eager to put an end to such a humiliation. It was Reza Shah, the founder of the succeeding dynasty, who eventually outlawed letters of immunity from foreign embassies.[53]

Initially the United Kingdom appeared to support the freedom fighters in Iran but then seemingly changed its policy and moved closer to the position of the Qajar ruler.[54] Russia, the other influential power in the country, was against the opening of parliament from the beginning and stayed that course; in fact it was a Russian officer, part of the Cossack Brigade, who was in charge of the shelling of Parliament building in 1907 under orders from the Qajar king. Eventually the Qajar dynasty was dissolved by an Act of Parliament and the new dynasty of Pahlavi with Reza Shah as its first monarch was established in 1925. Reza Shah's 16-year- reign was an attempt to catapult Iran into the modern world; an attempt that received much resentment and resistance from the clerical establishment.[55]

The second important event was the occupation of Iran by the British and the Soviet forces during World War II. The reasons for this were twofold: first was to secure easy access to oil for Britain, whose navy was now heavily dependent on this source of energy, much more than in World War I. Secondly, Iran was the best route to supply essential supplies to the Soviets, who were fighting the Germans at the time. In the process Reza Shah, whose development of a national rail network throughout Iran had made transport of supplies to the Soviets all the easier, was forced to abdicate in favour of his young son, Mohammad Reza. After the war Britain left Iranian territory but the Soviets refused to follow suit, and instead set up their puppet authority in the region under their occupation. It was the stewardship of the Iranian Prime Minister at the time, Mohammad Ghavam, supported by a stern warning from US President Harry Truman to Joseph Stalin that eventually made the Soviet troops leave Iran.

The overt support of the US President in forcing a Soviet withdrawal from Iran must have been viewed favourably by Iranian nationalists. For the first time in a long time a foreign power was actually helping to maintain Iranian territorial integrity. Having been through the humiliating Treaties of *Gholestan* and *Torkamanchai* in the early nineteenth century, whereby Russia had taken over much Iranian territory, and after the Anglo-Russian conspiracy to divide Iran in the early twentieth century, which was later foiled,[56] it must have been a welcome and surprising experience for Iranians to witness the intervention of a foreign power in the service of the territorial integrity of their country. The United States therefore would have had good grounds to foster good relations with the government and the new king.

That goodwill, however, did not last very long, which brings us into the third major development. The populist Prime Minister, Mohammad Mossadeq, nationalised the Iranian oil industry, hitherto under the control of Britain. He also openly challenged the power of the monarchy, taking control of all organs of government, an act well within his constitutional rights. His popular nationalisation of the Iranian oil industry had seemingly provided him with unconditional support, he believed, to formulate and execute domestic and foreign policy with impunity. That would explain his dissolution of the second Chamber of Parliament in the early 1950s (an unconstitutional act) because of the latter's disapproval of his treatment of the Iranian royalty. Along the same lines he asked deputies from his party, the National Front, to boycott parliament so as to prevent the quorum from being achieved for the conduct of parliamentary business.[57] One of the deputies later said:

> Statecraft has degenerated into street politics. It appears that this country has nothing better to do than hold street meetings. We now have meetings here, there, and everywhere – meetings for this, that, and every occasion; meetings for university students, high school students, seven-year-olds, and even six-year-olds. I am sick and tired of these street meetings.... Is our prime minister a statesman or a mob leader? What type of prime minister says 'I will speak to the people' every time he is faced with political problems? I always considered this man to be unsuitable for high office. But I never imagined, even in my worst nightmares, that an old man of seventy would turn into a rabble rouser. A man who surrounds Majlis with mobs is nothing less than a public menace.[58]

For Britain, the main issue was who would control the production, distribution, and the sale of oil. Iran had the world's largest refinery, was the second largest exporter of crude petroleum, and had the third largest oil reserves, all under the control of the Anglo-Iranian Oil Company (AIOC). The company provided the British treasury with £24 million in taxes and £92 million in foreign exchange.[59] Mosaddeq's move to nationalise Iranian oil not only gave control to Iran but it could also inspire other countries like Indonesia, Venezuela and Iraq to follow suit, which would radically shift control over the main energy market from Western oil companies to oil-producing countries.

The United States was initially unwilling to move against Mossadeq. But eventually it was convinced and a military coup, engineered by MI6 and the CIA, managed to topple the prime minister, and the monarch, who had gone to Italy at the time returned to Iran. In the words of the US ambassador at the time, 'only a *coup d'état* could save the situation.'[60] The defeat of Mossadeq and the triumphant return of the Shah marked a new era of friendship and alliance between Tehran and Washington, which broadened and deepened at many levels up to the Islamic Revolution of 1979. Some Iranian nationalists, however, felt betrayed by the US support for the coup and even viewed Washington as the main culprit.

Perhaps the most complex of all the political developments surrounding Iran was the religious-led uprising against the Shah of Iran, starting in 1978 with an article in a daily newspaper and culminating in February 1979 with the return from exile of Ayatollah Khomeini, by then a staunch advocate of abolishing the Iranian monarchy.[61] The clerical leader had gone into exile in Najaf, the city that houses the most prestigious school of Shi'ism in the world, after he had openly preached against the Shah in 1963. The multifaceted Iranian Revolution had been a blend of internal and external forces opposed to the kind and speed of change that Pahlavi II was eager to enforce. That process appeared to challenge much traditional, local and international sources of power, threatening to dislocate coordinates of social and regional status quo. There was in consequence a convergence of outside and inside forces to remove the source of that threat. The amalgamation of such divergent factors provided an umbrella of opposition forces, wherein all groups across the political spectrum were led to unite behind the religious leadership of Ayatollah Khomeini, who demanded the unequivocal ousting of the Shah. In effect, unlike the Tobacco Movement almost a century ago, religious establishment in Iran did not only compete with the state but actually campaigned, successfully as it turned out, to become the state. It was the culmination of political Islam that manifested at the time the increasing influence and control of the Shi'a hierarchy on Iranians.

The Shah's expeditious and ambitious modernising programme was not well taken by local institutions, who drew their identity and power from centuries-old traditions. The clerical establishment was the prime instance of such resentment, and resisted at every level its increasing distance with the society promoted by the state that seemed eager to force its own modernisation agenda. Internationally, the Shah's publicly announced plans at times implemented (like the price rise in oil in 1974) and to discontinue oil agreements with Western oil companies, did not win him any friends either.[62] His poor state of health, unbeknown to the Iranians and to the wider world at the time, hastened his programme for industrialisation, in turn exasperating further local and external opposition.

The attitude of outside powers to the four above-mentioned developments were different. The United Kingdom appeared to waver on the Constitutional Revolution of 1906–1909, supporting it initially but later changing sides. The Russians were against it from the outset and offered shelter to the beleaguered Qajar ruler, who abdicated in favour of his son. The forced withdrawal of Soviet forces from Iranian territory in the aftermath of World War II was greatly supported by the United States, without whose assistance the outcome could have conceivably been different. The United Kingdom also advocated the withdrawal of the USSR from Iran but fiercely opposed and undermined the nationalisation of the Iranian oil industry and subsequently enforced a boycott of Iranian oil. The United States also joined forces with Britain in deposing Mosaddeq, who, if nothing else, was the nominal architect of the nationalisation. And, lastly, on the Iranian Revolution of 1979, evidence now seems to suggest that the support for the Shah of Iran among the great powers was probably not as forthcoming as had been assumed by some.[63] What is certain, however, is that in all four developments there were overt and covert actions by outside interests to steer developments in a direction that suited their own perceived interests.

As for the attitude of the Iranians themselves, the first three developments have a striking difference from the fourth. While it appears that in the Constitutional Revolution, the forced withdrawal of the Russian troops from Iran and the nationalisation of the Iranian oil industry they were all aware of their specific aims and objectives, in the Islamic Revolution they appeared more keen on what they wished to reject without any certainty as to what their desired alternative/s were.

Internal challenges

The victory of the Islamic Revolution in Iran produced two inevitable challenges to the newly established religious authorities: first was the question of modernity in its political form with concepts such as liberty and sovereignty. The second challenge emanated from the claims of *shari'a* to be able to govern the temporal affairs of the people under all circumstances at all times.

On the first challenge, the liberties associated with modernity were more often than not anathema to the dictates of *shari'a*. While the former promoted freedom at individual, social and political levels permeating all aspects of intellectual, religious, and temporal life, *shari'a* had a very specific code of conduct that limited the manoeuverability of its followers. Therefore citizenship and all rights associated with it were subject to being a Shi'a Muslim first, an overarching status, which was decided for the individual and imposed from above with no control by him/her over its comprehensive and detailed doctrine and rituals, its dos and don'ts and the voluminous body of rules on social and spiritual life. At the core stood the question of sovereignty and its source. Does sovereignty emanate from God or from people? If from the former, then all that determines and shapes the social and political environment of people would have to appear to be in line with the parameters of the Divine defined and interpreted by official religious representatives institutionalised in an organised hierarchy of religious establishment. If, however, sovereignty emanates from people then popular will and the collective decision of citizens will sketch the social and political life of the community. Axiomatically then *shari'a* would be required to work within the context of the laws passed and executed by elected representatives of the people. The Islamic Republic in Iran, took on the formidable, and perhaps impossible, challenge of attempting to amalgamate *shari'a* with democracy and liberal practices. By elevating *shari'a* to the unassailable position it has assumed today in the country (in almost all aspects of social and political life), immune from popular likes and dislikes, the religious authorities (the state) have unwillingly but inevitably brought about a confrontation between the Divine and the people, a confrontation that people have reluctantly been forced to enter.

The second challenge, emanating from the first, addresses the ahistorical and absolute nature of *shari'a*. Both those qualities appear to defy the historicity and the relativity of humanity that have been the defining features of our development. Some of the rules of *shari'a*, formulated and compiled over a thousand years ago (long after the death of the Prophet), were in line with the requirements of life there and then, possibly to suit the expediencies of the caliphate.[64] However, the contemporary period has seen very poor examples of the rule of *shari'a* when applied in the context of a sovereign state. Sudan and Taliban Afghanistan are striking examples of the failure of political Islam.

Therefore the rational aspect of modern life, which adjusts modalities of the socio-political environment according to the needs of the time, cannot be sanctioned if *shari'a* is to be the overriding factor. The 'interest' on capital is one such instance, where religious rules forbid the institution of 'interest', whereas the whole banking system in today's world depends on it (paradoxically, however, Iran nowadays has one of the highest rates of interest of any country in the world – between 15 and 20 per cent). The Islamic Republic has thus clearly failed to resolve this conflict; while paying lip service to *shari'a* it has in reality been promoting a banking system heavily dependent on interest rates. The polarisation of the world into the arrogant (*mostakberin*) and the meek (*mostaz'afin*), as outlined by Ayatollah Khomeini, closing space for any middle ground, is another example of the incompatibility of radical religious outlook with modern political life. There are groups of people and countries who may belong to neither of those categories. Middle powers such as Canada and Sweden would have no place in this religious typology. This categorisation also flies in the face of Islamic injunctions exhorting followers to stay the middle course. One Quranic verse states, *We ordained you to be a people of moderation* ...[65] In their perceived polarised international environment, the Islamic Republic of Iran may appear to have shifted away from that course.

In order to meet these challenges a *reform movement* was formed inside the Islamic Republic that appeared to represent a less radical image of the religious rule in Iran. Personified in the figure of Mohammad Khatami, elected as president in 1998 and viewed then as the non-establishment figure, this movement advocated what was to be known as *religious democracy*. To date there is little written or spoken that can meaningfully present a convincing argument in favour of this new and vague concept. Religious democracy avoids debate on the question of the source of sovereignty (as referred to above) and evades important queries on its views on the relationship between popular will and religious rulings as practised in Iran. If popular will is the source of sovereignty and power then why should the Guardian Council assess the compatibility of laws passed by people's representatives in *majles* (parliament) with *shari'a*? And if it is the rule of religious laws (theocracy) can we call it democratic? The reform movement in Iran has failed to advance any substantive doctrine that would be able to justify the curious and seemingly self-contradictory concept of *religious democracy*.

In practice, too, the *reform movement*, though starting with promising beginnings, disastrously failed to move closer to any of its overused rhetorical goals. The much-publicised talks on civil society, for example, remained an empty slogan almost during the eight years that the reformist president was in power. Throughout most of that period, the legislature was also filled with reformist deputies, yet the net outcome was little more than verbal eloquence and inconsequential speeches.[66] In the international arena also this rhetoric was reflected in the Dialogue Among Civilisations initiated by Khatami and unanimously endorsed by the United Nations General Assembly in 2001. But again the rhetoric failed to be followed by any substantive doctrine, which hindered the project.

Political considerations, usually limited to periodic observations and passing expediencies, cannot usually be the foundation of philosophical and historical projects that require greater vision and a more holistic outlook. Nor can such an immensely significant task be carried out only rhetorically and only as a response to its adversary, 'the clash of civilisations'. There is a clear need for contextual analysis and intellectual engagement of the highest degree, usually past the patience of politicians.[67]

Reformist politicians failed to support the student protest of the late 1990s. In fact President Khatami labelled them 'seditious elements', which was more like an anticlimax to frustrated energies that had been near eruption point at the time.[68] The disappointed public, having experienced two terms of a reformist president and several years of a reformist parliament, were thus disillusioned with any notion of reform in the country. In short, the *reform movement* has appeared unable to win public support as a credible alternative in Iranian politics on two grounds: first, they appear to share much with those they are currently opposing. All leaders of this group have held the highest positions in the Islamic Republic: Mir-Hossein Mousavi was first the foreign minister and then the prime minister for eight years in the early formative years of the Revolution (1981–1989); Mehdi Karoubi has held numerous high-ranking posts including chairmanship of the Martyr Foundation for many years, head of Iranian pilgrims to Mecca, and the illustrious position of speaker of parliament for a total of seven years (1989–1992 and 2000–2004); Mohammad Khatami was a member of parliament and later a minister (1982–1986), followed by the headship of the Iranian National Library (1992–1997) and culminating later in his presidency for eight years (1997–2005). If the reformists had anything new to offer Iranian political life then some tangible results would have ensued in their years of having assumed high office.

The second reason why the *reform movement* has been rather unsuccessful in appealing to the general public, particularly the younger generation, is its inability to offer a clear agenda for reform. It has hitherto failed to publish a manifesto that would clearly outline policies or a programme of action that would address the grievances of all those whose aspirations for a better life remain unfulfilled. In the post-2009 election disturbances, Mr. Mousavi stated his goal to be a return to the golden era of Imam Khomeini.[69] That could hardly be an alluring objective when, after all, most of Khomeini's era was spent in a war with Iraq, which, though imposed by Saddam, could have ended sooner than it did; a war that failed to achieve its frequently stated objective of removing Saddam from power, forcing Iran's revolutionary leader to accept peace, which to him was 'a bitter chalice'. Mr. Mousavi failed to elaborate exactly what particular aspects of policy or life he was referring to when he stated his wish to return to the early revolutionary era. Similarly, none of the other reformist candidates have spelled out a clear programme that would address the demands of the protestors.

Added to the above was the political ineptness of reformist leaders to capitalise on their massive electoral majority in the late 1990s. With over 20 million votes, Khatami could have steered Iranian politics in a different direction. He and his colleagues failed spectacularly in this respect. The failure was so evident and embarrassing that Khatami, towards the end of his tenure, stated his office was no more than a formality and he should thus be excused for his inability to bring about change. The same could be said of Mr. Mousavi and Mr. Karoubi, who failed to translate the presence of millions in the streets of Tehran and other cities in support of new and free elections in 2009, into political gains. Perhaps an explanation for the above could be the strong conviction of the reformist leaders in the very structure of the Islamic Republic and that no protest should in their view be allowed to threaten the very existence of the system, which they served in prominent capacities for years.

Therefore in the wake of a questionable recorder in the past, a very vague agenda for the future, together with political ineptness to translate public support into political gains, it is not surprising that the *reform movement* has failed to effect any meaningful change inside Iran. In all likelihood it will not succeed in the future either unless it becomes part of a greater network of opposition or it begins to re-evaluate its past critically and face the future with a clear and pertinent programme of action.

External challenges

As for challenges that have beleaguered the Iranian revolutionary government since 1979, the most striking one is the pursuit of ideologised religious goals through the modern machinery of statehood. Statecraft is best suited for the pursuit of national interest and is normally utilised to that end. The efforts of Iranian authorities to pursue ideological objectives through statehood is a challenge reminiscent of the former Soviet Union, seeking to serve communist interests through the same mechanism. In this regard three aspects of Iranian foreign policy can be outlined: sources, means and goals.

While in the West the source of policy, the legitimising factor, is the popular will, in Shi'a Iran the source is the Will of the Almighty as interpreted by the religious jurist (*vali e faqih*). Usually conventional diplomacy, which does not necessarily exclude violence, in the pursuit of national interests (assessed rationally) are the means and goals of foreign policy in the West. However, in the Islamic Republic of Iran, jurisprudence replaces rationality and the pursuit of national interests is superseded by the fulfilment of religious objectives.

> Therefore, it can be observed that in terms of source, means and goals of policy, there are differences of some magnitude between Shi'ism and the Western conventional framework. Whilst the latter adopts the will of the people, rationality and national interests for source, means and goals respectively, Shi'ism adheres to the Will of God, jurisprudence, and ideology; rationality plays an important role, but only at their service.[70]

Another challenge (rather self-inflicted) has been a persistent course of anti-Americanism that has appeared in conflict with rationally defined Iranian interests. It started with the capture of US diplomats in Tehran lasting 444 days (4 November 1979–20 January 1981) by militant students calling themselves Students Following the Line of Imam [Khomeini]. This may have been an act to pressure the American government to extradite the Shah of Iran, who was undergoing medical treatment in the United States at the time. Abbas Abdi, one of the hostage takers, has claimed that the whole operation was a spontaneous action by students with a belief that the affair would end in just a few days.[71] A more probable reason for the hostage-taking, however, could have been to prevent a US-backed coup, like the one in 1953, to restore the Shah. Such a contingency was pre-empted by the taking of US hostages, who could have lost their lives in that eventuality.

But if the anti-American action and slogans were all just a reaction by militant forces to the US-oriented pre-revolutionary government in Iran, why has it been encouraged to continue 33 years after the Revolution? Does this animosity serve the ideological interests of the religious establishment in Iran? Even a casual observation points in the opposite direction, where on several occasions US interests and those of religious Iran have coincided. One striking example is the Bosnian question when the United States was the only powerful country that from the beginning spoke against the Milosevic regime in support of Bosnian Muslims. It was the Western Europeans, notably France and

Britain, together with Russia, that opposed military action against the Serbian forces.[72] In the end the US-led bombardment of Serbia triggered a process whereby Milosevic was deposed and eventually tried for crimes against humanity. Other instances of convergence of US foreign policy with the religious Iranian government have been the US ousting of the Taliban in Afghanistan in 2001 and the overthrow of Saddam Hussein's regime in 2003. The former were fanatic Sunni fundamentalists, considering Shi'ism heresy and executing a number of Iranian officials in Afghanistan, while the latter had started a devastating war against Iran in 1980 that lasted for seven years, killing hundreds of thousands, maiming more and costing hundreds of billions of dollars.

Even today, the greatest number of Iranian diaspora, numbering between one and two million, live in the United States. There has not been an instance of social unrest by them during their period of stay in the land dubbed by the founder of the Islamic Republic as 'the great Satan'. It seems Iranians have been able to find sufficient space to maintain their traditional values while conforming with the legal requirements of living there. The United States does not have a history of manipulation and interference in Iranian political life prior to World War II. In fact, one of the non-Iranians, perhaps the only one, who fought and died on the side of the Constitutional Revolution in the early twentieth century, was an American named Howard Baskerville.[73] There seems, therefore, little that should divide the people of the two countries historically, and national sentiments do not appear to justify the prolonged animosity that has bedeviled the relations between Tehran and Washington.

The continued hostility expressed by Iran towards the United States has also kept Iran out of the World Trade Organisation, which is a costly affair for all Iranians. Being deprived of the privileges of membership has been anathema to the Iranian economy. The shortage of spare parts for Iranian airplanes, including commercial ones, due to US sanctions, has added yet another cost to the ailing Iranian squadron of planes. Exorbitant prices have been paid to purchase those items on the black market. Iran has also been deprived of holding seats in important international fora such as the Security Council. And much of its assets in the United States have remained frozen for the past 30 years.[74] Why then adopt anti-Americanism despite such huge costs? Most certainly the Iranian government could not have benefited from it, nor could the Iranian people. It is a policy in need of serious re-evaluation.

The United States has not benefited from this state of affairs either. All US companies have been excluded from competing in the rich Iranian oil and gas fields. With the third largest discovered oil reserves and the second largest known gas fields in the world stakes must be high for all those investing, exporting and marketing Iran's natural resources. Accordingly, all US competitors in these fields must have been reaping the benefits of the rupture in ties between Washington and Tehran.

There have been reports that in 2003, the Islamic Republic of Iran, fearful of a US military advance into Iran, offered what is referred to as a Grand Bargain to Washington but was rebuffed by the White House.[75] Allegedly the deal offered the following three concessions on the Iranian side: first, Iran would stop supporting Hezbollah in Lebanon and Hamas in the Palestinian territories. Second, the authorities in Tehran pledged to recognise Israel if it withdrew from the occupied territories, and, finally, they would allow full and unhindered nuclear inspection of all Iranian nuclear facilities. The first two concessions were indeed monumental coming from the Islamic government in Tehran as they would have amounted to an almost complete reversal of its foreign policy since its coming to power in 1979. Even though this would not have been the first time such reversal had taken place, as the acceptance of an end to the war with Iraq in 1987 without any of Iranian pre-conditions having been met had already indicated, it nevertheless would have marked another significant change of direction in the rather short history of the Islamist discourse in Iran. The last concession would have removed the only potential barrier from Iran to deter the decisive military might of the United States. The experience of the former Yugoslavia, Afghanistan and Iraq had indicated, almost beyond any shadow of a doubt, that military confrontation with Washington with conventional weapons could only lead to one outcome: complete defeat and ousting from power. Only North Korea, armed with nuclear weapons, has managed to escape the wrath of Washington thus far. Perhaps that was why Tehran demanded the following concessions from Washington in return.

First and foremost among them was a security guarantee from Washington for the Iranian government, that is, that the United

States would not engage in military moves against Iran. The fate of Slobodan Milosevic, the Taliban and Saddam Hussein were sufficient to awaken the Iranian government to the realities of the hegemonic power of the United States (hence complying with US wishes in halting the nuclear programme in 2003 out of fear of US reprisals). This demand also indicated the vulnerability of the Iranian rulers vis-à-vis their domestic situation. For in all the three cases of US military assertion that ousted those political rulers it was the absence of internal support for their political establishment that made those outcomes all the more attainable. In the former Yugoslavia, the aerial bombardment triggered off a movement that led to the toppling of Milosevic. In Afghanistan there were organised and armed resistance groups to the Taliban that under US aerial protection moved against the theocratic rulers in Kabul. And Saddam Hussein, a tyrant hated by the vast majority of the Iraqi population, could hardly rely on popular support to defend his failing government in the wake of the US-led invasion and occupation of the country.

The second concession asked by Iran was the lifting of sanctions imposed on it by the United States since the days of hostage-taking in Tehran in the early part of the Revolution. This would have saved Iran a vast amount of money and would have allowed it to rearm, and perhaps renew, its rather old and US-based weaponry. Even commercial aircraft in Iran, largely American, were, and continue to be, short of spare parts, which they cannot obtain in the free market due to US sanctions. Politically such a move could have also helped boost the Iranian government internationally.

The third Iranian demand related to the removal of Iran from the list of Axis of Evil countries declared by then President George W. Bush in his State of the Union address in 2002, where North Korea, Iraq and Iran had been grouped together in this category. In the wake of the terrorist attacks in the United States in September 2001, Washington was then riding on the moral high ground and the inclusion of Iran in that infamous list was at the very least a diplomatic embarrassment for Tehran.

The last Iranian condition asked for a US green light to European investment in Iran. Understandably, Iran was in need of foreign investment, but one wonders why Iran did not seek direct US investment instead of European. A previous attempt by a former president of the Islamic Republic, Hashemi Rafsanjani, to bring the US oil company Conoco to Iran in 1995 had faced an executive order by President Clinton cancelling the deal; without the presidential veto this move could have perceivably opened the door to a renewal of Iranian–American commercial ties. Perhaps that explains why the Iranian government was not asking for direct US investment lest it face the same aborted outcome as before.

The Grand Bargain was delivered by a Swiss diplomat to Washington. It was, however, rejected and the diplomat concerned was allegedly later reprimanded.[76] Other such moves had similarly been frustrated in the past. In the early years of the Revolution President Reagan had sent a signed Bible in 1986 with the handwritten verse in the beginning: *And the Scripture, foreseeing that God would justify the Gentiles by faith, preached the gospel beforehand to Abraham, saying, 'All the nations shall be blessed in you'* (Galatians 3:8). That effort had been leaked to the media through relatives of the then deputy to Ayatollah Khomeini, Ayatollah Hossein Ali Montazeri, and had thus been foiled. The next known attempt, made by Rafsanjani, as noted above, was thwarted by the executive order of the US President in 1995. There is thus a history of failure on rapprochement between Tehran and Washington in the past three decades.

Current international challenge: the nuclear issue

The nuclear saga surrounding Iran has arguably been the most sensitive question that has concerned the international community. At its core is the anxiety over Iran's enrichment of uranium that has been the sticking point of negotiations between the two sides. Many rounds of negotiations are yet to produce any tangible results that would be satisfactory to both parties. Iran's quest for nuclear energy (the Iranian government contends it is only for peaceful purposes and that as a signatory to the Non-Proliferation Treaty it has a right to peaceful nuclear energy) started before the Revolution (the development of a nuclear site in Bushehr was due to be completed in 1980 but was halted by the Revolution) but the leaders of the Revolution had little inkling for nuclear technology at the time and did not pursue the completion of its final stages. Later, during the war with Iraq, Saddam bombed the nuclear site and it was only later that Iranian leaders realised that nuclear energy could have its own advantages.[77] In any event, peaceful nuclear energy is the right of any signatory to the Non-Proliferation Treaty, to which Iran has subscribed. Why should it then be a cause for concern for the international community?

Enrichment of uranium inside Iran has raised questions on why Tehran should need to invest so many resources for nuclear fuel when the same can be obtained from abroad probably at cheaper prices with certain advantages that would be granted by the international community. The only nuclear reactor in Iran, at Bushehr, has now been completed by the Russians and its fuel can be provided by Russia or other countries. The Bushehr reactor would hardly justify, it is contended by those opposing uranium enrichment in Iran, the vast and costly enrichment process that is going on inside Iran. The unease expressed by the IAEA (International Atomic Energy Agency) in Vienna regarding certain aspects of Iran's nuclear development has further fuelled the controversy.[78] The ultimate worry expressed is that once able to enrich uranium even for lower-grade peaceful purposes there is little that can prevent Iran from developing higher-grade enriched uranium for nuclear weapons in the future. Thus the enrichment process can transform Iran into a potential nuclear power.

Iran's response that it has never intended to, and will not, enter the military phase of nuclear technology has thus far failed to convince greater powers and the IAEA. The secrecy with which it went about the initial stages of nuclear development has not helped its claim either. The consequences of its continued work on this project have been several resolutions adopted by the UN Security Council, the last of which (at the time of this writing) in June 2010 has imposed biting sanctions on the country.[79] Considering the weak state of the economy in Iran and its desperate need for foreign investment, economic measures adopted against it can prove particularly painful.

The recent contamination of the nuclear computer network by a virus, Stuxnet, has appeared to considerably slow down the progress of Iran's nuclear development. The magnitude of the impact was apparent to the Russian scientists who stated that they could no longer guarantee the safety of the nuclear reactor at Bushehr, which they had completed. Consequently, after years of prevarication by Russia and billions of dollars invested in the project by Iran, the nuclear reactor had to be defuelled only two months after it had been fuelled. Though this may temporarily slow down the Iranian nuclear programme and thus delay a final showdown between the West and Iran it is doubtful it can be effective in the long term.

Nuclearisation of Iran will cause a shift in the balance of power in the Persian Gulf region. Traditionally, the West has been unwilling to accept the domination of the region by any single state even if the state concerned was considered to be an ally[80] let alone a country with strong anti-Western credentials. The international position towards Iran will be determined in great part by the way the nuclear issue develops. Perhaps this will remain the greatest global challenge revolutionary Iran will continue to face. However, the internal challenges noted above may be the determining force in shaping the future of the country.

Conclusion

Throughout this work we have attempted to address the three questions posed in the Introduction on the definitions of and circumstances for waging *jihad* and the importance of peace in Islam. In that regard different interpretations of the faith were outlined and it was illustrated that the Islamist radical reading of Islam does not reflect the totality of the religion. None of the schools in Islam outlined, whether conservative, radical, or liberal, can claim a monopoly on interpretation of the text. It was stated that the interpretation can and should vary with the historical development of humanity and that claims on the finality of any single reading can themselves be viewed as sacrilege for it would place the creature (humanity) equal to the Creator (God). The text remains constant and eternal but interpretation cannot and should not.

It was noted that the greater *jihad*, the internal battle for self-purification to overcome greed and to develop piety, is the more significant of the struggles encouraged and described in Islam. Without engaging in this all-important challenge it is naive and premature to expect a victory of good over evil just through the lesser, external *jihad*. The battle for justice and advancement of humanity starts within each and every single member of the human community, in their hearts and minds, before it can be extended outwards and take shape in the physical world. In this respect the teachings of Islamic Gnosticism championed in Islamic history by great mystics such as Rumi of Iran were narrated in the text to provide a more inclusive approach to temporal affairs. Rumi ascended to the lofty heights of transcendental spirituality by removing the zones of exclusion based on race, class, history, language, geography and culture. The spiritual empowerment of the individual, it was noted, may be the key to resolving much of the problems associated with a systems-based approach, as prescribed in Western liberal discourse. No system can be foolproof against corruption and injustice as long as the members of the community living in the system cannot control their internal desires to trample upon the rights of others. Gnosticism is a suitable guide in this respect.

Surrendering to the Will of the Almighty is the quintessential Abrahamic teaching, including Islam. But who knows and who interprets that Will? Two discourses in Islam with almost conflicting interpretations, the *conservative* and the *radical*, have a different take on this precept. Mysticism, however, challenges both. In the conservative school the acquiescence of many a follower of Islamic teachings in the developing world may discourage activism and delegate all to the organised religion represented in the clerical hierarchy. After all, their plight and the esteemed position of their religious leaders, they believe, must be the Will of God or else matters would have been different. The consequent apathy and lethargy that is associated with the absence of popular will for change in those communities may induce some thinkers and activists to distance themselves from religion and initiate a different narrative. Social and political inactivism, however, have never been the teaching of true mystics. The instance of the famous mystic Hallaj and his struggle against the establishment on the inhumane treatment of slaves was noted earlier in this work.

In the fundamentalist discourse, the radical and ideologised narrative of religion appears to banish reason from the faith. The belief that one has to fight injustice violently, wherever, whenever and however one finds it (as a responsibility bestowed upon us by the Divine) has itself propounded the question of the justice of the means applied to achieve justice. In this discourse justice is interpreted jurisprudentially and/or ideologically without reference to any notion of relativism that has defined humanity and has validated reason as a guiding and organising principle – if you know everything and can do everything do you still require reason (a relative concept in human terms)?

The importance of reason (as separate from mere rationality) in Islam was also noted stressing that faith in itself does not provide for the proper governance of communities. Jurisprudence as the codified maxims of the religion, named *shari'a*, cannot be a basis for political administration that has to assess, devise and implement in the context of the present conditions rather than the requirements of the then newly expanded Arab conquests over a millennium ago. Gnosticism also points in this direction. The spiritual aspects of mystic discourse and its preaching of selflessness does not detract from its locating reason as the focus of our temporal existence. One parable, among many, in the *Masnavi* of Rumi highlights this point. Three fish in a pond realised that they were about to be netted by fishermen. The first, the most thoughtful and intelligent, decided to escape to the vast ocean. Despite the difficulties and dangers in its way it headed for the safety of the edgeless waters of the sea. It did this without consulting the other two fish for that would have weakened its resolve. The second fish, having missed the chance to travel away with its more intelligent friend, decided to play dead and thus managed to sneak its way out of danger to find the way to the ocean. The third, however, that was bereft of reason and foresight, agitated in the lake to no avail and was netted. While being fried in the pan, it said to itself that if ever it was free again it would seek shelter in the vastness of the sea. Rumi concludes by stressing the centrality of reason and the importance of learning from memory:

> *From deficiency of reason the wretched moth does not remember the flame*
> *Or the burning and the pain but who's to blame?*
> *When its wings are scorched it begins to repent*
> *Yet cupidity and forgetfulness dash it (again) into the torment;*
> *Grasp, apprehension and retentiveness all part of the same season*
> *As they are all raised by the faculty of reason.*[1]

This reason (holistic wisdom), however, is not the same as rationality (pedantic rationality) as focused on in IR paradigms. The difference between the two was elaborated upon in previous pages. The most important of all teachings of Gnosticism, desperately needed in today's world, where individuals are at the mercy of undifferentiating systemic approaches, is the degree of care and empathy it encourages in everyone through the paradigm of selflessness that defies self-enhancing rationality but keeps in harmony with the holistic wisdom and the inherent intelligence in the world. It is self-lessness that can erode the sharp edges of rationality that prevent the emergence of a caring and solidarist human environment. The dictum of everyone for themselves without care or concern for the plight of others, as long as the law of the land is adhered to (and even that has apparently been a disappointment), has failed miserably to protect the lives of humans in society, in politics and in economics. The two world wars and the recurrent global financial crises are testimony to the terrific shortcomings of rationality. If, as postulated by Linklater,

> The discipline of International Relations has a deeper purpose [than the analysis of the elements of recurrence and repetition], which is normative and philosophical, and requires above all else the analysis of the potentials for the transformation of political community.[2]

and if, as Kant believed, the transformation of international relations and the safeguarding of peace must begin with the reconstitution of political community, a change in the organisation of society seems inevitable if meaningful transformation in international politics can come about. This change, however, is itself dependent upon the transformation of the individual, who is the main constituent of that community. The main agent of change, therefore, in the final analysis, is the individual himself/herself. Mysticism also alludes to the significance of changing within (being just to ourselves) before attempting to bring change without (spreading justice in the wider community). One verse in the Quran reads, *God will not change the destiny of any people unless they first change themselves* (their hearts and minds).[3] This verse is testimony both to the importance of inner greater *jihad* as noted above, as well as the significance of sociopolitical action (lesser *jihad*), in the discourse of humanity for advancement. As elaborated by Shari'ati, the most remarkable aspect of this particular verse is in its direct hint that the Will of God, in this instance, will be subject to the will of the people. Thus people are regarded as the primary source of change and the masters of their own destiny but only if they engage in internal (greater) *jihad* first and the subsequent external (lesser) *jihad* thereafter; to triumph over the self before they can triumph over others. The internal battle to fight the excesses of greed and human want is perhaps much harder than the outer struggle to engage and triumph over the external environment.[4]

The uncaring and standardising nature of the liberal peace, enmeshed in systematised treatment of human needs, regardless of time and place, history, tradition and circumstances renders it irrelevant to the everyday concerns of those for whom the peace is intended. Liberal peace seems to overlook difference, which is a universal trait of humanity. As narrated by Rumi when reporting God's instructions to Moses,

> *I have bestowed on everyone different modes of acting,*
> *I have given to everyone a peculiar form of expression.*[5]

This difference among traditions, customs, beliefs and behaviours, however, appears overlooked and rendered irrelevant in liberal discourse. Political rights alone do not in themselves allow for an all-inclusive peace permeating every level of society. It was noted that in the case of Iraq, for example, lack of recognition of local conditions could ill provide for the foundations of a durable peace (East Timor could be another instance). The post-liberal peace discourse points to the failings of the liberal peace project. Richmond describes the liberal peace as perceived by the locals of post-conflict environments: 'Ethically bankrupt, subject to double standards, coercive and conditional, acultural, unconcerned with social welfare and unfeeling and insensitive towards the subjects'.[6] The illusion of liberal peace discourse in considering itself independent of the local in establishing peace has also been highlighted by the same author:

> In the longer term, the notion that powerful states or even international organisations can independently create order, or even peace, without an intimate contract with the peoples who are part of that order and peace has proven to be a blind alley.[7]

The universal aspects of Islamic and liberal discourses were also discussed. Universalism, it was noted, should not stand in the way of difference, just as difference could not be an excuse to trample upon human rights. Nor should universalism be viewed as an absolute closing of the door to the hermeneutic practice of exchange between interpretations and teaching and/or learning from other traditions. There is no monopoly of knowledge and/or understanding and only the Supreme Being, in Abrahamic religions including Islam, has such Divine position. Pretending to the contrary is usually a political practice to instrumentalise the faith for the pursuit of power. The Taliban in Afghanistan and the regime of al-Bashir in Sudan are contemporary examples of exploitation of religion for political gain.

The battle between various strands of understanding in Islam will not come to an end. Nor should it. It is, however, incumbent upon the faithful, particularly the intellectual leaders of Muslim communities, to open up space for the variety of understandings of the text, all in the context of a world where reflexive dialogue and meaningful peace are not only a preferred option for intra-communal and international life but increasingly an indispensable imperative for the long-term survival of an embattled humanity.

> *Let us fall in love again*
> *And scatter gold dust all over the world*
> *Let us become a new spring*
> *And feel the breeze drift in the heavens' scent.*
> *Let us dress the earth in green*
> *And like the sap of a young tree*
> *Let the grace from within us sustain us.*
> *Let us carve gems out of our stony hearts*
> *And let them light our path to love.*
> *The glance of love is crystal clear*
> *And we are blessed by its light.*
>
> Rumi

Postscript: A Few Words on the Sweeping Changes in the Middle East

The popular movements in the Middle East, at the time of the writing of these pages in 2011, have overtaken all expectations with untold regional and international ramifications. Starting with Tunisia, and continuing with Egypt and Libya and now engulfing Syria, Yemen and possibly Bahrain, there is now justifiably talk of an Arab awakening that may well affect other countries in the area too. Interestingly, thus far, there does not appear to be an overwhelming fundamentalist factor that can effectively subdue all other moderate and secular elements in those societies. The killing of bin Laden by the US forces in Pakistan last year did not seem to trigger any substantial wave of protest among Muslims in the world either. These observations may point to a weakening of the grip radical Islamism has had on the minds and hearts of young Muslims. The monumental failure of political Islam, wherever it has been practised, may well have had something to do with that. So could the indiscriminate killings and carnage that has marked almost every step of the way along the fundamentalists' path. It may have dawned on the younger generation of Muslims that prospects for Islam and Muslims may in the end be better served by deposing Muslim dictators than by focusing on and attacking non-Muslim liberals.

Another flashpoint in the region is Lebanon. The underlying tension between various factions could be triggered by developments such as the inquest over the assassination of its former premier, Rafiq Hariri, in 2005. Hizbollah, the Shi'a militia group that has turned into a political party, but has refused to disarm, now controls much of the government. Supported by Damascus and Tehran, the group did apparently manage to play a decisive role in forcing the Israelis out of south Lebanon in 2000. However, now with several of its prominent members wanted by the international tribunal over Hariri's assassination, room for diplomatic manoeuvring can conceivably become more limited and a head-on clash may appear to some as a way out. Lebanon may be approaching yet another phase of bloody conflicts that have so often and so tragically characterised its political life in the past four decades.

Syria is now the most sensitive item in the Middle East. At the time of writing more than 6,000 have been killed in protests against the government, while the number of army defectors leaving the ranks of Bashar al-Asad is on the increase. Armed resistance is now seriously threatening the status quo and the expectations are that in the end Asad will not have a much different fate from Gaddafi in Libya. Once deposed, however, the political map of the region will have decidedly changed. One consequence will be the increased vulnerability of the Islamic Republic of Iran to outside pressure, including a possible military assault on its nuclear infrastructure. Another will be the isolation of Hizbollah in Lebanon and its exposure to local and outside opposition, including Israel, with possible military ramifications.

Iran, of late, has been of particular concern internationally. In the wake of mounting crippling economic sanctions and the increasing probability of a Western boycott of its oil, the Islamic Republic has threatened the closure of the Strait of Hormoz. Such a scenario would in all likelihood engender a military confrontation of Western powers against Iran with a predictable military outcome but rather an uncertain political aftermath. What, however, appears more certain for the country in general is the serious prospect for change, the nature and the speed of which will depend on the interplay of internal forces and external pressures.

Despite all the setbacks for radical religious zealots, it is far too early to view Islamist fundamentalism as a thing of the past. There is still sufficient frustration among millions of Ooperate and attract new recruits. The injustice that has affected the lives of so many in the Middle East has to be redressed before the final chapter of Islamism as a dogmatic ideology, as opposed to a liberating, enriching, elevating and caring religious discourse, can be written. The coordinates of power, however, may have to be shifted if such an outcome is ever to be achieved. Doing so requires, above all else, an examination of the self, an inward probing into the never-ending and ever-increasing desires that proportionally limit our scope for the improvement of human condition. Without containing the self and the consequent individual emancipation, it would be difficult to conceive of a trans-formed political community, which is a prerequisite to reconfigured international relations.

Notes

Introduction: Framework of Analysis and Setting the Questions

1. See Andrew Linklater, *The Transformation of Political Community* (Columbia, SC: University of South Carolina Press, 1998), pp. 77–100.
2. *From a whim springs their war and peace*
   On a caprice is based their honour and shame
   (Rumi, *Masnavi*, Book I, line 71).
3. Gnosticism is defined as knowledge of knowledge. Mysticism is the spiritual discourse that unlike philosophy seeks to mystify and not to clarify. Sufism comes from the word *suf,* a harsh fabric from which the clothing of some of Muhammad's disciples was reportedly made. They were known as sufis. Some have asserted that while Gnosticism emanates from love and knowledge, mysticism or Sufism can be based only on love. The obvious conclusion, however, is that there is an overlapping field of interest between them and in this work they are used interchangeably without implying that they are necessarily the same.
4. Even Hafez, one of the most celebrated Iranian poets and mystics, asserts that Hallaj was executed for his esoteric statements.
   That friend, who lost his life on the gallows,
   All because he let out the secrets.
5. See Herbert W. Mason, *Hallaj* (Surrey: Curzon Press, 1995), p. 79.
6. Otherwise known as Rumi in the West, Molavi or Molana (30 September 1207–17 December 1273) was born in a small province at the River Wakhsh in Iran. Due to political circumstances his family moved westwards. At the age of 37 he met Shams, later to become his sage, whose presence appear to have ignited a spiritual longing in Rumi. The impact of Rumi's association with Shams could hardly have been greater for it was their spiritual bond that led the former to produce one of the greatest works (*Masnavi*) in Persian and arguably world literature.
7. This point is made with reference to those who measure and assess the significance of any work in history in terms of the immediate upheavals it can create in sociopolitical systems. Shari'ati, for instance, though describing Rumi as being like a sun, criticises him for alleged political inactivism. He states that Rumi's presence in his society during his life was minimal. The greater and longer-lasting impact of Rumi's works, however, cannot and should not be analysed within the framework of his immediate sociopolitical structure as Shari'ati does. Trying to assess his influence in such terms would be like limiting his outreach to his own generation and depriving humanity of the allure of his discourse. Fundamentalists and revolutionaries appear to have a habit of getting

carried away in their views downplaying anything and everything that does not fit their radical interpretation of political activism.

8. When initials are capitalised (International Relations) the discipline is referred to and when not (international relations) it is an allusion to global relations.

9. Rumi, *Masnavi*, book VI, line 1967.

10. See in this connection Felix Guattari, The Three Ecologies (translation) (London and New York: The Athlon Press, reprinted 2005).

11. Herbert A. Simon, *Models of Bounded Rationality*, vol. 3 (Cambridge, MA: Massachusetts Institute of Technology, 1997), p. 293.

12. Andrew Linklater, op. cit., p. 123.

13. Many sources have referred to this but not necessarily in agreement. For one source that states but disagrees with this view, see Anthony Shadid, *Legacy of the Prophet* (Cambridge, MA: Westview Press, 2002), p. 156.

14. Works abound in this field. Amid a wealth of references see Fred Halliday, *Islam and the Myth of Confrontation*, (London: I. B. Tauris, 1995); John L. Esposito, *Unholy War* (Oxford: Oxford University Press, 2002 and Gilles Kepel, *Jihad* (London: I. B. Tauris, 2002).

15. One of the first maxims in the devotion of a sufi to God is to disregard the likes and dislikes of other people and focus oneself solely on God. This, however instead in turn, it is alleged by Islamic activists, discourages social and political activism, and instead promotes isolationism, passivism and inaction.

16. To give but two examples, see *Tahrir-ol-Wasila* [A Clarification of Questions] by S. Ruho-llah Khomeini and *Ma'alim fi-l-Tariq* [Milestones] by Seyyed Qutb. For the first, refer to the following websites for the Persian translation in four volumes (original in Arabic) http://www. hodarayaneh.org/files/obook/tahrir1.htm; http://www.hodarayaneh. org/files/obook/tahrir2.htm; http://www.hodarayaneh.org/files/obook/ tahrir3.htm; http://www.hodarayaneh.org/files/obook/tahrir4.htm.For the second, see the English translation (original in Arabic) on the website http://majalla.org/books/2005/qutb-nilestone.pdf. (All the sites were last visited on 4 June 2011.)

17. One can cite Rumi as the great Gnostic/sufi of Islam, Seyyed Qutb as the activist promoter of *shari'a*/legal Islam, Khomeini as a staunch supporter of clerical Islam and Mohammad Ghazzali as the great philosopher of Islam.

18. Others such as Al-Na'im of Sudan, Chandra Muzaffar of Malaysia, Abdulaziz Sachedina of Tanzania and Abdolkarim Soroush of Iran are also important figures and may be referred to in this book. However revivalists, it should be noted, are not necessarily fundamentalists.

19. This is a quote from Shari'ati. For easy reference see http://drshariati.org/ show.asp?ID=151&q=%D8%A8%D8%B1%DA%AF%D8%B2%D8%A7%D 8%B1. The site was last visited on 3 June 2011. The site is in Farsi.

20. One instance is that of Late Grand Ayatollah Borojerdi in Iran, whose views were diametrically opposed to those seeking a violent struggle against the Pahlavi dynasty.

21. It is interesting to note that one of the meanings of the word Islam is peace.
22. For one good source elaborating on this, see A. G. Noorani, *Islam and Jihad* (New Delhi: Leftword, 2002).
23. Islamic sources condemning suicide bombings are numerous; for one, see Muhammad Tahir-ul-Qadri's ruling in the UK in March 2010 (http://www.dailymail.co.uk/news/article-1254855/Muslim-leader-condemns-suicide-bombers-fatwa.html). The site was last visited on 27 May 2011. Also for Islamic juridical views against the death edict for Salman Rushdie, see A. G. Noorani, op. cit., p. 50.
24. For one source, see Seyyed Qutb, *Ma'alim fi-l-Tariq* [Milestones] at http://majalla.org/books/2005/qutb-nilestone.pdf. The site was last visited on 4 June 2011.
25. The Quran, 5:32.
26. Ali Shari'ati, *'Erfan, Barabari, Azadi'* [Gnosticism, Equality and Freedom], Collected Works, vol. 2 (Tehran: Hosieniye Ershad, 1978), p. 63; An electronic version can be seen at http://nimeharf.com/books/Erfan---Barabari---Azadi.pdf. The site was last visited on 3 June 2011.
27. *The Mathnawi of Jalalu'ddin Rumi*, vols. 1 to 6, ed. and trans. Reynold A. Nicholson (Cambridge: E. J. W. Gibb Memorial Series, 1990).

1 Islamic Discourses: Definitions and Background

1. There are many sources stating this. For one Western source see John L. Esposito, *Unholy War* (Oxford: Oxford University Press, 2002), p. 144.
2. The Quran, 28:77: *And seek by the wealth provided for you by Allah the eternal abode (the Hereafter) but do not forget and (and forsake) your share of this world. Be kind and good (to others) just as Allah was kind and good to you. And desire not corruption in the land. Indeed, Allah does not like corrupters.*
3. Abdolkarim Soroush, *Ghabz o Bast e Teorik e Shari'at* [The Theoretical Contraction and Expansion of Shari'a], 3rd edn (Tehran: Serat Cultural Institute, 1994), p. 86. This point has been dealt with deftly throughout the above-mentioned book.
4. See A. G. Noorani, *Islam and Jihad* (New Delhi: Leftword, 2002), p. 50.
5. Iran and Iraq are the two countries with a majority Shi'a population. However, it should be noted that up to the capture of Saddam Hussein in 2003 Iraq had always been ruled by a Sunni government.
6. For a comprehensive account of sects in Islam in Farsi see Dr Mohammad Javad Mashkoor, *Tarikh e Shi'e va Ferghehaye Eslam ta Gharn e Cheharom* [History of Shi'ism and Sects in Islam up to Fourth Century (Islamic Calendar)] (Tehran: Eshraghi Publications, 1994).
7. See, for instance, the report of an interview with the slain Al-Qaida leader in Iraq, Al-Zarqawi, by the Associated Press, wherein he refers to the highest Shi'a cleric, Grand Ayatollah Sistani, as Satan: http://www.freerepublic.com/focus/f-news/1751017/posts

8. For Sunnis see Al-Bukhari, *Sahih al-Bukhari*, Arabic and English, published by Dar Ahya Us-Sunnah, Al Nabawiya (nine volumes; no place or date of publication) and for Shi'as see Sheikh Mohammad Hassan Najafi, *Jawaher* (Tehran: Dar-ol-ketab al-Eslamie, 1392 [Islamic lunar calendar]). This edition comes in 43 volumes. Both books expound on jurisprudential dictums. At times the number of rules governing religious duties are astounding. For instance, jurisprudence in Shi'ism has over 4,000 ordinances regarding various aspects of the daily prayers.

9. W. Montgomery Watt, *Islamic Political Philosophy* (Edinburgh University Press, 1998, reprint), p. 125.

10. It is difficult to establish with certainty an approximate date for the establishment of clergy in Islam. It can, however, be assumed that during the Abbasids, when different schools of jurisprudence began to spread, clerical hierarchy started to emerge.

11. *Ijma'* meaning consensus is one of the principles of jurisprudence in Islam. Its importance compared to other tenets such as *qias* (analogy) varies according to different schools.

12. In Shi'ism, however, it is believed that *ulema* or jurisconsults emerged as a necessity in the aftermath of the Great Occultation of Imam Mahdi around 260 (Islamic lunar calendar). There are Hadiths in Shi'ism by the Infallible Imams stating that disobeying the rules of the representatives of the Hidden Imam is tantamount to polytheism; for two sources see Molla Hashem Khorasani, *Montakhabo-al-Ttavarikh* [Selected Histories] (Tehran: Ali Akbar Elmi Publications, 1973), p. 868; and Sheikh Abbas Ghomi, *Montahal-Amal* [The Ultimate End of Desires], vol. 2 (Tehran: Islamic Library and Printing House, 1942), p. 375.

13. Arthur Goldschmidt Jr and Lawrence Davidson, *A Concise History of the Middle East*, 8th edn (Colorado and Oxford: Westview Press, 2006), p. 81.

14. The radical branch of Islam, both Sunni and Shi'a, claims that in fact power must only be exercised in accordance with the rules of *shari'a*. In radical political Shi'ism, personified in the late Ayatollah Khomeini, this power should be exercised by the religious jurists themselves.

15. The word *caliph* literally means 'vice-regency', 'succession', or 'representation'. The immediate successor to Muhammad was Abubakr, his father-in-law. People began addressing him as *calipha-t-Allah* (successor to or representative of God). Abubakr himself is reported to have asked people to address him as *calipha-t-arrasoul-e-Llah* (successor to or representative of the Messenger of God). This tradition was kept after Abubakr.

16. For a powerful and perhaps unparalleled illustration of this principle see Ali Shari'ati, *Tashayyo' Alavi va Tashayyo' Safavi* [Alavid Shi'ism and Safavid Shi'ism], *Collected Works*, vol. 9 (place of publication unstated: Tashayyo' Publications, 1978). The book is in Farsi and to my knowledge has not yet been translated in its entirety.

17. An exception could be Judaism. For a reference to Jewish jurisprudence see Abraham M. Fuss, *Studies in Jewish Jurisprudence*, vol. 4 (New York: Sepher-Hermon Press, Inc., 1976). Vol. I, II and III were published

in 1971, 1974 and 1974 respectively; see also a critical view of the same in Israel Shahak, *Jewish History, Jewish Religion* (London: Pluto Press, 1994).

18. Note should of course be taken that Christianity, at least the Catholic and the Protestant sects, may claim a change in that regard after the Reformation.

19. For a fuller account of this incident see Arthur Goldschmidt Jr and Lawrence Davidson, op. cit., p. 199.

20. See L. Carl Brown, *Religion and State* (New York: Columbia University Press, 2000), pp. 52–9.

21. The Late Grand Ayatollah Boroujerdi of Iran, the undisputed Shi'a *marja' taqlid* (Source of Emulation) at the time (1875–1961), was known for his apolitical religious views. Mohammad Al-Shaltut (1893–1963), the Sheikh of Al-Azhar (1958–63), was also known for his sense of reason and moderation.

22. This is a widely reported quote; however, there appears to be no written reference.

23. Note should be taken that when in this work 'Islamic' is used, the adjective reflects the 'Islam for humanity' viewpoint as referred to earlier, whereas when 'Islamist' is mentioned the adjective denotes the 'humanity for Islam' viewpoint.

24. We are not including esoteric Gnostics such as Rumi or deep philosophers like Gazzali or Shabestari in this camp, even though others such as Abdolkarim Soroush have. Revivalists in our categorisation, belong to the *political Islam* approach, which does not see a gap between religion and politics.

25. Morteza Motahhari was the leading philosopher/intellectual cleric of his time in pre-revolutionary Iran and in the early days of the revolution, before he was assassinated. Recently attempts have been made to translate some of his works.

26. See Carl W. Ernst, *Following Muhammad: Rethinking Islam in the Contemporary World* (Chapel Hill, NC and London: The University of North Carolina Press, 2003), pp. 136 and 202. See also Graham E. Fuller, *A World without Islam* (New York: Little, Brown and Company, 2010), pp. 243–67.

27. This point is made by Huntington in Samuel P. Huntington, *The Clash of Civilisations and Remaking of the World Order* (New York: Touchstone, 1997), p. 51.

28. Ali Shari'ati, op. cit., p. 42.

29. There is in fact a Hadith from the Prophet of Islam stating that Muslims should seek knowledge even if it were to be found in China (the geographical distance of Arabia to China and its inaccessibility to Muslims at the time indicates the importance assigned to learning in Islam).

30. It is interesting to note, however, that many of the revivalists had actually received a Western education. For instance, Shari'ati and Iqbal had both studied in leading Western universities. The former had been to the

Sorbonne and the latter had attended Cambridge in the United Kingdom and Ludwig-Maximilians-Universitat in Germany.

31. See Abdolkarim Soroush, *Reason, Freedom and Democracy in Islam* (Oxford University Press, 2000), p. 30.
32. Jean-Paul Sartre, 'Preface', in Frantz Fanon, *The Wretched of the Earth* (Penguin Books, 2001, reprint), p. 7.
33. This is widely quoted. For one source see http://chss.montclair.edu/english/furr/pol/wtc/oblnus091401.html. The site was last visited on 1 August 2011.
34. *The Economist*, 15 September 2001, p. 5.
35. A. G. Noorani, op. cit., p. 52.
36. Persistence in revenge was even one of the principles of *Muruwwah* (code of conduct) among pre-Islamic Bedouin Arabs. See Arthur Goldshmidt Jr and Lawrence Davidson, op. cit., p. 24.
37. Pat Buchanan, 'Is Islam an Enemy of the United States?' *New Hampshire Sunday News*, 25 November 1990.
38. Abdolkarim Soroush, op. cit.; see note 3 above.
39. This point was ably made by Mohsen Mojtahed Shabestari in a keynote lecture at a conference on *Judaism, Christianity and Islam: Divinity in a Political World*, organised by the Centre for World Dialogue in Limassol, Cyprus, 1999.
40. See Katerina Dalacoura, *Islam, Liberalism and Human Rights* (London: I. B. Tauris, 1998), pp. 59–68.
41. This point was deftly made by Abdolkarim Soroush in a speech in Nicosia, Cyprus in October 1997.
42. This is an amazing story. Having successfully deceived Adam and Eve (in the Quran there is no report of Eve having been deceived first or Adam having been deceived via Eve) the Satan then asks God for respite until the Day of Judgement so that he can go about deceiving the children of Adam and Eve on Earth; a request that is duly granted by God. The significance of freedom and its cardinal place in the relationship between God and humanity and even Satan is indisputable. The Quran, 17:62–5 and 15:36–42.
43. In this regard there is a widely reported Hadith from the Prophet of Islam to the effect that people will have no religion if they are living in poverty; see Mohammad Bagher Majlesi, *Bahar-ol-Anwar* [The Seas of Colours], vol. 6 (Tehran: Maktab-ol-Eslamiye, 1964), p. 295.
44. For one source see Abdullahi Ahmad An-Na'im (February 1978) 'Religious Minorities under Islamic Law and the Limits of Cultural Relativism', *Human Rights Quarterly* 9(1): 15–16.
45. The Quran: *There is no compulsion in religion* (The Quran, 2:256). This is not just to say that there is no compulsion in accepting Islam. It is saying more than that. It is stating an inherent element of any religion, by stressing the freedom of humanity to choose. If it were to be imposed then it would not be by free choice; it would cease to be true religion.

46. Rights without corresponding duties are usually referred to as privileges.
47. Imam Ahmad Hanbal was the founder of the fourth main sect within Sunni Islam. He was born in Baghdad about one hundred fifty years after the Prophet and lived over seventy years (164–241 Islamic lunar calendar).
48. Wahhabism is known to interpret Islam in the tradition of Ibn Taymiyya (see Cyril Glasse, *The Concise Encyclopedia of Islam*, rev. edn (London: Stacey International, 2002), p. 469; although some believe that Abdul-Wahhab himself disagreed with some of Ibn Taymiyya's views (see Natana J. Delong-Bas, *Wahhadi Islam: From Revival and Reform to Global Jihad* (I. B. Tauris and Oxford University Press, 2004), p. 21. The 'anthropomorphist', or rather the literal, interpretation of the Quran, gave Ibn Taymiyya's view a political slant that appeared unwelcome in many circles. To this day there are supporters and those who disagree with his views.
49. See Natana J. Delong-Bas, op. cit., pp. 285–6.
50. Ibid., p. 201.
51. This term means different things to different people but to many traditional Muslims it implies a constant effort to purify oneself from sins (greater *jihad*) or at times when necessary to engage in defensive armed combat (lesser *jihad*). See Chapter 4 of this volume.
52. See Malise Ruthven, *Islam in the World*, 2nd edn (New York: Oxford University Press, 2000), pp. 299–300.
53. Ibid., p. 300.
54. Ibid.
55. A practice in Shi'a Islam, whereby Muslims are duty-bound to emulate a Grand Ayatollah.
56. There are four main schools in Sunni Islam: Maliki, Hanbali, Hanafi and Shafe'i.
57. For a comprehensive account of Abdu's philosophy see, Roxanne L. Euben, *Enemy in the Mirror* (Princeton: Princeton University Press, 1999), pp. 105–14.
58. Malise Ruthven, op. cit., p. 324.
59. Ali Shari'ati, *Ma va Eqbal* [We and Iqbal], *Collected Works*, vol. 5 (Iran: Elham Publications, 1982), p. 109.
60. See *Iqbal: Manifestation of the Islamic Spirit*, Two Contemporary Muslim Views: Ayatollah Sayyid Ali Khamene'i and Ali Shari'ati, trans. Mahliqa Qara'I and Laleh Bakhtiar (Canada: Abjad and Open Press Holding (Joint Publishers), 1991), p. 83.
61. Anthony Shadid, *Legacy of the Prophet* (Cambridge, MA: Westview Press, 2002), p. 53, n. 22.
62. Malise Ruthven, op. cit., p. 313.
63. Ibid., p. 314, n. 17.
64. Ibid., p. 330, n. 43.

65. See Ali Shari'ati, *Niyayesh* [Prayers], *Collected Works*, vol. 8 (Tehran: Hoseinieh Ershad Publications, 1979), p. 102.
66. Ibid.
67. Anthony Shadid, op. cit., p. 61.
68. Ibid., p. 89.

2 Contextualising Islam or Islamicising Context: Debates on the Role of Islam in Politics

1. Costas M. Constantinou, 'On Homo-Diplomacy', *Space and Culture* 9(2006): p. 359.
2. Susan Buck-Morss, *Thinking Past Terror: Islamism and Critical Theory on the Left* (London and New York: Verso, 2003), p. 42.
3. See the argument on the political activism of the famous mystic Hallaj in Herbert W. Mason, *Hallaj* (Surrey: Curzon Press, 1995).
4. Costas M. Constantinou, op. cit., pp. 351–64.
5. Rumi, *Masnavi*, Book I, lines 1373–4 and 1389. Translation as provided in Abdolkarim Soroush, *Reason, Freedom, and Democracy in Islam*, translated and edited by Mahmoud and Ahmad Sadri (Oxford: Oxford University Press, 2000), p. 103.
6. Note, for instance, phrases such as the 'killer instinct' or 'shark' amongst financial dealers.
7. The poem is by the famous Persian poet of the medieval era, Sa'adi. Translation is by T. C. Young, 'The National and International Relations of Iran', in T. C. Young (ed.), *Near Eastern Culture and Society* (Princeton University Press, 1951), p. 204.
8. Leonard Lewisohn, *Beyond Faith and Fidelity: The Sufi Poetry and Teachings of Mahmud Shabestari* (Surrey: Curzon Press, 1995), p. 257.
9. The Quran, 35:39.
10. Leonard Lewisohn, op. cit., p. 256.
11. Ibid., p. 255.
12. *The Mathnawi of Jalalu'ddin Rumi*, Vols V and VI, edited and translated by Reynold A. Nicholson (Cambridge: E. J. Gibb Memorial, 1990), p. 120, line 2012.
13. Emam Mohammad Ghazzali, *Kimiaye Sa'adat* [Elixir of Salvation] (Tehran: Peyman Publications, 2008), p. 40.
14. Mohammad Lahiji, *Sharhe Golshan e Raz* [Explanation of the Garden of Secrets] (Tehran: Zavvar Publications, 1992), p. 191. The book is a commentary on the famous work of the great mystic, Mahmud Shabestari, *Garden of Secrets*.
15. Mohammad Ali Movahhed, *Shams e Tabrizi*, 2nd edn (Tehran: Tarh e Noe Publications, 1997), p. 114.
16. Ibid.
17. See J. S. McClelland, *A History of Western Political Thought* (London and New York: Routledge, 1996), p. 24.

18. Emam Mohammad Ghazzali, op. cit., p. 77.
19. Heravi, HosseinAli, *Sharhe Ghazalhaye Hafez* [An Explanation of Hafez Poetry], vol. 3, 2nd edn (Tehran: Tanvir Publications in cooperation with Noe Publications, 2000), p. 2014.
20. Robert Cox, 'Social Forces, States and World Order: Beyond International Relations Theory', *Millennium: Journal of International Studies* 10(1981), p. 128.
21. This is by Mahmud Shabestarin in *Golshna e Raz* [Garden of Secrets]. For this translation see Leonard Lewisohn, op. cit., p. 258.
22. Costas M. Constantinou, op. cit., p. 352.
23. Ibid., p. 354, n. 1.
24. Ibid.
25. Ibid.
26. Reference for Persian speakers: the first line of this ghazal by Hafiz in original Farsi is

    Fash migooyamo az ghofteye khod delshadam
    Bandeye eshgham o az har do jahan azadam.

    I have not come across a published English translation, though there may well be one.
27. Ibid.
28. Translation as provided in Abdolkarim Soroush, op. cit.,, p. 96.
29. In the Nicholson translation *aghe joz'ee* has been translated as 'partial reason'. Here I have used 'partial wisdom'. See *The Mathnawi of Jalalu'ddin Rumi*, Vols I and II, edited and translated by Reynold A. Nicholson (Cambridge: E. J. Gibb Memorial, 1990), p. 107, line 1982.
30. Ibid., Vol. IV, p. 341, line 1258.
31. The Charter is in Latin but the Rector of the University made a reference to this very point in a speech given at the Annual Meeting of the Academic Council on the United Nations System (ACUNS), held at the University of Vienna in June 2010.
32. A. P. Martinich, *A Hobbes Dictionary* (Cambridge, MA and Oxford: Blackwell Publishers, 1995), p. 252.
33. Ibid.
34. Tom Campbell, *Seven Theories of Human Society* (New York: Oxford University Press, 1981), p. 75.
35. See Immanuel Kant, 'Speculative Beginning of Human History', in *Perpetual Peace and Other Essays*, translated by Ted Humphrey (Indianapolis: Hacket Publishing, 1983), pp. 49–60.
36. Ibid., p. 53.
37. This can be noted as *adl va ghest* in Islamic sciences. While the former refers to the norm in the society, the latter alludes to more fundamental underpinnings. For example, one may be paying the market price for a day's labour (*adl*) but that price may well be below what the labourer actually deserves (*ghest*).
38. Thomas Hobbes, *Leviathan*, edited by Michael Oakshott (Oxford: Basil Blackwell, 1955), p. 83.

39. Hedley Bull states the argument in his book *The Anarchical Society*, where order and justice are presented in a hierarchical fashion. Order is deemed as a prerequisite to justice for it is said that one cannot possibly aspire to establish justice in a state of chaos and disorder. Therefore, some kind of order, however imperfect, may be a necessary path to justice. An implication is that the status quo, for instance, however unjust it may be, is preferable to any alternatives because attempting to change it would lead to disorder, which cannot possibly serve the cause of justice. This is reminiscent of a saying by one of the famous gurus in the Islamist fundamentalist discourse. Ibn Taimiyya, of the fourteenth century, believed that, 'Sixty years with an unjust imam [ruler] is better than one night of anarchy.' Quoted in Malise Ruthven, *Islam in the World*, 2nd edn (Oxford: Oxford University Press, 2000), p. 171.
40. See Morteza Motahhari, *Adl e Elahi* [Divine Justice] (Tehran: Sadra Publications, 1982), pp. 59–67.
41. Abdolkarim Soroush, op. cit., p. 104.
42. Rumi, *Masnavi*, Book III, line 2435. Translation as seen in Abdolkarim Soroush, op. cit., p. 104.
43. Note should be taken that *aghe kol*, as previously referred to, is sometimes used by Rumi to denote the greater wisdom.
44. Mohammad Lahiji, op. cit., p. 46.
45. Rumi, *Mathnawi* (Nicholson), Vols III and IV, p. 245. Here I have trans-lated *hikma* as reason but Nicholson has used wisdom instead.
46. Rumi, *Masnavi*, Book I, line 2128.
47. See Leonard Lewisohn, op. cit., p. 227.
48. Ibid., p. 259.
49. Ibid.
50. Emam Mohammad Ghazzali, op. cit., p. 846.
51. See Leonard Lewisohn, op. cit., p. 227
52. Mohammad Lahiji, op. cit., p. 44.
53. This point is alluded to by many sufis including Rumi. See Leonard Lewisohn, op. cit., p. 224.
54. Reported in Mohammad Ghazzali, *Ehya' e Oloome-Ddin* [Revival of Religious Sciences], 6th edn, vol. I, translated by Mohammad Khawrazmi (Tehran: The Institute for Scientific and Cultural Publications, 2007), p. 35.
55. Mohammad Lahiji, op. cit., pp. 46–7.
56. Mohammad Ghazzali, *Ehya e Oloom-e-ddin*, vol. I, p. 43.
57. Rumi, *Masnavi*, Book II, lines 277–8; translation seen in Leonard Lewisohn, op. cit., pp. 223–4.
58. In the absence of any agreed definition of the term, terrorism denotes, in general, the use of terror and violence for political purposes, often involving non-combatants as the subjects of such acts. States as well as non-state actors can be terrorists.
59. Quran, 2:36.

60. Richard Falk, 'Manifesting World Order' in Joseph Kruzel and James N. Rosenau (eds), *Journey through World Politics* (Toronto: Lexington Books, 1989), p. 161.
61. See note 21 above.
62. See Martin Griffith, *Fifty Key Thinkers in International Relations* (London and New York: Routledge, 1999), p. 115.
63. Rumi, *Masnavi*, Book I, lines 3435–6.
64. Ibid., line 71.
65. Susan Buck-Morss, op. cit., p. vii.
66. Ibid., p. 2.
67. Fazlur Rahman, *Islam and Modernity: Transformation of an Intellectual Tradition* (Chicago: The University of Chicago Press, 1982), p. 19.
68. The Quran, 15:29.
69. The Quran, 23:12.
70. The Quran, 91:8, the translation is from Ibn Khaldun, *The Muqaddamah* [An Introduction to History], translated by Franz Rosenthal, edited and abridged by N. J. Dawood (Princeton, NJ: Bollingen Series, Princeton University Press, 1989), p. 97.
71. Ibn Khaldun, op. cit., p. 97. Many Western philosophers, such as Karl Marx, also believed that human beings have no fixed nature.
72. See Jean Paul Sartre, *Existentialism and Human Emotions* (New York: Citadel Press, 1987 [1957]), pp. 15–23.
73. Note should be taken that in Marx's view human beings have no fixed nature, but it is the system of production that can potentially corrupt human beings. See, in this regard, Tom Campbell, op. cit., p. 120.
74. Emam Mohammad Ghazzali, *Kimiaye Sa'adat,* op. cit., pp. 32–3.
75. In Islamic mysticism, the more elevated perceive the earth as ruins but can begin to build developments thereupon. *I was an angel and Paradise was my abode, Adam brought me to this ruined land I developed* (by Hafez) addresses this very point. Shari'ati also refers to this, narrating that he has only gone as far as perceiving the ruins but noting that Rumi was able to develop on the ruins; see two works by Ali Shari'ati: *Hoboot* [Descendence] and *Kavir* [Desert].
76. Andrew Linklater, 'The Achievements of Critical Theory', in Steve Smith, Ken Booth and Marsia Zalewski (eds), *International Theory: Positivism and Beyond* (Cambridge, Cambridge University Press, 1999), p. 281.
77. Rumi, *Mathnawi,* (Nicholson), vol. I, lines 1811–12.
78. See Tom Campbell, op. cit., pp. 73 and 75.
79. Thomas Hobbes, *Leviathan*, p. 81.
80. Tom Campbell, op. cit., p. 76.
81. The Quran, 2: 36.
82. Ibn Khaldun, op. cit., p. 97.
83. The Quran, 33:72.
84. J. S. McClelland, *A History of Western Political Thought* (London and New York: Routledge, 1996), pp. 233–6.

85. Ibid.
86. The Quran, 5:32.
87. J. S. McClelland, op. cit., p. 234.
88. Quoted in Sheikh Farid-eddin e Attar e Neishabouri, *Tazkarat-ol-Olia* [Biography of the Great], 5th edn (Tehran: Peyman Publications, 2008), p. 527.
89. For an interesting, but incomplete and possibly misleading account of Hallaj's esoteric discourse (in relation to Avecina's scientific and epistemological approach and Abuzar's forward and direct activism) see Ali Shari'ati, *Eslamshenasi* [Islamology] vol. I (Tehran, Iran: Shari'ati Publications, 1981).
90. Herbert W. Mason, op. cit., p. xii.
91. Ibid., p. 79.
92. The Quran, 55:7.
93. The Quran, 11:85.
94. Herbert W. Mason, op. cit., p. 7.
95. Rumi, *Masnavi*, Book IV, line 414.
96. See note 8 above.
97. Ali Shari'ati, *Baz Shenasi e Hoviyyat e Irani-Islami* [Rediscovery of Iranian-Islamic Identity], *Collected Works*, No. 27 (Tehran: Elham Publications, 1981), pp. 18–24.
98. This has been referred to above. But for another source see Mohammad Lahiji, op. cit., p. 191.
99. Ibid., p. 175.
100. Mohammad Ali Movahhed, op. cit., p. 74.
101. Emam Mohammad Ghazzali, *Kimiaye Sa'adat,* op. cit., p. 8.
102. Ibid., p. 20.
103. Rumi, *Mathnawi* (Nicholson), Books I and II, p. 206, line 3800. For the full account of the story, see pp. 202–8.
104. See note 76 above. This refers to the ability of humanity to transcend the limits of earthly life in search of a better and more refined existence.
105. The Quran, 7:21. This verse translates: *And he [Satan] swore unto them, Verily, I am of those who wish you well indeed!* Therefore, Satan did not persuade them with reason for if he/she had convinced them by reason there would have been no need for him/her to swear. Swearing (taking an oath) is exercised when there is neither independent evidence nor reason to advance an argument. One is thus asked to take someone else's word at face value, that is, have faith in him/her. It may be deduced from this that humanity can more easily be deceived through faith than reason.
106. The Quran, 2:36.
107. Ali Shari'ati, *Ommat va Emamat* [Religious Community and Its Leadership] (Tehran: Ghalam Publication, 1978), p. 30.
108. Ibid., p. 175, n. 1.
109. The Quran, 99: 7–8: *And whoso doeth good an atom's weight will see it then, And whoso doeth ill an atom's weight will see it then.*

110. St Thomas's Gospel, translated by Stephen Patterson and Marvin Meyer. See http://users.misericordia.edu//davies/thomas/Trans.htm, article 61, p. 7. (The site was last visited on 1 June 2011.)
111. The Quran, 49:13; the word appears in plural form.
112. The Quran, 4:13.
113. The Quran, 71:2.
114. The Quran, 2:49.
115. The Quran, 3:104.
116. The Quran, 49:13.
117. Ali Shari'ati, *Ommat va Emamat*, p. 74.
118. Ibid., p. 71.
119. Ibid., p. 75.
120. Quoted in ibid., pp. 84–5.
121. Ibid., p. 48.
122. Ibid., p. 160.
123. Ibid. p. 215.
124. Ibid. p. 194.
125. Ibid. pp. 196–7.
126. Ibid. p. 198.
127. Ibid., p. 104.
128. Ibid. p. 205.
129. The Quran, 3:110, 5:48, 6:108 and 7:38. Note in the last verse *Ummah* is used for those going to fire as a way of punishment.
130. Oscar Wilde (n.d.). http://praxeology.net/OW-SMS.htm. The site was last visited on 21 January 2012.
131. The Quran, 9:101.
132. See the Quran, 9:97–101. In those verses the Quran speaks contemptuously of at least some of those around the Prophet. The language is very specific and direct. And this is towards the end of the Prophet's life so if there were to be a utopia, it must have been at that time.
133. The Quran, 18:110.
134. See Ali Shari'ati, *Ommat va Emamat,* p. 201. The slain founder and former leader of al-Qaida, Osama bin Laden, also subscribed to the use of violence to further his goals.
135. The Quran, 5:32.
136. The Quran, 95:1–3.
137. See Andrew Linklater, *The Transformation of Political Community* (Columbia, SC: University of South Carolina Press, 1998), p. 28.
138. Susan Buck-Morss, op. cit., pp. 31–2.
139. See Hamza Alawi, 'The Rise of Religious Fundamentalism in Pakistan', *Secular Pakistan*, 10 March 2009, athttp://secularpakistan.wordpress.com/2009/03/10/the-rise-of-religious-fundamentalism-in-pakistan-hamza-alavi/. The site was last visited on 1 June 2011.
140. Susan Buck-Morss, op. cit., p. 29.
141. Samuel P. Huntington, *The Clash of Civilisations and the Remaking of the World Order* (London: Touchstone Books, 1998), p. 51.

142. W. Montgomery Watt, *Islamic Political Thought* (Edinburgh: Edinburgh University Press, 1998 [1968]), p. 24.
143. Ibid., p. 29.
144. Mohammad Ghazzali, op. cit. vol. I, pp. 28–9.
145. The Quran, 9:39.
146. See Cyril Glasse, *The Concise Encyclopaedia of Islam*, rev. edn (London: Stacey International, 2002), p. 278.
147. Charles Tilly, *Coercion, Capital, and European States, AD 990–1992* (Cambridge, MA and Oxford: Blackwell, 2000 [1990]), p. 5.
148. Martin Griffith, op. cit., p. 126.
149. Ibid.
150. Ibid., p. 121.
151. Richard Falk, 'In Search of a New World Model', *Current History* 92(1993), p. 149.
152. Rumi, *Masnavi*, Book II, lines 2328–32.
153. See L. Carl Brown, *Religion and State* (New York: Columbia University Press, 2000), p. 28.
154. The Quran, 61:10–11.
155. Rumi, *Masnavi*, Book I, lines 19–21.
156. For one source see Arthur Goldschmidt Jr. and Lawrence Davidson, *A Concise History of the Middle East*, 8th edn (Oxford: Westview Press, 2006), p. 74.
157. Rumi, *Masnavi*, Book II, lines 1770–71.
158. Malise Ruthven, op. cit., p. 363.
159. Susan Buck-Morss, op. cit., p. 43.
160. Quoted in Malise Ruthven, op. cit., p. 171.
161. Susan Buck-Morss, op. cit., p. 45.
162. Abdolkarim Soroush, op. cit., p. 56.
163. Arthur Goldschmidt Jr. and Lawrence Davidson, op. cit., p. 262.
164. The Quran, 20: 133–4. In these verses one is even allowed to complain to the Lord himself, however unjustified the complaint may be.
165. Abdolkarim Soroush, op. cit., p. 91. Note should be taken that in Persian language the word *haq* also connotes metaphysical truth and righteousness.
166. Ibid., p. 57.
167. This point is discussed at length in Abdullahi Ahmed An-Na'im, *Islam and the Secular State: Negotiating the Future of Shari'a* (Cambridge, MA and London: Harvard University Press, 2008). However, page one of the book states clearly an interpretation of secularism that corresponds to the point made here.
168. Mohammad Ghazzali, op. cit., vol. I, p. 45.
169. John L. Esposito, *The Islamic Threat: Myth or Reality?* (Oxford: Oxford University Press, 1992), p. 89.
170. See Emam Mohammad Ghazzali, *Kimiaye Sa'adat,* op. cit., p. 124.
171. This is a widely reported *hadith* from the Prophet of Islam. For easy reference in English see http://thinkexist.com/quotation/

seek_knowledge_from_the_cradle_to_the/162339.html. The site was last visited on 28 May 2011.

172. Mohammad Ghazzali, op. cit., Vol. I; Foreword by the editor, p. 22.
173. See Abdolkarim Soroush, op. cit., p. 29.
174. Quoted in Katerina Dalacoura, *Islam, Liberalism & Human Rights* (London: I. B. Tauris, 1998), p. 61.
175. Montgomery Watt, op. cit., p. 123.
176. This point has been made repeatedly by Abdolkarim Soroush in his writings and lectures.
177. Ali Shari'ati, 'Gnosticism, Equality, Freedom', in Ali Shari'ati, *Revolutionary Self-Construction, Collected Works*, vol. II (Tehran: Hoseineeye Ershad Publications, 1978), p. 64.
178. A. G. Noorani, *Islam and Jihad* (New Delhi: LeftWord, 2003), p. 52.
179. Olivier Roy, *The Failure of Political Islam*, translated by Carol Volk (Cambridge, MA: Harvard University Press, 1996), p. 196.
180. Ibid., p. 197.
181. Karen Armstrong, *The Battle for God* (New York: Alfred A. Knopf, 2000), p. ix.
182. See Abdolkarim Soroush, *Ghabz va Bast e Teorik e Shari'at* [Theoretical Contraction and Expansion of *Shari'a*] (Tehran: Serat Cultural Institute, 1994).
183. See Mohammad Bagher Majlesi, *Baharol-Anwar* [The Seas of Colours], Vol. 6 (Tehran: Maktab-ol-Eslamie, 1964), p. 295.
184. For an elaboration of this point see Abdolkarim Soroush, '*Tahlil e Mafhoom e Hokoomat e Dini* [An Analysis of the Concept of "Religious Governance"]', in *Din va Hokoomat* [*Religion and Governance*] (Tehran: Rasa Institute of Cultural Services, 1998), pp. 161–89.
185. Rumi, *Masnavi*, Book V, line 167.
186. Rumi, *Masnavi*, Book IV, lines 1434–35.
187. Montgomery Watt, op. cit., p. 3.

3   The Concepts of War and Peace and Their Comparative Positions in an Islamic Context

1. The Quran, 22:40.
2. The Quran, 2:36.
3. The Quran, 5:91.
4. Rumi, *Masnavi*, Book IV, lines 3261–4.
5. The Quran, 2:11.
6. The Quran, 11:117.
7. The Quran, 70:28.
8. Farid Mirbagheri, 'Islam and Liberal Peace', in Farid Mirbagheri et al. (eds), *Education for Sustainable Development: Challenges, Strategies and Practices in a Globalising World* (New Delhi: Sage Publications, 2010), p. 191.

9. Quoted in Chris Brown et al. (eds), *International Relations in Political Thought* (Cambridge: Cambridge University Press), p. 130. The similarity with an Islamic definition of justice is remarkable; see Morteza Motahhari, *Adl e Elahi* [Divine Justice] (Tehran: Sadra Publications, 1982), pp. 59–67.
10. The eight basic needs that have to be met for conflicts to end, according to Burton, are: 'a need for response, a need for security, a need for recognition, a need for stimulation, a need for redistributive justice, a need for meaning, a need to be seen as rational and a need to control'. See John W. Burton, Frank Dukes and George Mason, *Conflict: Resolution and Prevention* (Basingstoke: Macmillan, 1990), p. 95.
11. Johan Galtung, *Transarmament and the Cold War: Peace Research and the Peace Movement* (Copenhagen: Christian Ejlers, 1998), p. 272.
12. Galtung's perspective on violence consists of four types: 'classical violence' such as war and all the suffering associated with it, 'misery' such as deprivation of food, water, shelter and clothing, 'repression' such as loss of basic liberties like freedom of speech, 'alienation' such as violence against identity and non-material needs. The last three he categorises as 'structural violence'.
13. If peace is a unifying condition of life (as believed by Plato) and if peace is quintessentially just, it follows then that justice must be unifying.
14. The Quran, 49:9.
15. See Morteza Motahhari, op. cit., pp. 59–67.
16. For an elaborate account of various graduations of peace including 'victor's peace' see the conclusion in Oliver P. Richmond, *Transformation of Peace: Peace as Governance in Contemporary Conflict Endings* (London: Palgrave, 2006).
17. Immanuel Kant, *Perpetual Peace and Other Essays*, translated by Ted Humphrey (Indianapolis: Hacket Publishing Company, 1983), p. 107.
18. See ibid., p. 111; also see Thomas Hobbes, *Leviathan* (Oxford: Basil Blackwell, 1955 [1651]), pp. 80–4.
19. See note 16 above.
20. Oliver Richmond, 'A Post-Liberal Peace, Eirenism and the Every Day', British International Studies Association, *Review of International Studies* 35(2009), p. 560.
21. Ibid., p. 564.
22. Ibid., pp. 564–5.
23. Ibid., p. 563.
24. Report of the Secretary-General, 'The Situation in Afghanistan and Its Implications for International Peace and Security', UN Doc. A/62/345-S/2007/555 (21 September 2007), para. 24.
25. Oliver Richmond, op. cit., p. 571.
26. The Quran, 49:13.
27. Rumi, *Masnavi*, Book II, lines 1751–3.
28. Ibid., line 1785.
29. The Quran, 5:8.

30. For a hadith from the Prophet in this regard see Al-Tirmidhi, Hadith 1427, at http://www.islamfact.com/all_topics/moahmmad/3040.html. The site was last visited on 2 June 2011.

31. AbdulAziz Sachedina, *The Islamic Roots of Democratic Pluralism* (Oxford: Oxford University Press, 2001), pp. 43–4.

32. P. J. Stewart, *Unfolding Islam* (Reading: Garnet Publishing Ltd, 1995), p. xx.

33. Rumi, *Masnavi*, Book III, lines 1268 and 1270.

34. Anthony C. Thiselton, *Hermeneutics: An Introduction* (Michigan/Cambridge, UK: William B. Eerdsmans Publishing Company, 2009), Kindle Edition, location 5816.

35. Ibid. locations 5789–92.

36. Note should be taken that this is stated as a factual rather than an axiological point. In terms of values, the author would certainly agree with the universality of human rights.

37. Francis Fukuyama, *The End of History and the Last Man* (New York: Avon Books, 1992), Kindle Edition, locations 1424–26.

38. Rumi, *Masnavi*, Book I, line 3086.

39. The Quran, 16:93.

40. Rumi, *Masnavi*, Book II, line 3680.

41. The Bible, Matthew, 28:19–20.

42. Contrary to many who believe the Crusades were carried out by Christians more out of economic and other temporal conditions, there are those who hold the view that religious zeal was the more important factor in those wars. See Karen Armstrong, *Holy War: The Crusades and Their Impact on Today's World* (London: Macmillan, 1988), p. 3.

43. Quoted in Anthony C. Thiselton, op. cit., locations 4576–82.

44. Ali Shari'ati, Eslamshenasi [Islamology] vol. I (Shari'ati Publications, 1981).

45. The most noted work in that regard could be Francis Fukuyama, op. cit.

46. Johan Galtung, 'A Structural Theory of Imperialism', *Journal of Peace Research* 8(1971): 83.

47. Ibn Khaldun, *The Mugaddamah* [An Introduction to History], edited and abridged, N. J. Dawood, translated by Franz Rosenthal (Princeton, NJ: Bollingen Series, Princeton University Press, 1989), p. 129.

48. Perhaps the most notable Western scholar in this respect was Leone Caetani, whose work, *Annals of Islam*, was published in 10 volumes in Italian in the early twentieth century. To my knowledge, a complete translation of this pioneering work into English has sadly not been produced yet. Among those with Muslim backgrounds, the works of the contemporary writer and scholar, who passed away recently, Shoja'eddin Shafa, can be cited, though they also remain in Persian and untranslated; for one such source see *Iran Pas az Hezar o Chahar Sad Sal* [Iran after one thousand four hundred years], Vol. 1 (Farzad publications, 2003), two volumes. The book does not state place of publication.

49. See Shoja'eddin Shafa, *Iran Pas az Hezar o Chehar Sad Sal* [Iran After Fourteen Hundred Years], Vol. 1 (Farzad publications, 2003), p. 298. The book does not state place or date of publication.

50. The Quran, 49:13.

51. The Quran, 2:256.

52. Quoted in Chris Brown, 'Narratives of Religion, Civilisation and Modernity', in Ken Booth and Tim Dunne (eds), *Worlds in Collision: Terror and the Future of Global Order* (Hampshire, UK and New York: Palgrave Macmillan), p. 294.

53. Name cannot be disclosed.

54. Rumi, *Masnavi*, Book I, line 1911.

55. See John L. Esposito, *The Islamic Threat: Myth or Reality* (New York: Oxford University Press, 1992), p. 46.

56. The Quran, 2:213.

57. Dr Abdolkarim Soroush and *Hojjat-ol-Eslam* [clerical title] Mohsen Kadivar, *Monazere dar Bareye Pluralisme dini* [Debate on Religious Pluralism], 4th edn (Tehran: Salam Newspaper Publications, 1999), p. 31.

58. Anthony C. Thistleton, op. cit., locations 266–8.

59. Ibid. location 228–9.

60. Ibid. locations 245–8.

61. Ibid. locations 759–60.

62. Friedrich Schleiermacher, *Hermeneutics: The Handwritten Manuscripts*, edited by Heinz Kimmerle, translated by James Duke and J. Fortsman (Missoula: Scholars Press, 1977), p. 42.

63. Anthony Thistleton, op. cit., locations 238–85.

64. See, on the uncertainty of theoretical knowledge, Karl Popper, *Popper: Conjectures and Refutations* (London and New York: Routledge, 1963, reprinted 2002), p. 125.

65. Abdolkarim Soroush, *Ghabz o Bast e Teorik e Shari'at* [The Theoretical Contraction and Expansion of Shari'a], 3rd edn (Tehran: Serat Cultural Institute, 1994), p. 86.

66. Mohammad Ghazzali, *Ehya e Oloom-e-ddin* [Reviving Religious Sciences], 6th edn, Vol. I, translated by Mohammad Kharazmi (Tehran: The Institute for Scientific and Cultural Publications, 2007), p. 75.

67. Mohammad Lahiji, *Sharhe Golshan e Raz* [Explanation of the Garden of Secrets] (Tehran: Zavvar Publications, 1992), p. 22. The book is a commentary on the famous work of the great mystic, Mahmud Shabestari.

68. Rumi, *Masnavi*, Book IV, lines 2126–43.

69. Unit of currency at the time.

70. Rumi, *Masnavi*, Book II, line 3691.

71. Mohammad Ali Movahhed, *Shams e Tabrizi*, 2nd edn (Tehran: Tarh e Noe Publications, 1997), pp. 45–6.

72. Rumi, *Masnavi*, Book II, line 2927.

73. For an elaborate discussion on this point see Dr Abdolkarim Soroush and *Hojjat-ol-Islam* [clerical title] Mohsen Kadivar, op. cit.

74. For one excellent source citing commonalities in spiritual dimension and prayers see Kenneth Cragg, *Praise, Penitence and Petition, Common Prayer: A Muslim–Christian Spiritual Anthology* (Oxford: Oneworld Publications, 1999).

75. Leonard Lewisohn, *Beyond Faith and Infidelity: The Sufi Poetry and Teachings of Mahmud Shabestari* (Surrey: Curzon Press, 1995), p. 244.
76. See Abdolkarim Soroush, 'Relationship between Islamic and Western Civilisations', manuscript of a lecture delivered at a conference entitled *Political Islam and the West*, Nicosia: Centre for World Dialogue, 31 October 1997.
77. See Fouad Ajami 'The Summoning', *Foreign Affairs*, September–October 1993, pp. 2–9.
78. For instance Huntington's depiction of the imprecise concept of civilisation, describing it as the ultimate human tribe (see Samuel P. Huntington, *The Clash of Civilisations and the Making of World Order* [London and New York: Touchstone Books, 1998], p. 207) and yet giving it the central place in his discourse is rather a broad brush that overlooks differences and nuances within and between civilisations. Huntington's treatment of the vague and human-constructed concept of civilisation, utilising it in the way he has, is an oversimplification at times.
79. For a difference between the *Mo'tazele* and the *Asha'ere* see Farid Mirbagheri, 'Shi'ism and Its Impact on Iran's Politics: A Theoretical Perspective', in Farid Mirbagheri (ed.), *Islam and the Middle East: An Insight into Theory and Praxis* (Nicosia: University of Nicosia Press and Daedelos Institute of Geopolitics, 2009), p. 41.
80. These questions were part of the Distinguished Lecture Series on Dialogue Amongst Cultures and Civilisations organised by PRIO (Cyprus Centre) and the Dialogue Chair in Middle Eastern Studies, University of Nicosia. My learned friend, Costas Constantinou, and I were the co-organisers of this series of lectures and these questions owe much to his contribution.
81. Abdolkarim Soroush, 'Relationship between Islamic and Western Civilisations', pp. 1–5.
82. Farid Mirbagheri, 'Narrowing the Gap or Camouflaging the Divide: An Analysis of Mohammad Khatami's "Dialogue of Civilisations"', *British Journal of Middle Eastern Studies* 34(3), p. 316.

4   The Question of *Jihad*

1. See, for instance, www.fas.org/irp/world/para/docs/980223-fatwa.htm. The site was last visited on 11 June 2009.
2. This is quoted by many. For one source in English see Tariq Ramadan, *In the Footsteps of the Prophet: Lessons from the Life of Muhammad* (Oxford and New York: Oxford University Press, 2007), p. 194.
3. The Quran, 2:255.
4. Tariq Ramadan, *The Messenger: The Meanings of the Life of Muhammad* (London: Allen Lane, Penguin Group, 2007), p. 99.
5. Ibid., p. 98.
6. Majid Khadduri, *War and Peace in the Law of Islam* (Baltimore: John Hopkins Press, 1955), p. 18.

7. See Maulvi Chiragh Ali, *A Critical Exposition of the Popular 'Jihad'*, (Delhi: Idarah-i Adabiyat-i Delli–Jayyad Press, 1984), p. 138.
8. See Oliver P. Richmond, Introduction, *Peace in International Relations* (London and New York: Routledge, 2008), pp. 1–18.
9. This point has been alluded to by Ali Shari'ati. He observes that the Quran begins with, and in, the name of God (*Allah*) but ends with the name of the people (*naas*).
10. Of course, the establishment of an institution does not necessarily mean successful realisation of its goals.
11. Reported in Bruce P. Lawrence, *Shattering the Myth: Islam Beyond Violence* (Oxford: Oxford University Press, 2000), p. 182.
12. Reported in Glen E. Robinson, 'Can Islamists Be Democrats? The Case of Jordan', *Middle East Journal* 51(3), pp. 378–9 (Summer 1997).
13. T. P. Schwartz-Barcott, *War, Terror and Peace in the Quran and in Islam* (Carlisle, PA: Army War College Foundation Press, 2004), pp. 273–4.
14. See Ali Shari'ati, *Az Hejrat ta Vafat* [From Migration Until Death], back cover (the book has no publication details).
15. Binyamin Abrahamov, *Islamic Theology: Traditionalism and Rationalism* (Edinburgh: Edinburgh University Press, 1998), Appendix I, point 17, p. 55.
16. W. Montgomery Watt, *Islamic Political Thought* (Edinburgh: Edinburgh University Press, 1998 [1968]), p. 91.
17. Majid Khadduri, op. cit., p. 143.
18. Ibid., p. 56.
19. Abdolkarim Soroush, *Reason, Freedom, and Democracy in Islam* translated and edited by Mahmoud and Ahmad Sadri (Oxford: Oxford University Press, 2000), p. 27.
20. T. P. Schwartz-Barcott, op. cit., p. 274.
21. Note should be taken that any war fought during the life-time of the Prophet by Muslims, when authorised by the Messenger, is considered a military *jihad* by all Muslims.
22. T. P. Schwartz-Barcott, op. cit., p. 298.
23. The following is widely believed to be a principle in Islamic philosophy amongst *Osooleeyoon* (a school that believes in the ascendency of principles over tradition): *Kollama hakama behe-shshar', hakame behe-l-aghl wa kollama hakama behe-l-aghl hakama behe-shshar'* [Whatever religion commands so does reason and whatever reason commands so does religion].
24. T. P. Schwartz-Barcott, op. cit., p. 271.
25. Majid Khadduri, op. cit., pp. 60–1.
26. Ibid., p. 86.
27. Muhammad Abdel Haleem, *Understanding the Quran: Themes and Style* (London: I. B. Tauris, 1999), p. 63.
28. See Imam Mohammad Ghazzali, *Kimiaye Sa'adat* [Elixir of Prosperity/Salvation], 3rd edn (Tehran: Nash Publications, 2007).
29. Natana J. Delong-Bas, *Wahhabi Islam, From Revival and Reform to Global Jihad* (London: I. B. Tauris, 2004), pp. 201–2, n. 47.

30. T. P. Schwartz-Barcott, op. cit., p. 273–4.
31. W. Montgomery Watt, op. cit., p. 17.
32. Ibid.
33. Ibid.
34. Ibid., p. 15.
35. Ibid., p. 17.
36. Mohammad Abdel Haleem, op. cit., p. 65.
37. The Quran, 18:110 and 41:6.
38. See Abdulkarim Soroush, *The Expansion of Prophetic Experience*, translated by Nilou Mobasser (Leiden and Boston: Brill, 2009), pp. 3–13.
39. Majid Khadduri, op. cit., p. 81.
40. Ibid., p. 95.
41. Mohammad Abdel Haleem, op. cit., p. 66.
42. Note should be taken that defensive war is not necessarily the same as a preventive or pre-emptive war. The latter do not constitute what in the West is usually referred to as just war. Some scholars claim that the Quran is rather vague whether offensive or defensive war is permitted for the faith; see A. G. Noorani, *Islam and Jihad* (New Delhi: LeftWord Books, 2002), pp. 43–4.
43. Hadith reported in Muhammad Nasr ad-Din al-Albani, *Al-Jami as-Saghir wa Ziadah* (Beirut: al-Maktab al-Islami, 1988), 2: 948, quoted in Tariq Ramadan, *The Messenger*, p. 102.
44. Quoted in Tariq Ramadan, *The Messenger*, p. 102.
45. See J. S. McClelland, *A History of Western Political Thought* (London and New York: Routledge, 1996), p. 24.
46. One notable exception is the late Iqbal Lahoori, who was not fond of the connection of Islamic and ancient Greek philosophy.
47. Quoted from Ali Shari'ati, *Ma va Eqbal* [*We and Iqbal*], *Collected Works*, Vol. V (Tehran: Elham Publications, 1971), p. 247.
48. Leonard Lewisohn, *Beyond Faith and Fidelity: The Sufi Poetry and Teachings of Mahmud Shabestari* (Surrey, UK: Curzon Press, 1995), p. 229.
49. Abolghasem Payande (ed.), *Nahj-ol-Fesahe* [The Way of Eloquence], 19th edn (Tehran: Javidan Publication Organisation, 1985), p. 2059.
50. William Blake, *Blake: Complete Writings*, edited by G. Keynes((Oxford University Press, 1972), pp. 96–7.
51. See Leonard Lewisohn, op. cit., p. 239.
52. Mahmud Shabestari, *Gulshan-i Raz* [The Mystic Rose Garden], translated by E. H. Whinfield (Lahore: Islamic Book Foundation, 1978), p. 78.
53. Rumi, *Masnavi*, Book I, lines 1373–8.
54. Molana Jalledin Mohammad Balkhi Rumi, *Masnavi Ma'navi*, translated by Coleman Barks et al., in *The Essential Rumi* (New Jersey: Castle Books, 1997), pp. 221–2. The whole allegory can be seen in Reynold A. Nicholson, *The Mathnawi of Jallalu'ddin Rumi*, Vols 3 and 4 (Cambridge: E. J. W. Gibb Memorial, 1990), pp. 56–61, lines 976–1076. The translation, however, is mainly provided by the author.

55. Ali Shari'ati, *Niayesh* [Prayers] (Aachen: The Office for Collecting and Publication of the Works of Martyred Brother Dr Ali Shari'at in Europe, 1979), p. 99.
56. Ibid., p. 101.
57. See the entry on 'Just War' in Graham Evans, *Dictionary of International Relations* (London: Penguin Books, 1998), pp. 288–9.
58. Michael Walzer, *Just and Unjust Wars*, 4th edn (New York: Basic Books, 2006), p. x.
59. Muhammad Abdel Haleem, op. cit., p. 62. Also see in this regard Montgomery Watt, op. cit., p. 18.
60. Ibn Khaldun, *The Muqaddamah* [An Introduction to History], edited and abridged N. J. Dawood, translated by Franz Rosenthal (Princeton, NJ: Bollingen Series, Princeton University Press, 1989), p. 223.
61. Ibid., pp. 223–4.
62. The use of the term 'holy war' here is the choice of the translator, and in the interest of keeping faithful to the translation, I have reported the same. However, in editorial brackets I have stated what is meant is actually lesser *jihad*.
63. Ibn Khaldun, op. cit., p. 224.
64. Ibid., p. 96.
65. Ibid.
66. Rumi, *Masnavi*, Book II, lines 3109–10.
67. Ibn Khaldun, op. cit., pp. 96–7.
68. Ibid., p. 183.
69. The Quran, 55:7–9.
70. The Quran, 57:25.
71. The Quran, 2:35.
72. Khadduri, Majid, op. cit., pp. 65–6.
73. 'Iraq Rewards Family of Suicide Attacker', *The Providence Journal*, 31 March 2003, p. A5 (from the Associated Press), quoted in T. P. Schwartz-Barcott, op. cit., p. 256.
74. Many have written on the abuse of this precept. For one authoritative source see W. Montgomery Watt, op. cit., pp. 15–16.
75. Haleem, Muhammad Abdel, op. cit., pp. 62 and 63–64.
76. Majid Khadduri, op. cit., p. 62.
77. Ibid., p. 18.
78. Arthur Goldschmidt Jr and Lawrence Davidson, *A Concise History of the Middle East*, 8th edn (Oxford: Westview Press, 2006), p. 210. See also Montgomery Watt, op. cit., p. 19.
79. Arthur Goldschmidt, op. cit., p. 140.
80. Montgomery Watt, op. cit., p. 18.
81. Ibid., p. 15.
82. T. P. Schwartz-Barcott, op. cit., p. 301.
83. Shoja'eddin Shafa, *Pas Az Hezar o Chehar Sad Sal* [After Fourteen Hundred Years], Vol. I (Farzad Publications, 2003), p. 132.

84. The Quran, 60:8.
85. The Quran, 2:190.
86. Maulvi Chiragh Ali, op. cit., p. 138.
87. Reported by Al-Bukhari, reported in Tariq Ramadan, *The Messenger*, p. 112.
88. The Quran, 2:143.
89. Rumi, *Masnavi*, Book II, lines 3511–12.
90. A. G. Noorani, op. cit., p. 49.
91. Ibid., p. 50.
92. *The Jerusalem Post*, 'UK Muslim Leader to Put Fatwa on *Jihad*', by Jonny Paul, 3 February 2010.
93. Report by Chaiwat Satha-Anand (Qader Muheideen), quoted in Noorani, op. cit., p. 48.
94. Ali Shari'ati, *Niayesh*, p. 107.
95. For example, Montgomery Watt and Fred Halliday both believe that *Shari'a* was put together at least 150 years after the Prophet had passed away. For one source, see Montgomery Watt, op. cit., p. 125.
96. Leonard Lewisohn, op. cit., p. 201.
97. For the Persian text, see Mohammad Ghazzali, *Ehya' e Oloom-e-Ddin* [Revival of Religious Sciences], trans. Mohammad Khawrazmi (Tehran: Institute for Scientific and Cultural Publications, 2008), p. 753; for the English translation as quoted in this work see Muhammad Isa Waley, 'Contemplative Disciplines in Early Persian Sufism', in L. Lewisohn (ed.) *Classical Persian Sufism; from Its Origins to Rumi* (New York: Khaniqahi Nimatullahi Publications, 1994), pp. 412–13.
98. Imam Mohammad Ghazzali, op. cit., p. 49.
99. Rumi, *Masnavi*, Book VI, lines 53–4.
100. Pat Buchanan, 'Is Islam an Enemy of the United States?', *New Hampshire Sunday News*, 25 November 1990.
101. Buck-Morss, op. cit., p. 30.

5 Current Conflicts and Muslim and Islamist States: Two Contemporary Cases

1. Subsequently there were two more major Islamist terrorist attacks in Madrid and London, in 2004 and 2005 respectively.
2. See Robert J. Delahunty and John Yoo, 'The "Bush Doctrine": Can Preventive War be Justified?', *Harvard Journal of Law & Public Policy* 32(3),p. 844.
3. Ali A. Allawi, *The Occupation of Iraq: Winning the War, Losing the Peace* (New Haven and London: Yale University Press, 2007), p. 28.
4. Saddam Hussein used poison gas against Iranian soldiers in Iraq's war with Iran on several occasions and also on Iraqi Kurds in Halabja on 16 March 1988.

5. For a detailed account of the background to this conflict see, among others, F. Ogboaja Ohaegbulam, *A Culture of Deference* (New York: Peter Lang, 2007), pp. 104–5.

6. Condoleezza Rice, 'The Promise of Democratic Peace: Why Promoting Freedom is the Only Realistic Path to Security', *The Washington Post*, Sunday, 11 December 2005.

7. There was reportedly an assassination attempt by Saddam's operatives on former President Bush (senior) in 1993. For details and US response see David Von Drehle and R. Jeffrey Smith, 'US Strikes for Plot to Kill Bush', *Washington Post*, Sunday, 27 June 1993, p. A01. Whether or not this could have been a factor, however minor, in the invasion and occupation of Iraq in 2003 has not been ascertained.

8. See on this a very interesting article: Shahrbanou Tajbakhsh and Michael Schoistwohl, 'Playing with Fire? The International Community's Democratization Experiment in Afghanistan', *International Peacekeeping*, 15(2), pp. 252–67 (2008).

9. See Sara Baxter, 'America Ponders Cutting Iraq in Three' *The Sunday Times*, 8 October 2006.

10. See Irvin M. Wall, 'The French–American War over Iraq', *The Brown Journal of World Affairs* X(2), pp. 123–39.

11. One point should be borne in mind regarding the debt that Iraq had to France and other countries. At the time of US military action against Iraq in 2003 the country owed some $120 billion, $40 billion of which was to the Paris Club, a 19-nation group that defines itself, on its website, as 'an informal group of official creditors whose role is to find coordinated and sustainable solutions to the payment difficulties experienced by debtor nations.'

12. See 'Iran: Nuclear Intentions and Capabilities', *National Intelligence Estimate*, National Intelligence Council, Office of the Director of National Intelligence, United States of America, November 2007, p. 6.

13. The sensitivity of some Arab countries in this regard could be seen in that a summit of the Arab League on regional political and economic reform in Tunis in March 2004 was abandoned because several members did not wish the word 'democracy' to be used in reform proposals. See http://news.bbc.co.uk/2/shared/spl/hi/middle_east/03/after_saddam_popup/html/2.stm. The site was last visited on 12 June 2011.

14. See in this regard Ali A. Allawi, op. cit., p. 15.

15. Michael W. Doyle, *Ways of War and Peace* (New York: W. W. Norton & Company, 1997), p. 206.

16. Ali Rahnema, *An Islamic Utopian: A Political Biography of Ali Shari'ati* (London and New York: I. B. Tauris, 2000), p. 94.

17. Ali A. Allawi, op. cit., p. 15.

18. Ibid.

19. Ibid.

20. See Tom Campbell, *Seven Theories of Human Society* (Oxford: Clarendon Press, 1981), p. 79.
21. In one of the most secular Western countries, the United Kingdom, for example, the first function of the Queen, the Head of State, is to protect the Faith (Protestant, Church of England). Many political parties in the West are named after religious affiliation, for example, Christian Democrats in Germany.
22. Michael W. Doyle, op. cit., p. 217.
23. Ibid., p. 209.
24. J. S. McClelland, *A History of Western Political Thought* (London and New York: Routledge, 1996), pp. 235–6.
25. Michael Doyle, op. cit., p. 207.
26. One seasoned journalist in a Middle Eastern country had once observed satirically that there was absolute freedom of speech in his country. But there was, however, no freedom after the speech.
27. Michael Doyle, op. cit., p. 207.
28. Charles Tripp, *A History of Iraq* (Cambridge: Cambridge University Press, 2007), p. 16.
29. Arthur Goldschmidt Jr and Lawrence Davidson, *A Concise History of the Middle East*, 8th edn (Oxford: Westview Press, 2006), p. 24.
30. Charles Tripp, op. cit., p. 260.
31. Ibid., p. 261.
32. Ibid., p. 260.
33. Arthur Goldschmidt Jr. and Lawrence Davidson, op. cit., p. 24.
34. For a recently written source on Iraqi tribal life see Sam G. Stolzoff, *The Iraqi Tribal System* (Minneapolis, MN: Two Harbors Press, 2009).
35. Ali A. Allawi, op. cit., p. 14.
36. See ibid., pp. 13–14.
37. See ibid., p. 13.
38. See ibid., p. 15.
39. See ibid., p. 16.
40. Ibid., p. 14.
41. See S. M. Farid Mirbagheri, 'Shi'ism and its Impact on Iran's Politics: A Theoretical Perspective', in Farid Mirbagheri (ed.), *Islam and the Middle East: An Insight into Theory and Praxis* (Nicosia: University of Nicosia Press, 2009), p. 40.
42. Titles such as Grand Ayatollah were not in use then.
43. As a result of cancelling the concession, Iran was forced to pay £500,000 in compensation.
44. S. M. Farid Mirbagheri, op. cit., p. 46.
45. Ibid., pp. 46–7.
46. For one source on this issue see Johanna Mcgeary, 'Ayatollah Sistani: Iraq's Shadow Ruler', *Time* magazine, 18 October 2004.
47. In this respect see Paul Vallely, 'Grand Ayatollah Sistani: The Real Face of Power in Iraq', 6 March 2004; see http://iraqdinar.us/forum/viewtopic.php?f=8&t=1141. The site was last visited on 21 January 2012.

48. For those outside the discipline, it is noted that International Relations with initials capitalised refers to the academic field of study.
49. Oliver P. Richmond, *Peace in International Relations* (London and New York: Routledge, 2008), p. 74.
50. See Stuxnet virus attack: 'Russia warns of "Iranian Chernobyl"', *Telegraph*, 6 June 2011. See also Yaakov Katz, 'Stuxnet Virus Set Back Iran's Nuclear Programme by Two Years', *Jerusalem Post*, 15 December 2010.
51. For an account of the role of clerics in the Constitutional Revolution in Iran see Homa Katouzian, 'Liberty and Licence in the Constitutional Revolution of Iran', *Journal of the Royal Asiatic Society* 8(July 1998), pp. 159–80.
52. It should, however, be noted, that the founder of the dynasty, Agha Mohammad Khan, brought back centralised command in Iran albeit through cruel methods.
53. Mo'tasemmo-Ssaltane, *Khaterat e Sisasi e Farrokh* [The Political Memoires of Farrokh] (Tehran: Entesharat e Javidan), p. 59.
54. See Edward G. Browne, *The Persian Revolution of 1905–1909*, Elibron Classics Series (Cambridge University Press, 2007 [1910]), pp. 148–9 and 174–90.
55. Ervan Abrahamian, *A History of Modern Iran* (Cambridge: Cambridge University Press, 2008), Kindle edition, locations 1456–61.
56. Ibid. locations 892–900.
57. Ibid. locations 1819–24.
58. Ibid. locations 1797–1802.
59. Ibid. locations 1826–32.
60. Quoted in Abrahamian, op. cit., locations 1858–63.
61. The article appeared under a pseudonym, Ja'far Rashidi Motlagh, wherein Khomeini was described as an agent of repression. In protest people demonstrated and the police reaction led to deaths and spiralling violence gripping the whole country.
62. The Shah of Iran first made this public in a speech on 23 January 1973; see 1970–9 world oil market chronology, Wikipedia, at http://en.wikipedia.org/wiki/1970–1979_world_oil_market_chronology. The site was last visited on 7 June 2011. Also for an enlightening account of the impact of the shah's oil policies on his demise, see Andrew Scott Cooper, 'Showdown at Doha: The Secret Oil Deal that Helped Sink the Shah of Iran', Middle East Institute, Washington DC: *Middle East Journal* 62(4), pp. 561–91.
63. One writer with such a belief is Mike Evans; see Mike Evans, *Jimmy Carter, the Liberal Left and World Chaos* (Phoenix, AZ: Time Worthy Books, 2009). The author contends that Carter's administration was conspiring to remove the Shah of Iran from power.
64. For more discussion on this point see Chapter 2 in this work.
65. The Quran, 2:143.
66. It may be noteworthy that the speaker of Majles (parliament) at the time was Mehdi Karoubi, now a *reformist* leader. As the Speaker, Karoubi, based

on a written letter he had received from Iran's Supreme Leader Ayatollah Ali Khamenei, refused to allow deputies to vote a bill into law for the freedom of the press. Farsi speakers can see a brief account of the debate at http://mazrooei.ir/post/241.php. The site was last visited on 7 June 2011.

67. Farid Mirbagheri, 'Narrowing the Gap or Camouflaging the Divide: An Analysis of Mohammad Khatami's "Dialogue of Civilisations"', *British Journal of Middle Eastern Studies* 34(3), p. 315.

68. This was made public by Mohammad Khatami in a televised interview on 13 July 1999; see http://irangreendemocracy.persianblog.ir/page/18tir78. The site was last visited on 7 June 2011. The site is in Farsi.

69. This was widely reported. For one source see http://www.mideastyouth. com/2011/06/29/movement-continues-in-iran/. The site was last visited on 21 January 2012.

70. S. M. Farid Mirbagheri, op. cit., p. 51.

71. Abbas Abdi made this claim at a meeting with one his former US hostages, Barry Rosen, at UNESCO headquarters in Paris on 31 July 1998. The meeting was organised by the Centre for World Dialogue.

72. See an incisive article on this by Marshall Freeman Harris, 'Clinton's Debacle in Bosnia', at http://www.barnsdle.demon.co.uk/bosnia/clindeb. html. The site was last visited on 3 June 2011. For the religious dimensions of the conflict see David Storey, Michael A. Sells, *The Bridge Betrayed: Religion and Genocide in Bosnia* (Berkeley: University of California Press, 1998).

73. Information on him is readily available on the Internet. For one source see http://www.howardbaskerville.com/. The site was last visited on 3 June 2011.

74. The amount of these assets varies according to the source of reference. Iran, however, claims they are in the tens of billions of dollars. A point of contention in this regard is the money granted by US courts to US citizens for claims made against the Islamic Republic of Iran. This factor can potentially complicate matters further before a final settlement is eventually reached.

75. See Guy Dinmore 'US Rejects Iran's Offer for Talks on Nuclear Programme', http://www.mideastweb.org/log/archives/00000467.htm and Barton Gellman and Dafna Linzer, 'Unprecedented Peril Forces Tough Calls', *Washington Post*, 26 October 2004, http://www.washingtonpost.com/ ac2/wp-dyn/A62727-2004Oct25?language=printer. The sites were last visited on 3 June 2011. Also see Donette Murray, *US Foreign Policy and Iran* (Abingdon, UK and New York: Routledge, 2010), p. 126; and also Semira N. Nikou, 'Timeline of Iran's Political Events', in Robin Wright (ed.), *The Iran Primer: Power, Politics, And US Policy* (Washington DC: United States Institute of Peace, 2010), p. 235. Even though some have disputed the actual contents of the proposed deal, due to the reticence of Tehran and Washington on media reports, there seems little doubt that some kind of a deal may have actually been proposed.

76. Guy Dinmore, 'Washington Hardliners Wary of Engaging with Iran', http://www.mideastweb.org/log/archives/00000467.htm. The site was last visited on 8 June 2011.

77. This is allegedly stated in a letter in which Khomeini cites the opinion of military commanders on the need for atomic weapons, released by Rafsanjani in recent years. See http://www.bluelight.ru/vb/showthread. php?t=272583.

78. The latest report by the International Atomic Energy Agency (IAEA) reflects that. See Report of the Director General to Board of Governors, IAEA, 'Implementation of the NPT Safeguards Agreement and relevant provisions of Security Council resolutions in the Islamic Republic of Iran', GOV/2011/7, 25 February 2011.

79. Security Council Resolution 1929, adopted 9 June 2010; see Security Council document SC/9948.

80. This was particularly so after the Shah, against the wishes of the West, quadrupled the price of oil in 1970s. See in this regard Andrew Scott Cooper, op. cit.

Conclusion

1. Rumi, *Masnavi*, Book IV, lines 2291–3.

2. Andrew Linklater, *The Transformation of Political Community* (Columbia, SC: University of South Carolina Press, 1998), p. 216.

3. The Quran, 13:11.

4. Shari'ati refers to this in a publication entitled *Chehar Zendan e Ensan* [Four Prisons of Humankind] in which he outlines the limitations of biology, society, history and the self on the individual. He concludes that the last limitation is the most difficult and most limiting of all.

5. Rumi, *Masnavi*, Book II, line 1753.

6. Oliver Richmond, 'A Post-Liberal Peace, Eirenism and the Everyday', British International Studies Association, *Review of International Studies* 35(2009), p. 558.

7. Oliver P. Richmond, *A Post-Liberal Peace* (manuscript), (London and New York: Routledge, 2011), p. 112. This book is a well-argued narrative of post-liberal peace in IR.

Index

Lightning Source UK Ltd.
Milton Keynes UK
UKOW05n0832061016

284605UK00017B/414/P